BAX SEAT

BAX SEAT
Log of a
Pasture Pilot
by
Gordon Baxter

Ziff-Davis Flying Books
New York

For Robert B. Parke

CONTENTS

First Words, by Stephan Wilkinson
Chapter 1   The Birds that Brung Me
Chapter 2   Back to Saint-Ex
Chapter 3   Never Take Pictures at Noon
Chapter 4   Too Many Engines, Too Much Dixie
Chapter 5   Without Looking out the Window
Chapter 6   Why Pilots Sweat in the Winter
Chapter 7   A Little Orange-and-White Airplane
Chapter 8   Just One More Hour Solo

First Words

by Stephan Wilkinson

Since he's going to have all the last words in this confrontation, let me tell you now about Gordon Baxter before he does— which he rarely misses an opportunity to do.

Gordon Baxter is a singer of songs, though his songs have no notes. (Neither does his straight reporting, more often than not.) Many of those songs are in this book, and you'll see that they do, nonetheless, have a music of their own, including a rhythm that you'll recognize at once and realize you've never heard so clearly. Bax has something that writers lust after—an Ear, one of the things that made Mark Twain great and are doing the same for Gordon: Bax hears things that nobody else notices, remembers them in a way no tape recorder ever could, gets it all down with a spare style that makes many a writer think, "If I could do that, I'd be rich and famous."

Well, Gordon may not be rich yet, but among pilots he's as famous as an aviation writer can be. He sees airplanes as the rest of us think we do or wish we could: as magic carpets that defy common sense and reward their masters with insights no ground-pounder could ever have. He sees airplane people not as the businessfolk, braggarts and conspicuous consumers that the rest of us think we recognize but as mystics, magicians, secret children with the world's biggest toys in their hands. He sees what aviation once was—an adventure that lifted its partakers out of the commonplace—and rejoices that what made it so indeed still exists in isolated pockets and patches, which Baxter seeks and finds.

Gordon has always sought adventure and the adventuresome. A Merchant Marine officer and Torpedo Alley survivor (not without getting his feet wet) during the War and a Mississippi riverboatman after it, a car freak and hot-rodder almost before the terms were coined, Bax himself invented the profession of creative disc-jockeying with a program that for decades was an East Texas radio combination of Arthur Godfrey, Wolfman Jack and the *Today* Show. Gordon Baxter is also a TV performer and a movie actor—he starred in a film version of "One of the Missing," by Ambrose Bierce, that won the equivalent of an Academy Award for small, independently made films. He also happened to put together a collection containing a specimen of every model of rifle issued to the U. S. Army from the time of General Washington to that of General Westmoreland. It was so complete that he finally had to give it to the Government. He is also the world's worst photographer.

Bax tries to pass himself off as a pilot, but don't believe him. He never could fly worth a damn. You'll read some libel in this book about my own touch at the controls, but that just goes to prove that he wouldn't recognize class east of Natchez if it were an international-orange rudder lock. But Gordon *feels* airplanes, loves and honors them in ways the rest of us are ashamed to admit. (The man still makes *models,* forgodsakes.) And he's certainly one of the few romantics who can express what he feels so perfectly.

Some of what you'll read in this book deals with the relationship between Baxter The Writer and me The Editor. It should be said up front that the abilities of a successful editor are vastly overrated, a mistake that Bax rarely makes. The writer's work is the loneliest kind, and all that an editor can bring to soothe the agony is a suspicious ear and an open mind. He's somebody for the writer to talk to. All we editors have to do is make believe that we're the audience, which isn't hard, since that's what we are; it's just that we get there first. We try to tell the writer if his words are on straight, hoping to do it in a way that he can understand and accept. There's nothing worse than an unspecific editor, unless it's an unwilling writer.

In any case, a good editor is only a tiny pilotfish for the omnivorous talent of a Gordon Baxter. Some day, I will be able to stand up and announce, "I worked with Gordon Baxter," and people will buy me another drink or ask me to tell inside stories about our tempestuous partnership or inquire whether Bax is truly as brilliant a pilot as legend holds him to be. So I am honored that in this book, Gordon has given me portable proof of our relationship, legal tender easily carried in a Jepp bag to any line shack, cockpit or saloon frequented by pilots who are also flying romantics. Heaven knows we'll always need such romantics around. Heaven help us if Gordon Baxter is the last of them.

1.

The Birds that Brung Me

I would go out to Pappy Sheffield's grass airport and get the yellow J-3 Cub and go fly it in the heat beneath puff-ball clouds as their shadows drifted across the field and do touch-and-goes. I would throttle back and do long, delicious side-slips back to earth. With the side open, the window pinned up under the wing and the door let down on the landing gear strut, I would feel the warm wind on my face as I looked out and saw when the wheel touched. If you bring the Cub in just exactly right, descent rate, speed, pitch, all of it just exactly right, the three wheels will touch at the same instant, and that fat tire never lifts an inch from the first contact. There is not an ounce of lift left in that wing, and the little airplane just starts rolling, if you do it just exactly right.

And with your head out like that, you can smell the tires crush the clover.

One night, in a Third Avenue bar, my friend and mentor at *Flying* Magazine, Stephan Wilkinson, leaned across the table to me and cried out, "Baxter, for over eight years you have been writing the same story for me!"

"But Stephan," I explained, "you keep buying it."

And so have my readers. As you go through this book you will hear a certain constancy in these stories, brought back in the same order that they appeared in *Flying.* They are all love stories, pure as the Elizabethan ballads sung by Mamma Maybelle and the Carter Sisters from deep in the valleys of the Great Smoky Mountains. First come the trials and sorrows, then satisfaction to a heart that is true. Stories of a life-long love affair with airplanes.

I guess that, if anything, I am the romance writer for *Flying.* Once, after one of our few attempts to have me do a pilot report on a new product, Stephan sent the fourth rewrite attempt back to me with a sizzling "Baxter, the trouble with you is that you never met an airplane you didn't like!"

I was one of those lucky kids born in the Golden Age of Aviation. I caught the twilight of barnstorming. Paid a 1933 fortune of five dollars to ride with Clarence Chamberlin in a Curtiss Condor, a gigantic old fabric box kite. Filled out my log book with rides in an OX Robin, a Stinson trimotor that belonged to Billy Rose. Travel Airs, Wacos, a Lincoln-Page, a spin in a Fleet. Once at a recent product breakfast at the Reading Air Show an avionics company president introduced his new line by starting out with "Now that we can dispel all the romance and view the airplane as a useful tool . . ." That's all I stayed for. I not only did not like the way that Yankee pronounced it "useful tew-el" but I really have no reason to stay in the same room with a man who believes there is no more romance in flying. Even if he just bought me breakfast.

The ruination of my boyhood ambition to be an Army pursuit ship pilot and then fly for the airlines had been accurately forecast by a high school math teacher: "If you don't pay attention and stop drawing airplanes, you will not be smart enough to even get in the gate at Randolph Field." And that's exactly how it turned out. But the germination of my ambition to be a pilot never died. By 1957 I could afford to solo a headstrong Luscombe, which circled me three times on the ground and then mowed itself out of sight in a sorghum field, where my instructor, A.M. Vanneman, eventually located me and said, "Well. We ain't gone leave it out here, are we?"

For the next few glorious years I had the fun of flying Cubs, "Airknockers" and Stearmans before such evil inventions as nosewheels, radios, and VORs. The tower at Houston would give you a green light to land amidst the hustle of an occasional DC-3 or a big, sleek Connie.

I filled in the long spaces between flights by reading about flying. During the '30's I spent lunch money for the dime pulps, *War Birds, Flying Aces,* and *G-8.* The writings of Arch White-house and all those paperback writers laid the undercoating for my own skills, I still wish I had some reason to write, "The instrument panel of G-8's Spad exploded before his eyes. Blinded by hot oil, wires screaming in the turn, G-8 whipped his helmeted head around and stared into the coffin nose of the Fokker. Sunlight glinted evilly off the square goggles of the Boche pilot, his twin Spandaus began to flame in their dance of death. G-8, with seconds left to live, slammed the stick over and firewalled the throttle. The Hisso bellowed with power and his wings drummed tight as the shell holes of no-man's-land grew in his center section. His only hope, nothing could outdive a Spad." Man, I just gave myself cold chills writing that much of it.

I also nearly memorized and completely wore out my first copies of Ernest K. Gann's *Fate Is the Hunter* and Saint Exu-péry's *Night Flight.* Those two were my graduate school, and I still go back to them when I feel a dryness of the soul.

I read *Flying* and *Air Progress* during the late '60s. *Flying* was read in a scholarly manner, *Air Progress* because it then still carried the vestiges of my beloved War Birds tales. I wanted to write airplane stories, and they kept bubbling to the surface like tar in summer, but it would have never occurred to me to send any of that stuff to a real magazine. So I printed it in the *Kountze News.*

The *Kountze News* came out every Thursday, ready or not, in the little Eastex town of Kountze, with a press run of about 1,400 papers. The shaggy old editor, Archer Fullingim, paid me in mayhaw jelly and gourds. There was not an aviator in town.

Now *Flying* is put together in Manhattan, but most of the writing traditionally has come from little fields, far west of the Hudson River. I commented on this once to Robert B. Parke, then my editor-in-chief. That urbane New Yorker's explanation was: "to avoid the Manhattan syndrome." Were it not for that practice, I would never have begun my long, loose and mostly happy relationship with *Flying* Magazine. *Flying* found me down on the Gulf Coast of Texas where for 25 years I had produced my own radio and TV shows. Sort of the morning mouth of Beaumont.

One day in early 1970, Archie Trammell, then Senior Editor for *Flying,* came to town to address the local Rotary Club. I snared Archie for an interview on the morning broadcast. He was in a hurry, but I caught him in the door and pressed some of my *Kountze News* airplane stories into his hand. Archie scanned them, standing on one foot, then looked up at me and spoke the words that became my contract with *Flying:* "Why aren't you writing for us?"

Archie Trammell started as a line mechanic with American Airlines, joined *Flying* in 1966, made Senior Editor in 1970 and moved to New York, and then was given the Editorship of *Business and Commercial Aviation* in 1972. When I last saw him, Archie was still greeting the world like a kid on Christmas morning.

Archie was then being dragged out of Indiana for the first of a long line of promotions. He said to me, "I'm moving into the head shed soon, and my first piece of official business will be to take you with me."

The editors decided to hang my stuff out the back of the magazine, sort of like a friendly brakeman waving to you from the caboose after the serious part of the train has gone by. Archie tagged the column "Bax Seat," a name nobody has ever seen any reason to change, even when my column runs in the front.

I sent them three stories, "Hound Dog," "Cross City" and "The Wide Job" and started haunting the newsstands to see if I was really a writer for *Flying.* Then, as now, I find out if Bax is in the magazine the same day you do; when I get the thing. So I went out and bought a subscription, and the subscription department treats me the same way they do you. I even get all that "Save Now! Early Subscription Offer!" stuff. They never

have figured out that I work there. After three or four years the
New York office began to send me clip-cornered freebies. A
sure sign, they say, that you work there.

In May of 1970 I found my first story in print.

Houn' Dog

I don't recall how we came to acquire this god-awful aircraft. I just
went out to the airport one day and there it was, severely chained
to earth way at the end of the line, looking like a torn-down Air
Force recruiting poster, with brightly colored Cessnas sticking up
their pointy tails at it.

It drew me like a magnet. All weird airplanes do—the halt, the
blind, the lame, the oddballs. Even as I drew near beneath its
decrepit but still fierce gaze, I knew with sick certainty that I would
have to fly it. And that it would be a hair-raising, humiliating
experience, one I would cherish forever.

I walked slowly around it, gazing at its old bones stretching a
scarred hide, being careful not to touch it or get too close. Patches
on the wings; alligatored tires; a long, flat snout with flared, hairy
nostrils. It looked like an old rodeo bronc standing deceptively
still.

Lee Sheffield crept up behind me. "Alright Lee, what is it? Or
was it?"

"The Houn' Dog. Yeah, Houn' Dog."

"Alright. Why Houn' Dog?"

"You'll find out."

According to an old brown folder that something had wet on,
it was an L-5E, built by the Stinson Division of Vultee Aircraft,
Wayne, Michigan in 1944. The Army ordered 558 of them—a
life-time supply. This one was still wearing the uniform it got
mustered out in. Crash silver, with a broad, orange belly band
bordered in black, and a big orange square painted on the side
of the nose. For high visibility, I guess, although I don't see how
anybody could lose a thing like that.

I can't believe Stinson had anything to do with this. I never saw an ugly Stinson in my life. It must have been designed by a committee of captains bucking for major.

"Give them anything they want, we got to get us some wartime contracts."

"They want unsurpassed visibility."

"Okay, put windows in the top, the bottom, all the way around the sides. Slant the windows way out, so you can lean outside and look and still be in the airplane."

"They want to carry bodies in it."

"Okay, hollow it out and put a six-foot door down the side so you can put a stretcher in it, sideways."

"It ain't gonna fly, full of guys like that all the way back to the tail."

"The hell it won't. Give it a 190-horse Lycoming, slots, flaps, drooped ailerons, and make the gear out of truck parts. It'll fly. Something'll give."

I peered inside to where they close you up in that canvas coffin on a stretcher. If I was wounded bad enough, they might have got me stuffed in there, but they'd never have got the claw marks off the sides.

Bill Teddlie came out to give me a check ride, licking his lips and wiping his palms on his pants. Teddlie noticed that there was no control stick in the back. A short piece of three-quarter-inch pipe was inserted into the socket. The regular stick had a dogleg in it; this one pointed right at where Teddlie was sitting. I tested for freedom of movement. Teddlie cringed back as far as he could get.

A brave man propped it over and it bellowed to life. Everything set up a lively, chattering rattle. Vultee, alright. I peered out the front: nothing but cowling and tubing. I looked up the skylight: more tubing. Back at Teddlie through a maze of pipes and turnbuckles. It was like driving a plumbing-supply truck.

Later, after the Houn' Dog was gone, we tried to remember what instruments it had in it. Sheffield claimed three of the holes were filled. Altimeter, oil pressure, tach. Wayne Gregory said, "No, it was oil pressure, airspeed and tach." I don't remember any of them. The Houn' Dog told you what you needed to know right up your spine.

It loved to fly. It gave you the feeling that you wanted to knock down houses with it like in an old Paul Mantz movie. It was all Stinson in the air, all steady balance and ball bearings in the control rods. It kept whispering in my ear, "Go on, do a loop." I did a little dive, eased back, then I had a vision of them trying to sort me out from all that plumbing, and faded the loop into a sort of a chicken wing-over.

The day it finally houn' dogged me was coming back from a CAP search mission with Howard Bracht, a TV cameraman and a very fine aviator, in the back. I was set up on one of those whispering approaches, holding the flap handle down because it would some-times jump out of its notch and dump you. With the leading-edge slots sucking air, I painted one on and settled back to enjoy the glory. It went wild just at the end of the roll-out—screeching and leaning, right between a pair of runway lights and out into the gumbo. Betrayed and dismayed, I grabbed up big fistfuls of Houn' Dog, blew up a mudstorm back to the runway, and let it go on and take off with my neck burning red.

I turned around to face a leering Bracht and told him we couldn't let a landing like that stay on the books. This time around, I was ready for it, sitting up tight, armed. It did it again. Same thing, only it nearly made it all the way out to the fence, then stopped in a hurricane of mud, bogged to the axles. I heard a rapid clicking sound in the back and figured Bracht for the fastest Rosary I ever heard. Turned around and there he was, filming the entire episode. And he filmed the part about my losing my shoes in the mud, and throwing my helmet at him from the runway, and wading off like a marsh bird to go get the tractor.

I told the tractor boys I was going to do it one more time. They said, "Then we'll just wait out here." And evermore when I came out to fly the Houn' Dog, the boys would ask me where I wanted the tractor spotted.

One by one, the Houn' Dog let all the good taildragger pilots sign their initials out in the high grass. It became a great un-builder of confidence.

I was determined to find out what was going on under there to cause these crazy roll-outs. I shot crosswinds, wheelies, flaps, no flaps, roared around with the tail up. I studied the weird arrangement of the way the gear spread out on landing, compressing oleos inside the fuselage. I came up with the theory that because of its remarkable slow-flight characteristics, the wing unloaded onto the gear so slowly on a gentle landing that the oleos compressed at different rates, causing one wheel to scoot out, and then the other. This subtle changing of wheel camber and tread width would catch a pilot in mid scramble, correcting the wrong way. The only way to land it was to spread the gear firmly. Slam it a little.

After the Houn' Dog left us, we heard from the man who had it, over in Orange, Texas. From out in *his* high grass, he claimed the tailwheel control cables were crossed, but they said it was an alibi, just like mine. Last we heard of the Houn' Dog, some guy in Indiana owned it and was trying to sell it back to Lee. Claimed it was barking at night, disturbing the peace, and his neighbors were going to sue.

Lee "Pappy" Sheffield is a continuing thread through this book. Up until the day my wife, Diane, and I bought our Mooney, nearly all these stories took place in his planes and at his famous "grass airport." Even though Beaumont Municipal was paved and lighted under his management in 1977, it is still a family airport. A place of wives and daughters. Lee is not much for lip, but his secret pride is his line boys who made good. If they could all come back home on one day it would be a heart warming scene of Army and Air Force pilots, corporate and Line pilots. The process is still going on for any school kid who wants to fly bad enough to work hard enough.

Pappy's airport is truly open. On a typical Sunday a unicom field advisory might sound like this: "Caution, a stick of sky divers just came out at 10,000 feet over the field, three students in the pattern, ag planes operating at the north end, radio models flying near the terminal, and there is a glider on final." The only guy I ever saw Pappy run off the airport had an American flag sewed to the seat of his jeans.

Another operator who figures strongly here is George Mitchell, who operates M&M Air Service from a single turf strip a few hundred yards west of Beaumont Muni. With a 35-plane, three-state operation, Mitchell is one of the nation's largest ag applicators. His uncle, Poley, and his father, Fields Mitchell, gave me privileges to the company's old two-holer, old N59977 of nearly all the Stearman love stories here. George and I sort of grew up together and I became involved in the lives of his men and their beautiful biplanes.

Two pilots are mentioned in "Houn' Dog," Wayne Gregory and Bill Teddlie. Wayne was one of Pappy's line boys and at this writing is a Houston insurance broker and corporate pilot. Teddlie was dealt a different hand. Shortly after checking me out in the Houn' Dog, Teddlie hired out to M&M. He went straight in while working his Stearman in Arkansas.

Loyd Hood was one of Mitchell's mechanic-pilots. He was highly instrumental in building the "wide job," laying out her lines in chalk on the cement floor of the shop. Just before "The Wide Job" was printed in the August 1970 issue of *Flying,* Loyd was killed instantly in a mid-air between two Stearmans. I gave the meager proceeds from this story to his widow.

The Wide Job

If you had seen and heard the big biplane working the rice fields along Interstate 10 on the Texas coast, you would have known that it was not a Stearman. If you had stopped to watch it, the sound that beat against your ears would have confirmed your suspicion. The melody of a 450 Pratt & Whitney snoring out of a short, open stack is music enough, but nothing else in the world sounds like the unbridled horses of a 600-hp P&W.

Look now, as it passes low, in profile. No Stearman this. The memory comes of photos of the chesty little Boeing shipboard fighters of the 1930s. But no, those biplanes were narrow hipped behind their great engines. In this one, the bulk of the rocker boxes and cylinders and crankcase continues, flows on back, the silhouette deepened by the hopper bin slanting from the high-seated pilot down toward the engine.

He flashes by fast, with that nosedown, hungry look that a Stearman gets when it's riding those California highlift wings. Now he zooms up for the turn, showing a fat belly. He rolls it out and you see the topside, and the shock comes. It's as broad as a boat. There's room for two guys in the cockpit, side by side, engineer and fireman.

It wasn't a Stearman. More than anything else it was a Mitchell. "Something we built with our own hands"—that's how the men who built it for Poley Mitchell described it. And if you had seen it die along that same Interstate 10, seen it go in from 300 feet, seen it part all those thick power lines, thunder into that ditch and slew around and destroy itself and perform its last design function—to save its pilot from even a scratch—you would have understood the gloom that hung over M&M Air Service for weeks afterward.

Crop dusting is a hard business. It breeds hard airplanes, hard men and hard sayings like, "You cain't make any money with the hopper shut." If, while sitting around the coffee table in the pilots' room, you were to dream up the idea of splitting a Stearman down the middle and making it just 10 inches wider, you could increase the hopper capacity from 1,700 pounds to 2,500 pounds. That figures out to less turn-around time, more time over the rice fields with the hopper wide open.

For M&M Air Service, one of the nation's largest ag operators, the money motivation might have been reason enough. But it wasn't. Nobody could remember keeping any dollars-per-acre figures on "the wide job," as they called it. Instead, these big-dollar ag operators would get a faraway look in their eyes and a soft, wistful tone in their voices, and start talking about the way it looked, the way it flew, and the time they all had in building it.

"I'd been wanting to build my own airplane for a long time," said Poley, gazing out over the ranch spread where he lives now. "With another 18 inches of wing, it would have been a real good airplane. But it was too big, too heavy with its payload for the wing. But it flew just like a Stearman."

Earl West, who flew it most of the 956 hours it logged, remembered the wide job differently. "It wasn't an airplane for just anybody to fly. With heavy loads, it flew on horsepower, not lift. On a hot day, with a full tank of 300 gallons, it made you talk to that engine. 'You be good to me, and I'll be good to you.' "

I started asking West a lot of questions about the wing loading, weights and stall speed. "Wait a minute, I'll have to go look in the files." But none of this was to be found. Nobody had ever written it down; there wasn't even a set of blueprints. There was only a copy of the application for certification, a weighty document that read in full: *2/16/66: Increase width of Boeing fuselage & installation of P&W R-1340 engine. Note: Modification for Boeing E-75 #75 6015 only.*

"We carried 2,500 pounds in the hopper, 12 gallons of oil, 46 gallons of gas, and me," Earl recalled. "That comes to a little over 3,000 pounds. And I do remember that the airplane would lift more than its empty weight, so I guess it grossed out at something over 6,000." Yes, and so does a seven-passenger Cessna 401, or a Piper Navajo, for quick comparison.

The GI Stearman weighed 2,200 empty and was rated for a 600-pound load. With approximately the same wing area and about three times the original horsepower, the Mitchell carried five times the original load. A tidy piece of aeronautical engineering? Well, yes and no. Not a man in the shop was encumbered with a college degree. All they had was about 20 years of experience in building ag planes.

"We worked it by itself whenever we could," Earl said. "It didn't pair up with anything else in the loading and spraying cycle because it stayed out so long. We used it mostly on long hauls and big fields. We only used full power on takeoff; we worked it at about 45 percent, even in the turns. It didn't flare out too good on landings, though it just came over the fence and said, 'Okay, I quit.' It wasn't a good airplane to fly. There was no indication of a stall, no kick-off either way. It just started going down, settling fast, and when it did that, you better have plenty of room."

To this, Poley added, "We all knew it didn't have enough wing, but it was within the capabilities of my pilots. We were going to put a longer wing on it as soon as we got a chance. The engine quit the day it went in, and it was carrying a load, but the pilot had control all the way down."

Earl's words came very softly "Something you build with your own hands . . . and now it ain't here anymore. A lot of original ideas, a lot of work . . ."

"Earl, do you think they will ever rebuild it, or make another one?"

"I don't know. I wouldn't say we never will . . ."

The Reading Air Show of June 1970 was my first time to meet anyone from *Flying* except Archie Trammell, and I had only seen him for five minutes. I didn't know what to expect.

I ordinarily dress like a bum, but I went out and bought me a going-to-New York suit, complete with fire-striking shoes. I was standing out on the flight line at Reading among the flags and all the hoopla, all gussied up in that awful suit and tie, when the company Shrike Commander wheeled around in our slot and came to a stop. The worst looking bunch of hippie chicks and bearded freaks and weirdos you ever saw came tumbling out. I decided the airplane had been stolen and these were the hijackers.

It was the New York staff. They swarmed round me and the other staffers already there with much hoo-hahing, grabbing and hugging. Right quick I learned two things about us: that *Flying* is produced by a touchy-feely group who are not much for hiding their affection . . . or rage . . . or despair; and that they are sharply divided by the choice of threads and hirsuteness into the straights and the freaks, Brooks Brothers and blue jeans. I quickly returned to my room, dug out my jeans and thus cast my lot.

Right off I was typed as the one to send out and do the weird, gamey stuff. "You will ride with Bob Hoover when he does his aerobatic show in the Shrike," they said. And I didn't dare admit to anyone that I get airsick. Learned to fly with a bucket between my knees with Ray Gannoway in the old Aeronca. Hoover is a gentleman and a hero. When he saw me turning the same color green as the upholstery he said that he gets airsick too when somebody else is flying this kind of stuff, and if I could last five minutes more we would be at the chocks. We got to the chocks before the chucks.

Infright Report

Everybody wonders what it would be like to be with Bob Hoover when he does his thing in the Shrike Commander. What does Hoover's face look like when he dives for the deck, feathers both engines, and puts the plush, heavy "Stag Ship" through an eight point roll, loops it, flares for a dead stick landing, kissing first one wheel then the other, and rolling in silent triumph to the ramp while the stands go wild . . . What's it like in there? Hah! Let me tell you. I was just there.

I'm the new boy on the *Daily,* see? So when our fiendish editor told me he was arranging a ride with Hoover I figured that was just part of the initiation. Word got back that Hoover seldom does this sort of thing. Various legalities, etc. Cool heads would prevail. I began to relax, counting on the good sense of Hoover and North American Rockwell. Right up until the time that Hoover held the door open and invited me in, I kept believing that at the last moment I would hear from the Warden or the Governor.

Bob Hoover looks like your kindly neighborhood obstetrician. Very tall, lean as a slat, salt and pepper grey hair and a neat doctor's mustache, slender delicate hands, and an air of crisp professionalism and concern for the patient.

The entire episode was conducted with an air of clinical detachment and accompanied by scholarly classroom remarks from Bob. Not once did we exceed redline, or even crowd the yellow, or pull over two G's in the stock Shrike Commander. The only clue to the business at hand was before takeoff. Bob tactfully asked if I tended to "get uneasy." No use lying about it at a time like this. I told him I could do it for a time, but that it would eventually get to me. And that good and gentle man said, "Me too. It never bothers me unless I'm a passenger."

Hoover described the takeoff, which ran flat out on the deck to the edge of the woods, and a zoom climb for a thousand feet or so as, ". . . these engines are meant to be used like this. You can leave them at 100 percent as long as you want to. You don't have to worry about the engines."

Outside Reading traffic, Hoover made two careful clearing turns while in max climb. From where I was hanging, I thought this was part of the aerobatics, then he announced that we would now see the stall characteristics of the big pointy-winged bird. "Straight up and down, zero airspeed, riding the props, no tendency to tail slide. Just look out there." I looked out there, just in time to see Pennsylvania pitch over and return to normal attitude without spilling a pretzel.

"Now we'll do some wind-up turns," said Bob, eyes starting to gleam. Up on edge, yoke full back, chasing our tail in a deadly tightening circle. Horn blowing, control wheel shaking, wings starting a hard buffet, every fiber of the Shrike was shouting "Stall! Stall!" and Bob Hoover sitting over there describing it like a classroom professor at the blackboard. "Anything else would have snapped by now. I have full control, all three axes." Brushing the chalk dust from his hands, the professor rolled level and said, "Now, same thing into a dead engine. Either way. This would put anything else over onto its back. I can force the nose up in this turn and it just tries to fall straight through. A person enjoys flight characteristics in the Shrike not available anywhere in its class. Notice that I'm holding it as tight as it will go."

I noticed we were funneling right down into the gorgeous hills that were swirling past the windshield. The big high-winged bird had its back arched, trembling, pounding, sinking, but under control, in a flight attitude that would have made a good ole Stearman or a nimble Luscombe snap like popcorn.

"Now for a two-G loop." The big plane went whooping, laughing over the top. "Same thing, power off." Up and over again, sleek belly sunfishing in the sky. ". . . and the Shrike also remains completely stable in an eight point roll . . . One . . . two . . . three . . ." Bob using short, abrupt but smooth control movements, the Shrike snapping its wings, and all those engines hanging out there, to the precise point in the sky and holding it there. ". . . four . . ." I am floating lightly in the belt, the mountains are hanging overhead, the Shrike is purring softly. Everyone should fly twins inverted. Relieves the burden of a long flight, better than stereo and unclogs the biffy.

We did more things. The land and sky keep swirling past each other changing places. I say "Stomach, don't do that. We are riding with Bob Hoover." Stomach says, "I been telling you, in a minute you are going to be a Hoover's heaver. This is your final notice."

Bob is enjoying himself hugely, "Wonderful. Such a wonderful airplane . . ." He looks around to see if I'm still in there. I am limp, green as asparagus, slick and shiny with sweat, sliding slowly down, down, in the big leather seat. He levels up, gives me a comforting pat, "That's about all of it. Making notes and pictures like that will get you every time. Let's see if we can find the airport." What a prince of a guy.

We were way out and high. Hoover reaches over to the Shrike's pedestal, grabs the big iron levers and shuts it all off. Yes, he did. He calls it "level flight, zero power." After a time of ghostly silence I ask, "What's our sink rate?" "We haven't started sinking yet. Isn't this something?" Hoover says.

Hoover twiddled the radio, I could hear the soft clicks in the quiet. Then he asked Reading if they would approve a dead stick landing on three-one. The tower makes sounds of disbelief. Almost apologetically he tells them, "This is Bob Hoover." Oh. So they ask him to take a holding pattern. I mean really holding, in 5,700 pounds of slick glider. We just sort of hung around up there. Hoover, hugging the yoke in happiness, chortled, "Look how long we been sitting up here. Isn't this unbelievable?" We were whispering along at 130 mph, seemingly in a flat attitude, both shiny props knife-edge to the winds. When Tower finally cleared us to land, Hoover had to kill off altitude even with wheels, full flaps and me all puckered up. He came downstairs on final in a classic falling leaf, dousing gallons of altitude. The yoke was going full right, full left, the rudder crossing up. Biplane stuff. "Bob, I thought you weren't supposed to slip a modern plane like this with full flaps down." "It's ok for the Shrike. Now we land. First we do this wheel . . . chirp . . . now we do this side . . . chirp . . ." The Stag Ship, hurtling down the runway, one sharp wing pointed heavenward, was a bird in his hand.

We rolled out, made the turnoff, coasted to a stop halfway to the ramp. "Now comes the tricky part," muttered Bob, reaching overhead, and to the pedestal and panel to hot start the fuel injection engines. Remember that, too, when you see him fly by with both feathered next time, and then restart at the top of a stall.

Hoover gave me a ride back to the North American pavilion. Shirttail out, stained dark with sweat, hair plastered to my green face, dragging my camera in the grass. He brought me in like some kind of game he had just bagged.

I asked Bob how he ever got started doing things like that in the Shrike Commander. "The first time I flew it I liked it. I thought it would be wonderful for the show. Precision flying like this is one of the best ways to convince people that an airplane is great. And it is a great airplane."

I came away thinking the only thing more honest and beautiful about Bob Hoover's flying, is the fact that he enjoys it and believes in what he's doing.

The "they" who put me up there with Hoover was Bob Parke. Robert B. Parke, with *Flying* since 1953, ran the magazine from 1967 to 1977. He won the DFC and two Air Medals as a B-17 commander in World War II. Dapper, grey and immaculately mannered, he looks like a prototype Westchester County manor lord who lunches at the exclusive University Club in Manhattan. He is. Parke was the once-removed overseer of my career with the magazine. After I was taken into the fold at Reading, Parke sent me a follow-up memo saying that while our association would not preclude my writing for other aviation publications, *Flying* would want first refusal, "and it is unlikely that we would encourage you to do stories for other competitive magazines." In later years, after I had built a reputation through *Flying,* Keith Connes, of *Air Progress,* Dennis Shattuck, of *Private Pilot,* and Hugh Whittington, of *Canadian Aviation,* all explored with me the possibility of their printing some of my stuff. I approached Parke about this, and he was, as always, kind, gentle, understanding. He said, "Of course you can—once." And once, when I thought I had been taken unfair advantage of by his company, I raged, "Bob, I am going to write a book and expose this whole rotten deal!" His eyes twinkled as he answered, "Sounds good. Give us first look at it."

Thomas H. Block has had about the same experiences. Tom and I have agreed that since anywhere from *Flying* Magazine is down, we would settle for being "captive freelancers," which is a non-phrase, like "virile impotence."

Now Tom Block was the street-wise kid who used to stand in the garbage and smog of the LaGuardia Airport approaches and watch the airliners appear out of the clag, and he would say, "One of these days I'll fly one of those things." He does, for Allegheny Airlines. Big, boyish Cap'n Block has taught many staffers his gentle touch with airplanes. The author of "Pro's Nest" in the magazine, Tom, like myself, is one of the outside insiders. He laughs, he lasts.

For a time, Tom and I enjoyed the swaggering title of "Associate Editor," until the company lawyers sniffed that out and said, "These guys are not on the payroll; no titles." So we got down-statused to the dull-sounding "Contributor." What we really are is a more respected journalistic form of "stringer." I now send my stuff to New York under a self-appointed title that comes closer to describing my years with and affection for *Flying:* "Senior Executive Stringer."

In November of 1970 the magazine carried the first story they bought from me, "Cross City". One way an author can judge the worth of his writing is to look back on it after it gets old and see if there is any truth still in it. By that standard "Cross City" is a keeper. The place is still my entry point for my many trips into Florida, and I am about convinced that the Cross City Thunderstorm is permanent. I have looked down upon that place in sunshine only one time, and it has really changed: a thriving, alive little airport with what appears to be a going FBO with full services. They must train some of the world's best instrument pilots there.

Cross City

I called aviation weather from Central Brevard and they said, "It's good out of here, but there's a front with thunderstorm activity at . . ." Guess where. Cross City. If there's ever going to be bad weather in Florida, it's gonna be at Cross City. That's what the line boy told us when we came in. Never forget anything a line boy says.

The sun was shining, the sky was high and clear, wings bent back. It was gorgeous. We were smoking good tobacco, leaning back in the seats. Roney, the Navy guy, was already asleep all over the back seat. We knew it couldn't last.

We passed Cross City, and came into what you might call a declining sky. It looked like a tunnel that had caved in. Now, there is a little hook in the Florida coastline here, formed by Apalachee Bay. Out on the point of this bay is the town of Apalachicola, and the only place up in the middle of this empty coastal curve is the Saint Teresa Light & Mud Flats. It's a little Catholic lighthouse and mud flat, and there's not a thing out there—not even Saint Teresa, who checked out a long time ago.

By the time we got to Saint Teresa, we were in light rain. Let's say heavy rain. We looked up ahead and there was nothing but water. The curving coastline had disappeared. The Gulf of Mexico was standing on edge. Vertical.

I had been listening to all those depressing weather reports from all over the Florida panhandle. Tallahassee was saying, "Ceiling, three inches. Visibility, nine millimeters. Fog. Bubonic plague. Do not land here for six months."

Alan cried out, "Hey, there's an airport!" Trying to dump speed and altitude at the same time, I made a tight 180 at about 100 feet, thanking the old Stearman for all it had taught me and turning slightly gray at the temples.

The G load woke up our hero, returned from Danang, who was sleeping it off in the back seat. He fell into the window. He opened his eye, expecting to see the sky, and was looking down into a pine tree.

I said, "Alan, we are going to have a look at that little airstrip." The only difference between it and the rest of the swamp was that it had a windsock.

He was looking from his side on the pass. "It's very wet. I think it has fish." We flew on.

"Alan," I said, in a very casual, offhand manner, "we will try that highway to the lighthouse, but I can't seem to find it now."

"You went right over it."

"Why didn't you say something?"

"I didn't want to disturb you. Anyway, you couldn't have got into it with a torpedo."

We were flying back now, only there was no back to go. Tallahassee was saying, "Cross City, ceiling three feet. Visibility nothing. Heavy rain and high grass."

We continued back-tracking the coastline in our little slice of wet, gray sky. I decided to consult Tallahassee. The man in the safe cement tower said, "What is your exact position?" I told him I was down on the coastline by Saint Teresa and that I was about snookered. He said, "Call Tyndall Field."

Tyndall yawned and stretched and threw aside his comic book and said, "Fly arrgh rowr-rr, raarrh niner nar nar-r . . ." fade, fade, last we heard of Tyndall. Probably vectored some pelican in and left us out there on the Saint Teresa mud flats.

Speaking close to the windshield, I said, "Let us avoid any hasty decisions or gloom and look upon the brighter side of this matter. We are not lost. We have plenty of gas. We are just a little low on sky. We will proceed in an orderly, cautious fashion back in the direction of Cross City, a sound decision based on there being no other choice."

I noticed that the omni was beginning to respond to strong urgings from Cross City. A beautiful airport, abandoned, I think, the concrete checkered in rich grass. The landing was not too bad for a pilot in such a high state of thankfulness.

A little old man came out of a small hut, the only building in sight. I asked, "Is this a public building?" The little old man said, "The door is 40 inches wide. If you cannot get through it, it is no fault of mine." I knew we had a contest going.

"Where can we get the weather?"

"This is a United States Weather Bureau facility."

"Well, what's the weather?"

"I don't know. I don't give out the weather. I just record it on these instruments, for which I am paid to do by the Government."

I walked in and all around. There was a ton of weather equipment humming to itself, but no readout. "But how can we get the weather?" I asked the elf of the machines. "Well," he said with a cackle, "you could get in your airplane and spiral up and call Tallahassee, except that the weather is too bad for that. Tee hee hee."

2.

Back to Saint-Ex

After the heady business of being accepted and becoming insy with real aviation writers, I sort of lost my taw, became disoriented, sent in bad stuff that they couldn't use. Along in here Managing Editor Stephan Wilkinson got out a memo about his yet ongoing struggle to get contributors to clean up their work. The main thrust was to *not* send him 1,600 words of copy for an 800-word space, "or your copy will be subjected to my butchering, and I can't even carve a roast." I wrote back and suggested that if my copy was too long they should run it with a "continued next month," or maybe print it on a fold-out page, or better yet, run two last pages in the magazine.

Sometimes Stephan Wilkinson looks like TV's Barney Miller. In other light, he looks like a fox in a hen house. Stephan is what you could expect from sending a high-born Upstate kid to Harvard. But Stephan can't be handled here in a few glib lines. It takes the rest of the book. And then all you will know will be a few dippings into the surface of what went on between us. Nothing about why he went to sea on tankers awhile, or when the FBI was on his case because he cared about the screwing that the White Man is still giving the American Indian, or that he lives in a house empty of inside doors and full of art, a house perched high atop Storm King Mountain, where he can stand on the porch when the wind is right and piss on Manhattan, or that he rides dangerously pure motorcycles, or that he builds model airplanes, but none with machine guns on them.

The interplay between Stephan and me is much of the fun of what is going to go on from here. We were onstage with each other, playing out our roles; the Eastern literatus versus the raw Texan. What the Wilkinsword did to my copy is real enough. It was stony ground he dragged me over. But somehow, in all of it there was a sense of delight between us. Stephan is that one editor out of so many, who can cut a writer's work by half in such a way that when the writer sees it in print months later, he thinks, "Boy, I don't remember writing this that good!"

I was really floundering and saved it for a while by going back to page one of the same story I am still writing. I tapped the roots and sent Stephan "The Last Barnstormer," which *Flying* ran in February of '71. I really wanted this to be *the* story about Glenn Parker. He was the last barnstormer. He built a little tin shed and stayed and became the first FBO. In the Beaumont-Port Arthur area if you can say, "Parker taught me how to fly," it is the equivalent of saying you learned from Orville or Wilbur. Today an aging Parker comes out and sits in the sun on the bench in front of the pilots' building at BPT and watches the airplanes come and go, and it's a local honor if you can say, "Hello Mr. Parker," and he nods and calls you by name. Parker is notorious for his dry wit and for being close-mouthed. His story is rich, and legends have grown around him and his pilot son, "Bucket" Parker. But he discouraged the only foray I ever made at picking at his story. I said, "Glenn, where did you come from before you came here?" He smiled at me with those mild, twinkling blue eyes and said, "Baxter, it's been so long that even I don't remember." And his son, Bucket, is no better a source. I saw him climb out of an old Lodestar on the ramp at Lafayette one day and went up to him grinning and said, "Hi, Bucket, that your Lockheed?" To which he raised his brows and said, "What Lockheed?"

The Last Barnstormer

We were boys in the twilight of barnstorming. Maybe twice a year Jimmy and I would hear what we had been listening for—the sound of an airplane engine. "Airplane! Airplane!" Running, shouting, grabbing up the kit and bicycling down the empty country road to the long pasture . . . If the pilot was hunting a pasture, we knew he would make a pass at our field, and we knew it was best. The hungry pilot would see several that might do, but on one of them, a low windsock would suddenly appear, and two small figures marking the ends, waving white flags. We captured at least half the pilots that came to Port Arthur, and being first boys there, we automatically claimed crew rights: handing up gas and oil cans, buckling in the passengers. For this, we got at least one free ride, usually the one where the pilot "advertised," beating up Main Street with tree-top passes, Jim and I clinging in the cockpit like squirrels.

We met Pop Johnson this way, and when springtime cleared the Gulf Coast skies, we started listening for the beat of that J-5 and the straight-wing Waco. To see him slip into our field, delicately fishtail and alight on the grass filled us with ecstasy. He treated us as a lord should treat his vassals—seldom speaking, but allowing us complete freedom in touching the cream and red Waco and keeping anybody else from touching it.

We stayed in the cockpits all night, Pop warning us, "Don't let the cows eat the fabric." We had never seen any fabric-eating cows, but never doubted that they would. That Waco was so beautiful that I imagined any creature would eat it if it could. For me, flying began under the canvas cover of that Waco, slick with sweat and oil of citronella, listening to the mosquitoes and the dum-dum dit-dum of dew rolling off the trailing edge of the upper span and drumming on the lower. Holding the stick and staring at the glowing instruments, Jimmy and I followed Lindbergh across the Atlantic, flew Spads with Captain Eddie and landed F4Bs on the Saratoga with James Cagney.

To have been one of Pop's sons would have been all that life

could give. They were tall, lanky and handsome, and wore boots
and whipcord britches. They followed the plane on the ground in
a yellow Cord roadster, which was always parked near the Waco
in a circle of beautiful girls.

The Johnsons came back nearly every year. Others we saw only
once. We paid five dollars to ride in a clamoring Ford Trimotor.
We solemnly shook hands with balding, courteous Clarence
Chamberlin and rode aloft in that fabric-covered barn, the Curtiss
Condor, with its box-kite tail and bellowing Conqueror engines.
We read the magazines and built the models; we could usually
name the plane before it landed, but there were odd ones we
found hard to believe, and some questions were never answered.

One pilot landed a strange, silver-gray biplane in a bad pasture,
narrowly missing the weed-covered grave of a bootlegger. He told
us his plane was an OX Lincoln-Page. It had a radiator hung right
out in the breeze. And the first Travelair 2000 was another unknown to us. We finally asked the pilot if it was a Fokker; it looked
just like the ones in the movies. But we never asked him why he
kept a loaded revolver jammed into the tubing by the throttle.

We knew about the Liberty-engined flying boat that used to land
on Lake Sabine; we had seen them unload the heavy cases into
the speedboat, and we understood that some of the things a man
had to do to keep an airplane simply were not to be openly dis-
cussed.

And we never understood why Billy Rose would paint pictures
of scantily clad girls all over a beautiful red Stinson trimotor. We
compared the sensuous-looking Stinson, with its fat wheel pants
and bulging cowlings, to the austere Ford, and rejected it as not
being a serious airplane. But we loved the guy who always landed
his Curtiss Robin by coming in under the wires.

Then, one day, a soft-spoken man with mild blue eyes landed
a dark green cabin Waco. He built a shed, and bought a house,
and he stayed. His name was Glenn Parker. Around the Waco,
there sprung up a wiry little bird's nest of airplanes—a razor-
backed Aeronca, which crashed on the beach one day; and a
barking *eindecker* called a Buhl Pup; and a Porterfield that looked
like a fat fish; and a lean, handsome unknown that claimed to be
a Davis and looked like a biplane with no bottom wing and soon

crashed, as we fully expected it to. And then there were yellow Cubs on Parker's airport and Parker was teaching the young men of the town to fly. And after that, no more barnstormers came from out of the empty skies to the north.

    The things that just seem to happen always work out better for me than my efforts at a carefully contrived story. The night I unexpectedly got to land a Fokker-Fairchild F-27 on a short narrow strip in the forest is a prime example. In the original copy I left out all the names for fear that I might get somebody in trouble. Figuring that the statutes of limitations have surely taken effect by now, and just itching to share these characters more fully with the many people in the aviation world who should know them, let me tell you who they are. The pilot of the F-27 is the legendary "Big Deal" Goodwin; his copilot, that fair red head, is Mike Boyette; and the scene was the Eastex-Time-Life private strip at Evadale, Texas. Mike and "Deal" still fly side by side, same company, only the Fokker is a jet now, and Mike keeps his old blind Cessna 195 and a Stearman hid out at Kirbyville. Evadale is just a few miles straight through the wooded swampland from my wilderness home on Village Creek, and on a clear, still morning I can hear them fire up the Fokker jet or the turbo Beech and depart for faraway places.

As a barefoot boy with cheek, I would stand beside the airport fence and watch the mighty DC-3 airliners come boring in from faraway places and land with a chirp and a puff of smoke and taxi up to the gate. And I would look at those cool heroes way up high in the nose and wonder how they could do it. And now in my middling years, having landed many lovely Cessnas, (If you can drive you can fly), and floated to grass in Cubs, and even come down bareback astride snorting Stearmans, I still marvel at those heroes sitting way out there in the nose who can gently land tons of airplane with the wheels way back there behind them feeling for the cement. I have always wondered, how can they do it? Could I do that? What a great thing it must be.

And so it came to pass that I was deadheading home one dark night in a Fairchild F-27 of the executive configuration. In its airline suit the F-27 is a great goose of an airplane, high of wing, long of leg, twin Rolls turbo props, and about 40 people at about 40,000 pounds.

This F-27 has seats for about half that many within its paneled compartments. Each seat a reclining, swivel throne attended by stereo, monogramed lap robes, playing cards and napkins and 12-year-old Scotch. The captain is a wise old bird with miles of skies behind his eyes about whom legends have sprung up; that when he rings his cowbell over the mike certain Texas towers automatically give him clearances and terminal forecasts.

I was fast asleep on a soft lounge, barefooted and weary when the last VIP deplaned and the captain invited me to the flight deck for the home base leg. It was the copilot who stood up while I, murmuring very small protests, sunk into the deep leather of the right seat and curled my bare toes over the broad cool rudder pedals. To my sleep-fogged mind the instrument panel seemed to come over the top of my head and looked like the Las Vegas Strip on New Year's night. Lots of bright, squirrelly lights, but no message.

We roared away on takeoff and in a climbing turn over the pitch black forest the captain said, "You got it."

Rather than disturb a professional airplane at its work, I just pretended to fly. The Fairchild, that great honest stable long-necked high-tailed goose of a Fairchild, just kept at its business, a normal climb and turn. A regular Eagle Scout of an airplane. As altitude and heading came up I apologetically rolled it into level cruise, and was rewarded with a bonus balloon of an extra thousand feet of altitude. The thing was bubbling with lift.

As we approached home plate, which is about a 3,000-foot gash in the piney woods, the captain told me to descend to pattern altitude and set up a 180-degree overhead approach. It looked awfully black and bottomless down there, but I employed all my great skill as an eight hour instrument student and started letdown, listening for the scrape of tree limbs. But by the time we had rolled through the turns and woke up the forest creatures for miles around, I was starting to enjoy myself. It flew just like an airplane.

On final I looked at those awfully short rows of converging yellow lights on the horizon and I was glad it was him and not me that was going to have to get all this whistling slick tonnage stopped in that little notch in the pines.

I kept waiting for him to take it, instead he asked if I was going to let the crosswind carry us over into the next county. Without thinking I crossed it up a little, a slight slip, a little skid. It responded just like a wayward Stearman. The copilot had done the flap and gear things, the captain was milking off power, the short rows of lights were rushing up at over 100 knots. "C'mon fellas, enough!" "You got it. Land it. It's just an airplane."

What happened next took just a few seconds. I know I never tried to look at the panel, but all of the feel of flying that I have ever done was flowing out of me and into that thick control wheel, and the F-27 is a feel airplane. I felt the sink begin and it felt just right to land short. I eased the off rudder and she swung a little, matching centerline to center of runway. I let the wing stay down for the drift, we were rushing over tree tops. The captain was crooning to me like a mother to her baby, "Nose up a little, that's a good boy, little more, hold now. . . ." I lifted the wing to level and from somewhere way back down there and behind us the tandem gear went "chunk-chunk!" We were on, solid and short. I wanted to cheer, to dance in the aisle. I don't know when I have ever felt such elation in my life.

It was a shoo-in, of course, with them managing the power, and I bet his hands were curled around that yoke, but I had done it. Landed a transport plane, and in the dark, crosswind, short field and barefooted at that! When we got to the barn I said, "Do you know what this has meant to me?" And the captain said, "Why do you think I wanted to share it with you?"

June of 1971 saw my first real feature story, about Reading, and I was still off stride. Archie Trammell sent it back about four times, as I recall, and patiently worked with me until I got it right. His comment was "It sounds more like a compilation of facts and figures. Go on, loosen up, have fun with it." The story here got a few cheers from the New York office but brought down the wrath of Harold Serpas, the DC-3 pilot featured therein. Harold knew I was stretching the truth about his activities at Reading and thought I was poking fun at him. This is as good a time as any to offer Serpas the olive branch and publicly say that he is a most widely respected pilot, heads up the flight operations of the Aviation Office of America, knows more FARs by heart than a whole room full of ATC controllers, and woe to the hapless controller who gives Serpas a sloppy vector as he steers AOA's showcase BAC 111 across the nation. What I am trying to say is I was only kidding in the part here about the biffy.

Reading

There I was, down in Texas writing about airplanes in a shopping guide for bewildered housewives. "Come with us," said FLYING Magazine, "and write about the Reading Show."

And so it came to pass that in the month of June Serpas was bringing us up over the mountains to Reading in the DC-3. I flew a leg over the Pennsylvania farmlands and thought of Ernie Gann's writing about this historic route in the early chapters of *Fate is the Hunter.* I was sort of reliving it; Ernie didn't have the smog or the traffic then, but I had the rest of it. I had Serpas, who kept looking pointedly at the compass and over at me, and finally said, "This is as far south as I want to get on this heading."

I lost Serpas and the -3 in the crowd on the ground. The last I saw of him, he was walking across a field of 10,000 airplanes trying to get his biffy emptied. Then I was up against the rope with the crowd, head back, gaping at a little yellow biplane in the sky, twisting upward like a leaf in smoke.

At the top of it, the biplane died and jerked and flip-flopped like a hooked perch; then it came twisting down very close to the grass, and the crowd let out a sound like the falling plane. The Expert turned to me and said "That's Mary Gaffaney. Now she's really in it. She always starts cold, too high. She's ground-shy at first, but she's in it now. God!"

I watched the little Pitts going for more, listened to it sing, tried to imagine what sort of a woman Mary Gaffaney must be to do that. With man-logic, I decided that she must be flat, muscular, perhaps with a faint mustache. When I met her later, I was too embarrassed to think of anything to say. She reminded me of my Mom at the peak of her pie-making and singing-in-the-kitchen days. She looked more like a contestant for a Betty Crocker prize than a member of the U.S. National Aerobatic Team. Whom can you trust?

Later, I went out to where Art Scholl was getting ready. The de Havilland was parked in the grass; Art was standing on the wing root. There was a wind coming down off the mountains. The lesser men in clean white shirts were indistinct in the background. I got the feeling that Art and his airplane were alone, always.

I was struck with how much he resembled the de Havilland. Both were hard-framed, muscles stretching to cover. The broad forehead and bulbous canopy; the wide-apart, deep-set eyes; the wings grown long to catch the last vestiges of lift. They were oiling each other. His words were few, and they rang like tools dropped in an empty hangar at night.

There was a cold fury in his passage across the field inverted, holding it down until the engine rattled and smoked. The Expert turned to me and shuddered. "He always does that, holds it down until the engine rattles and smokes." I'd rather think it was Art's laughter, cold and hard through bared white teeth, drifting back across the field.

Then the company pilots were doing it for Cessna and Citabria, and they were excellent pilots. Anyone is who can take a training plane that is the end product of 30 years of trying to achieve flight stability and coax it to roll over on its back. The gallant announcer gave the various maneuvers proper names, but they were all just different ways of falling. Stripes do not a tiger make.

I turned my head and in my mind I pictured a Citabria with open cockpits—a parasol monoplane like the old Davis. And had fantasies of a two-hole Cessna Agwagon with wheel pants. (I design a lot of sporty airplanes for these giants of America's aviation industry, but they aren't ready for me yet. I even have one for Beech; it's a biplane, called the New Travelaire 2000.)

It seemed as though there was always an F-4 Phantom off the end of the runway at Reading. The Thunderbirds were having their troubles getting their big jet fighters planted on Reading's short, curly, early-American runway. There's nothing that looks so embarrassed as one of the world's most versatile fighter planes sitting among the cabbages.

After the third day, they did not rise again. Nobody said much about it, because the Thunderbirds are honestly among the Unknockables. Anyway, with the present budget crunch upon the Air Force I suspect they were taking all those blown tires out of a captain's pay. And anyone who has seen those Phantoms coming droop-snooted out of the haze from the four points of the compass can never forget it. They meet at midfield with a clap of thunder in your belly and go straight up on a thick column of smoke that flares into a *fleur de lis* at the top. Then one more screeches up the stem and leaves a climbing corkscrew of spiral white smoke that grows out of the center of the lily and upward into the infinity of the sun.

One day, I caught the T-Bird act from out in midfield with their official photographer.

"You film everything they do?"

"Everything. And it ain't film, it's video tape. We can't afford film any more."

"What do you do with the tapes?"

"That, my friend, is what famed Thunderbirds do at night. They look at these tapes. And you ought to be a fly on the wall and hear one of those sessions. Oh, boy!"

An F-4 had landed and taxied up within nudging distance of us. "I think he wants to turn around where we are standing," I said.

"Hell with 'im. He knows I'm ordered to be in this spot."

The video camera stayed skyward, and the giant, slab-sided fighter groaned on by, roaring like a boiler, wheels gouging up asphalt. It slowly turned around us, the pilot fixing us with a steady glare, as though he wished his guns were loaded. The photographer smiled at him. Some things never change.

Now, I have not left out Bob Hoover. When they hear the moan of Hoover's P-51, it empties the tent. The pitchmen stare at each other awhile across empty aisles, and Hoover rattles the hangar roof, then even they abandon their posts to come out and watch. Those middle-aged death-wish guys who flew in their own WW II fighters stop polishing chrome and stare up too, and somebody says, "There goes Bob Hoover," and they watch, licking their dry lips, knowing in the gut that if they had the airplane to do this and if they tried it they would die in it.

After Hoover has done all those symphonies and painting in the P-51, he drops briefly to earth and ascends again in that big twin-engine Shrike, and he does it all over again—only more so, because your mind just can't accept a light twin coming in on final with both props feathered and suddenly pulling up into a loop, and a slow roll, then flaring out to land delicately on one wheel.

I rode with Hoover and wrote a story about it for the daily newspaper published by FLYING at the Reading Show. Bob Parke, editor and publisher of FLYING, stood me in front of the editors and writers whom I had only admired from afar, and he laid hands upon me and intoned, "This is my beloved son, in whom I am well pleased." He presented me with a hastily scribbled name tag showing all the world that I belonged to FLYING. All the famous writers began to speak to me with "Hiya kid," and things like that, and they let me borrow their typewriters and flasks. I went forthwith into the great exhibit hangar and swaggered around, indicating that if the various manufacturers played their cards right, I could do great things for them.

At the close of the first day, this new power had gained me a litter bag full of plastic trivets, key chains, color fold-out brochures, and the undivided attention of Jim Bede.

Hoping for a quick follow-up to reinforce my narrow foothold as a sure-'nuff writer, I kept reporting in at the FLYING snake pit, where, among other things, the official *Reading Daily* was crammed into print.

"How about a story on the homebuilt guys? They're all way down at the other end of the line in the orphan's compound with those beautiful little airplanes, giving away homemade cake and just dying for a little affection."

"Yup, yup, we'll see about it, if we got room after the big story on the new Grandiose Turbo Bizjet."

"How about this one? I saw Mr. Piper himself sneaking into the

Windecker Eagle. He got inside and looked all around and bounced up and down on the seats."

"Sure kid, sure . . ."

Finally, I got my big break: "Go find Jim Bede and do us a bit on the BD-4, his first production model. It's due here any minute."

Knowing best-seller material when I see it, I headed out of the Ziff-Davis trailer, past all the weird-looking types that cluttered up the place. Shoved my way through throngs of middle-aged Midwesterners wearing walking shorts and those funny little caps that private pilots are supposed to wear. They were strolling around looking at million-dollar Grandiose Jets and $5,000 transponders with the keys to T-crafts in their pockets. I made a mental note to do a brilliant article on how general aviation's great show is county-fair exciting.

I found Bede, still under the tent, sweating, talking, with a fair-sized tip standing around watching him instantly assemble a wing for the BD-4. Artfully insinuating myself into Bede's confidence, he let me in behind the counter, where I stood smiling, holding up one end of the wing spar while we assembled it for a new group.

Bede agreed to let me be the first writer to ever fly the first production BD-4. He said there had been a slight delay, but that the plane would arrive in two hours. Additional delays consumed the rest of the afternoon, but I had a firm appointment for a flight in the early-morning dew.

I skipped the big party that night, to be fresh for Bede, marveling that FLYING would let a beginner handle the risky assignment.

The days drifted by. I spent a lot of time hanging around the runway watching skyward for my BD-4 to come in. At last, I hurried to the FLYING trailer, and found it dark and empty, a crew taking down the beach umbrellas where we'd had all the good times, the stacking of metal chairs echoing like laughter.

The last air show ended, leaving shreds of smoke and thunder drifting across the valley, and suddenly I saw thousands of guys running. They were running across the grass and deserted runways to all those little planes parked out there, each wanted to be first to get out. The sound of ten thousand Continentals and Lycomings and Franklins began to fill the air, and the shapes and shadows were moving across the field like a kicked-over ant nest. With a chill, I realized I was watching the greatest show of all, the tremendous movement of the little guys, actually visible at last! Together, they could have swarmed and carried off a 747, vortices and all; or an upside-down FAA wedding cake, leaving not a crumb. It was awesome!

There was nobody left at the fence but me and the Expert, who turned to me and said, "You should have been here in the good ole days when they used to turn them all loose at once."

"Tell me, Expert," I said, "who are you, anyway?"

"Only a pilot for the whiskey company that always wins the trophy for the best corporate airplane. I just ferried in next year's winner for storage. They'll start to wax it as soon as they get the hangar cleared out."

Then, high over the mountains, I saw the winking lights of the old DC-3. It was Serpas. He'd been gone a week; he'd missed the whole show.

"Serpas, where have you been?"

"To Pittsburgh."

"Why Pittsburgh?"

"To get the biffy emptied. Why else would anybody go to Pittsburgh?"

We flew grandly off to Texas, and I told him stories about the Reading Air Show for the next eight hours until he had tears in his eyes and had to open the window, so great was his desire to get back to Reading this year.

After Reading '71 I was still dried up. After New York kindly but promptly rejected a few more wrong stories I got the great "Bax, where are you?" memo from Wilkinson. Now all the New York staff will work with a writer to help him improve his stuff, but mostly they use the blue pencil so quietly and make my writing flow so smoothly that when I read it in the magazine later I think I did it. Not Stephan. Like Zorro, the Wilkinsword always leaves his mark on the body. He is the one in ten thousand who can razor my work or razz my mind and get improvement. He is, in a word, an Editor. The bastard.

In the memo Stephan began by saying, "Perhaps you are trying to write like you think we want you to write . . ." He had nailed it. In my identity crisis after the string of rejections I had gone back through and carefully read back issues of the magazine to try to find out what a writer for *Flying* sounded like. And that is not what they ever wanted of me. Stephan wrote, "We miss the wind in the wires, the prop blast and the oil on the windshield, we miss the scent of when the clover kisses the tires. Bax, where are you? Come back, we miss you."

Right after that I went out to M&M Air Service and asked George Mitchell if I could fly the old two-holer. Walked softly out through the springtime and into the big shed full of Stearmans and climbed into old N59977, thinking that this plane was born in the '40s, during the war, and here, 30 years later, it was still doing the job it was designed to do: teach pilots how to fly. I strapped on my helmet and goggles and called "contact!" and the big radial coughed and rumbled and came smoking to life. Same 300 Lycoming that Loyd Hood had been installing in it when I made the last picture of him. I warned up the oil a while, then plumed a long tail of dust down Mitchell's dirt strip and climbed for the heavens. Got up to where it was cold and clear, cinched down the belt one more time and snapped it over and wrote glory in the sky.

We came sighing back to earth after a time. I felt like I had been to church. You really *can* smell the clover crushed from the tire. I swung round, let it idle a while just hearing, then shut her down and listened to the tink tink of the cooling manifold joints. Climbed down and came foot scuffing up behind M&M's sheds where they keep all the scrap, the junk and empty chemical drums. I walked past the pitiful little pickup truckload of what had been Loyd's Stearman. For the first time I stopped and looked at it. There was blood, darkly dried in the crumpled sun and rain weathered cockpit section. And the story welled up in me. "Dear Loyd . . ." It was almost like the printing of most private thoughts. A communion between pilots. I didn't think *Flying* would print it because we don't like to run stories about crashed airplanes or dead pilots by name. But they never changed a word of it.

Dear Loyd:

They started planting rice this week, and I thought of you. The clover is up, and the wheels leave tracks in it, and the smell of fresh clover comes up into the cockpit with the exhaust. Everybody was up. There were Stearmans all over the sky, clean and yellow, fresh from the winter shop. It was one of the first warm, sunny days, and all the engines were good.

I took the two-holer up to 5,000. Just let her take her own good, sweet time, watching the black shadows of the N struts move across the lower bay. Just sat there resting my hand on the laced leather cockpit rim. Once, I put my hand down and felt her fabric against the stringers. She's alive. I looked at her as though I had never seen her before. Sunlight in the cockpit, the lower wing-fitting bolt that you can see from inside, the lift curve of the bottom of her wing, light and shadows on the stitching.

At five, in the fresh cold, I laid her over. Put the center-section strut flat on the horizon, and she went around very tightly and bobbed in her wake. It was better to the left. We were all alone. I pushed her nose over, floated up against the harness, held her, looking at farms until I heard that sound in the wires, then pulled about two Gs in a great, glorious loop.

Then I guess I just lost myself in being a part of it all. The roar, the shriek, the taut wings full of lift. Chain-looped until I lost count, then inverted wingovers, then all-the-way overs, letting her die off at the top with a plume of gas off the center section. She would float up there, belly up, with her arms out, and then we would be diving again. In the pull-outs, I would lay my head back and yell "Yaa-zooooo!" It wasn't anything out of the book, it was just smooth ups and overs, whatever she wanted to do. I lost track of time and place until the needle went below two, then I just closed the throttle and curved it around in a long dive home, listening to the wires. God, it was beautiful. It was flying.

I parked behind the hopper truck and laid under the wing in the grass and watched the guys in the 450s come and go. Some came over and had a quick smoke, with goggle prints deep on their faces and first sunburn. Everybody felt good.

Later, I went into the pilot's room and had coffee with Earl, listening to the big 450s shake the building. You remember my story about the Wide Job that they printed last year? Well, George cut it out of the magazine, and had it framed with the cover of FLYING, and it's hanging on the wall. It reminded me of you. Between the time you helped me write it and it was published, you went in.

It seemed strange to hear your name in the pilot's room. You know how we never talk about a guy that's gone in. I mean, everybody will kid you for pranging one—they'll even come out to the hospital and kid you. And old Orine in the fabric shop will save a piece of the wreck and write a poem about you on it, and hang it up in his "Hall of Fame." But when a guy is gone, well, what can you say?

It was kind of strained, but Earl and I tried to remember. We know you came out to the airport as a real young kid, and Poley hired you as a flag boy, and he grew to love you. And that your Daddy had died and you had quit school very early to earn wages. We were not sure how much you could read or write. We got to wondering how you passed your commercial. Somebody said your wife read the book to you and you memorized the entire FARs. It doesn't matter. At the funeral, your pastor said you came to him when you were troubled and he would read you scripture and you memorized it on the spot. And he loved you. Hell, we all did. You were so good-humored and good-looking, and such a good mechanic and loved flying so much.

When we got to talking about the work you did on the Wide Job, everybody remembered. Earl said you did most of the engineering and all of the welding and metal work. We remembered you laying chalk lines on the shop floor and designing and building an airplane that successfully worked an almost double payload. And the day the FAA came out to jack a six-G load on your engine truss ring, and all the tubing stood up until the jack raised the hangar roof and bent the girders.

It was an all-new airplane that was in perfect rig from the day it rolled out of the shop. Loyd, when I think of it, I wonder what you could have done if you had lived, and had a college degree.

But you had five seasons of flying them in the summer and building them in the winter. And you had the love of Gerry and the kids. A lot of guys exist for a lifetime and never live that much.

Anyway, they're planting again, and the clover is green on the strip. You can smell it taxiing. We wanted you to have this. George will put it on the wall beside the story of the airplane you built, with your name at the end. Loyd Hood, Pilot.

Still feeling disenfranchised and moon-eyed, I later went out to the grass airport and flew Pappy's old 172 in the dark. You can tell I had been reading Saint-Exupéry again.

Nighthawk

The night was hushed, soft as velvet. One tall window in the old airport building was yellow-lighted. The rotating beacon on top swept its light across sleeping airplanes on the flight line; metal glinted cold.

By flashlight and by touch I crept around the friendly old bird, then sat awhile in the dark cabin, in the musty aluminum-tobacco-gasoline smells, reaching out.

I remembered the story about the student who carried a flashlight with a magnetized base and carefully laid it on the cowl beside the compass, and for the rest of that night all he could find with his compass was his flashlight.

I remembered my first night flight. My instructor and I got lost. We flew toward Lufkin, which is about north, and the lights of Lufkin grew and grew until they filled the horizon and became Houston, which is about east. Nonetheless, we seemed closer in the dark cockpit than two men do in the daylight, and his voice carried clear as he passed along the hard-earned lessons of pilot lore. About the hidden night clouds, and how one light on the ground will betray you into vertigo, and to "curve in a little on final, and carry a little power till you're in."

The first time alone when the edge of night came forbidding,

like flying into wrongness. Dusk deepening on the earth below while I was still aloft in distant, lonely light. And of how cities hundreds of miles apart glowed upon the horizon, and how easy it was to find other planes. Delta cleared down to six was that winking red beacon descending, and Braniff reporting on frequency was that distant star. Once, in a bunch of them, I said, "and that's me, the low and slow one." And a big voice chuckled softly and said, "Gotcha." Even the voices are softer on a clear night.

Our grass airport is black as the pits of hell. Coming home when the beacon is out, you steer for the only place in town where there are no lights at all and tell yourself clearly that you do know how to let yourself down into there.

You know because you have practiced. Practiced going to coal-black on takeoff, practiced landing with the light until you are good enough to pretend the landing light has failed, then practiced with it switched off, feeling all your flying senses prickle alive as you settle dark between those pale runway eyes.

And practicing tonight, yes—and for the love of it, too. Taxiing slow, watching nested nighthawks start up and swerve away on bladed wings. On takeoff, the old Cessna is enveloped in lift at once; the wings feel as though they grow out from my shoulders. The night air is full of lift.

I am a tiny green light and a red light droning softly over my sleeping city. Even the junkyards are lovely. It's all so peaceful and orderly from here, like God had stayed over from Easter morning and got it all together for once. The wings are so fat with lift, there is no sense of motion. I may park it here and climb out and stroll up and down on that broad wing and have a good cigar and contemplate the ancient stars.

In the summer of '71 Stephan went through another of his spasms to try to clean up the literature in our trade paper. In a memo to all he put his sword to buzz words and clichés. Banned were: name of the game, state of the art, would you believe, verrrry interesting, beautiful downtown anywhere, "and any other TV birthed catchphrase," no way, and ball of

wax ("unless you are writing about Madame Tussaud's"), department (as in a vast improvement in the airplane's roll department), wise (as in roll-wise). I memoed back to the Wilkinsword and told him I thought he had the courage of a lion to set foot where the hand of man has never trod in such shark infested waters.

3.

Never Take Pictures at Noon

For February of 1972 I had reverted to type again and had sent Stephan the Basic Bax Story—about Stearmans, grass airports and the love of it all. He bought it and even paid for some art work to go with it. Since grown men must not risk too much show of affection, he later sent me the original painting of the Stearman with an offhand memo saying that they just happened to be helping Creative Director Bud Loader clean some junk out of his office and found this picture and thought I might want to hang it in my war room. That is the equivalent of awarding a matador the ears and tail. I hung it on the wall with my autographed pictures of Minnie Pearl, Roy Clark and Al Mooney.

Graduation Day

I have graduated, I have grown antlers, I have soloed a 450 Bull Stearman at last! After all those good years flying Mitchell's two-holer—that lovely, muley 220 Stearman—flying it until we wore out the 220 and replaced it with a Lycoming 300. That made it hornier, but did not unlock the secrets of what happens when you line up one of those stubby, big-engined blind bats on the strip and open the throttle on 450 horses. But most of the 450s are working airplanes, single-seaters, and there are some manners to consider before asking a man to let you go out and play with a $20,000 ag plane just to see if you can hack it.

Then there appeared a brand-new 450 two-holer, the Bull Stearman, built in a Winnie, Texas, bowling alley by Jeff Jenkins and Ronnie Langlois—Jeff who was begat of Mitchell, Ronnie who was begat of Spartan and Glen Parker (who was the begatter of us all). Winnie is a wide spot in the Gulf Coast rice fields, a place of 2,500 souls and six airports and three ag operations, where these two young men have built a dozen immaculate ag Stearmans, and where American Dusters sends students to graduate.

The 450 two-holer is for graduation day the Homecoming Queen.

Ronnie said, "She's a cherry—the last of Glen Parker's new ones. She was still in the cosmoline. We built our jig from her frame." Ronnie and Jeff say they'll never run out of Stearmans. "We got 10 more hid out in barns, and all the jigs and dies and fixtures. With a load of pipe and a handful of welding rod, we can build them from scratch."

She stood there in the grass and the sun at the end of a double row of single-seat sisters. Chrome yellow, white side panels, looking short-coupled and deep-chested like they do when they put in the 450 P&W and set it well back to keep the balance. Sun danced off the wires and chromed engine parts. That engine, its naked roundness standing out beyond the lines of the fuselage: It was scaring me to death just looking up at it.

In the cockpit, wood-grained panels, new leather-laced coamings, polished wooden stick and even a "self-commencer," as the Cajuns say—a starter. Down the line of planes, pilots were climbing into cockpits, engines starting, wings rocking, cocky, brave, blatting away. Cherish this: Few men yet look down a row of biplanes from the cockpit.

Jeff was telling me the power settings. The blown P&W will rave up to 38 inches and nearly 3,000 rpm on takeoff, but you only need 27 inches and 1,900 for fast cruise. I was writing it on the back of my hand.

"Let me give you a piece of paper."

"No, man, I want it where I can find it." I asked Jeff what to expect, what to use over the fence. He just grinned. "She'll tell you. You'll really be surprised." That's what I was afraid of.

The starter whined, the big, flat Hamilton windmilled, caught, chopped smoke and the engine settled down, going "bloopa, bloopa, ker-bloopa" deep in her throat, rocking the biplane on her tires. I touched the throttle like it was a serpent, taxied the thing like it was made of blown glass.

The mystery of takeoff had always been how much swerve to expect. The surprise was the unbelievable roar and force of the prop blast. My Bell was trying to fly my head off my neck, I was wishing I had the seat a notch lower, and we were long gone, a pursuit ship, climbing on solid power, wings angled up where other planes stall.

Level now, a feeling of tearing along, airspeed reading 125, the big P&W rumbling, loafing. She sailed up in wingovers like a kite, begging to barrel roll. She nibbled at stalls, burbled, then said "oh, well" and sunk flat. Power-on stalls were pointless, prop-hanging being such an awkward feeling. Jeff tapped his helmet, took it, slowed down and gently snap rolled. Gently. Right around that big engine. But there was no use postponing the moment of truth. Sooner or later, I was going to have to try to land all this.

I arced around for the grass, slipping to find it, to see past Jeff and all those wings and wires and engine parts, feeling her, never looking at the panel. She told me what she needed. We slipped over the fence, lined up true, and she came to nest like a warm dove in the hand. I couldn't believe it. Two more and Jeff made the four-oh sign with his hand and I stopped and let him out. "She's yours. Go up and use her."

Alone, my heart was a song. We climbed up to where it was cold. The sun was low and red, bathing the cockpit, glinting off the windshields and wires. Earth and sky tumbled, we sang, we roared, we made music and love until we were drunk with it all.

Then we chain-looped down, and sighed in over the grass and met our long shadow. I parked her in the row with her sisters, hating to turn off the sound of that great-hearted horse of an engine. The 450 is for the Stearman made. I just sat there. A pilot came by and grinned at me, knowing. I reached out my arms, hugging and patting the round of her fuselage. He laughed.

In the pilots' room with coffee and the strong, lean faces, I felt I had graduated. I was one of them. And now I want to share it with you. I hope you can come out of your flying Chevrolets someday and know all of this, for this is not business, not transportation, or towers or concrete or numbers. This, dear hearts, is flying.

In March I sent Stephan the same story again. Only this time, along with the love of it and flying being more than anything else, an experience in beauty, the main thrust of "The New-comer" is to note the peculiar leveling effect that little airports have on all persons, regardless of what social or economic status they come through the gate with. I think if I ever had anything to say about flying I said it here.

The Newcomer

The low-time student pilot curves forward over the controls as if diminishing the inches between his nose and the windshield will bring the answer he is seeking a few moments sooner. Within the past hour, he has found his way 50 miles beyond the horizon and successfully landed at a strange airport and located the men's room and then the coffee pot, holding his cup with shaking hands, hoping no one would guess that this was his first cross-country solo.

Now, before him lie the fields of home, dappled in sun and shadow. The pasture where he hunted rabbits and looked up with longing at planes in the sky is passing below. Now it is he who has the view of the hawk. He wipes his palm on his thigh and reaches for the mike, rehearsing his speech. On the ground, he will play it like Ernie Gann said pilots are supposed to. He'll stroll in and hand over the keys and they will say, "Where you been?" And he will say, "Don't know. I was lost the whole time." And they will grin and his heart will swell around the word inside his chest. "Pilot. Pilot. I am a pilot!"

Spring will be approaching as you lay aside this magazine, and if you are lucky and live in Nowheresville, as most of us do, you'll drive out to that little airport where you'll find an old building and an assorted group of very contented-looking men, perhaps a girl or two. They will ignore your arrival, so you must announce to no one, "Who do I talk to about learning to fly?" Conversation will cease, and they will turn and smile upon you warmly, and the hungriest-looking one of the lot will introduce himself and take you at once out to the airplane.

In time, you will come to know that there is a separate, distinct and never fully described social order that begins and ends at the edge of little airports. First, you will find a total honesty, found elsewhere only among small boats and men who take them to sea. The reasons for the honesty are the same: The element is hostile to the unfit men and vessels. They perish.

Secondly, you will find democracy as Jefferson dreamed of it. The plant manager you couldn't even get an appointment to see will sit and talk with you for hours in the shade of the wing of his proud Bonanza. And have you ever wondered who cures the doctor? You'll know when he invites you to come with him in his Mooney on his Tuesday off. Finally, the neighborhood barn-raising spirit of frontier America still lives when the guy gets the cowling off his Piper and finds himself in a circle of eager eyes and willing hands.

So now you and the hungry-looking man are standing beside an innocent little Cessna. On this very first ride, you will be in the pilot's seat, and he'll be telling you the things you need to know as you need to know them. "Now first, this here is what we call the fuselage . . ." In the beginning—even as it was told to him, years ago.

When you have descended from the skies on this first day, and on all the days thereafter, you will no longer be able to remember whatever it was that troubled you before you left the ground. And you will come to know that flying little airplanes from grass fields is, more than anything else, an experience in beauty.

Stephan finally gagged, and I suffered the withdrawal pains of not being in the April and May issues, I also got this memo from the Wilkinsword:

Steer clear of conventions and dusters for awhile, though; what with Flying Farmers, and those broads who race (the 99's), plus the dusters, we've had enough of the former to hold us, and you know what a hard time we have getting you to talk about anything but Stearmans.

How about some pieces on the little guys—the Aeronca owner who owns a piece of an Esso station, the man who manages to keep a Luscombe in license on a $7,000 a year salary (or am I showing my New York naiveté by quoting a figure that most people find sufficient to fly a 182), the friendly 50 year old out at the airport who has only seen a transponder when he pressed his nose up against the side window of the twin that got lost and landed by mistake at his field one day last summer? I don't know what pieces, or how, but this is an area comparatively untapped by us Eastern snobs. Have at it.

Best,
Stephan Wilkinson
Managing Editor.

Actually this was the germ of a long running and happy new series that we were to call "Life At Little Airports," but here was my immediate reply to Stephan, who responds coolly, if at all, to being called Steve:

Right, Steve-o, but I sure will miss doing the Flying Morticians. . . . 'Well, for one thing, sir, the passengers don't keep settin' up asking whur we are . . .'

But how is this? I got a line on a Mr. Sam Smite, paraplegic operator of a septic tank cleaning firm, owns a single engine Cessna 310. Said, 'Line boys always look so surprised when I taxi up with that empty nacelle, but as I always say, handicapped airplanes for handicapped folks, eh?' Smite's plane is equipped with a hand cranked Narco, says his lifelong ambition is to fly into JFK at the six-P.M. rush hour, says he wants to assert his Constitutional rights.

Went up to an old codger peering in the window of a twin, like you said. Asked him if he had ever seen a transponder before. Answer was short. Two words. Last one was "off!" Turns out he was a retired Braniff captain, come to repossess the airplane.

Best,
Bax.

Then, somewhat in anger and resentment, I went into the most cold, sterile, scientific atmosphere I could find and did Stephan a story called "Flight (Simulated)."

Flight (Simulated)

The tour bus took us over gray, anonymous freeways, past windowless factories and curved rows of suburban boxes, out to where the deer and the antelope used to play, and where today Dallas begins to flow into Fort Worth. There lies an unfinished superairport, roughly the size of Ohio, bearing the unworkable name of Greater Southwest International. Located somewhere in its cement maze, via tunnels under the runways, is the American Airlines Flight Academy. It's about the size of Dayton.

They set us down in front of one of those instant-landscape complexes of low, white, space-age buildings—the sort of place where, as you drift soundlessly down endless corridors, trailing germs, you keep listening for the theme music from *2001.* I fought off the strange sensation that we were all done in HO gauge and mounted in silhouette on plywood.

Our hostesses, uniformly beautiful little Barbie Dolls, spoke in throaty recorded messages as they led us by vast white rooms filled to the ceiling with surgically removed nose sections of familiar old jet-transport friends, now called CPTs (cockpit trainers); the human is installed for the required hours until his hands can find fuel, flaps and fubar as surely as they used to fly to cigarettes and mouth. Prior to this eerie simulator stage, the human is preprogrammed in an automated, push-button, tape-readout, failsafe classroom, where he gets feel-see-hear hours learning each lever in the cockpit.

But the classroom concept and its mocked-up millions of dollars of aircraft systems is already obsolete. The new pilot-teaching system will be *mano a mano*: a little cubby with two projection screens for eyes, so that each member of the new generation of males, preconditioned to group-think, can travel at his own speed, under his own little hood. At designated intervals, the glassy-eyed one is removed and seated at a tandem console with the instructor, who sets the student on fast rewind, then plays him back to determine if he's retaining the required percentages.

During his confinement at the Academy, the human is under constant surveillance by the Health Maintenance Building. "We have too much invested in our people to wait until they get sick to do something about it." So Big Brother in a white coat catches samples off your tongue on Monday morning and measures the intensity and duration of the gleam in your eye on Friday afternoon.

The hostess reeled off a list of airlines who have contracted to have crews trained at the Academy. I think she named them all but Ajax, Pan Am and Aeroflot. The list did include Air Force One, and if you buy a Cessna Citation, part of the package is the Academy course for two pilots and one mechanic. They are returned to your home town with an I.D. card that tells you who they were. Actual specimens sighted in the corridors were early middle-aged, tummy up, chin out, 1942 haircuts and wearing company raincoats inside the building. The faces were all Clark Kent.

Final processing comes in the flight simulators, which cost more than the entire Army Air Corps of 1939 and fly better. The crew enters a complete nose section of a 747 and it unports. Standing free over a yawning pit of criss-crossed hydraulic legs and swaying an elephantine umbilical cord beneath, the skull of the 747 flies away, humming, wagging, yawing.

As the pilot taxis out onto the active and takes off to fly the pattern, he gets all the sensations and sights of actual flight. What he sees is projected onto a white screen hung out in front of the windscreen like a bulldozer blade. Projectors on the cabin roof are showing pictures taken by a battery of cameras, in a separate room, with more eyes than a mad spider. This device is grazing over a scale-model relief map of the airport and surrounding terrain, which can produce its own weather conditions, fog and low ceilings, and can light up and twinkle at night.

We saw a from-the-cockpit film of a simulated missed approach; fog rolled in and the airport went to zero just as we passed the middle marker. It was so real that several instrument-rated pilots in the audience had to be excused. I fled the place after a

747 cabin-evacuation demonstration. With more people in the cabin than Travis had in the Alamo, and just as much bad news, they plan to get everybody over the wall in 90 seconds. I couldn't find my shoes in that much time.

Back home, I slipped into the hangar and went up to my Stearman. I stood in the puddle of oil under the engine and put my arms around her. "Baby," I whispered, "Hold me close. Our days are numbered."

The June '72 issue also carried my last feature on the Reading Air Show. The way we get out a timely June story about a June event in a magazine that has a 60-day lead time is that the story is about last year's show. This one was about as much fun as I ever had being with our people at Reading.

There was a side-bar story attached to this one, in what we call a "box". It was a prophetic little account of my being charmed by Jim Bede and hanging around waiting for Bede to do what he said he was going to do. Jim is an aviation entrepreneur, a man of projects and promises long known in aviation.

At the Reading Show

The Reading show may be the only place in the world where you can look up and see the world's only turboprop DC-3 flying formation with a P-51 while a Hawker Sea Fury makes a pursuit curve on them and nobody's paying any attention. Reading may be the only airport where you turn base so far out you get lost on final; or be number 15 to land behind a de Havilland and a Messerschmitt and have the tower advise you of jet traffic landing to your right on a converging runway, and never mind the frequency change, just break left and finish your rollout on the grass—NOW!

I came to Reading last June in the Windecker because there was one going my way, and I wanted to find out if it really is a 200-mph airplane. It really is. Seamless and plastic like it was carved out of one piece of Ivory soap, it slipped along at 208 mph. Atlanta Center, watching the blip scoot across their radar, said, "Say again yo type aircraft?"

Bill Lowrey, chief pilot for Dow Chemical, made his little speech again: "It's a Windecker, all plastic, made in Midland, Texas."

"Oh yeah, I read about that in FLYIN'. Y'all like it?"

"It's a beautiful airplane."

"Well, s'long, y'all."

Lowrey turned and grinned like a happy elf. "If General Lee had one of these, we'd have to get a visa to get into Pennsylvania."

The Reading Show gets itself together and opens on a Tuesday, and then roars along like a Mexican fiesta until Friday. On Friday, everybody flies away—except for a mysterious little group that meets somewhere in the night and later announces which million-dollar corporate jet is this year's Flagship of the U.S. Industrial Fleet. Nobody pays any attention to that, but they also name such good things as Best Antique, Mossiest DC-3, Best Military, Best Classic. It's a shame they don't do all that earlier and go hang ribbons on the airplanes, so you know what you're looking at when you see them. The EAA boys were there, too, with a few examples of the last of real American hand craftsmanship, but they are not allowed to come in and sit at the big table or win any of the awards yet. Pity.

The Reading Show runs four days every June. It makes no difference which day you get there; the pattern repeats daily. The mornings begin with Important People in Aviation conducting Meaningful Seminars in the big striped tent, but when they cranked up that twin-row radial on the Sea Fury and it coughed to life, rippling the canvas, it sucked me right out of the tent. And there was Flt. Lt. Ormond Haydon-Baillie up in the Hawker's cockpit, right out of the Battle of Britain, with the sun shadowing his patrician cheek bones and glinting off his goggles.

After he had powdered us and gone, I got lost in the exhibit hangar among all the things they have invented to separate an airman from his money. A pitchman's paradise: "See the black dirty ole oil? See it coming clear after passing through our filter which contains only a roll of toilet paper? Yes, sonny, the toilet paper is certified by the FAA . . . a dual purpose bargain. . . ."

Then there were the flight simulators, measuring their success
by how long it takes to make you airsick on the ground (not long)
. . . and the companies with icy blondes in long-legged miniskirts
saying, "lookee, come see, register here, take a free booklet.
. . ." I was wishing the Confederate Air Force booth didn't remind
me so much of the Ku Klux Klan . . . and Continental had its
gold-painted Tiara display engine hung out again, as familiar as
last year's station wagon . . . and what a sad thing, the occasional
unmanned booth, an advertisement for a failure . . . oh fun . . .
shucking along with this good-natured crowd in all this carnival
midway huckstering, and black boxes with flashing lights, and
grab-yous, and all this good airplane stuff!
    At noon, the sharks are separated from the little fishes. The
sharks pass into the Private Area, where tinny trailers called "cha-
lets" are aligned in an exclusive clubmanship of the Big Ones. The
game is the same as in the carny booths, only the chips are blue.
A few ho-hos over scotch or bourbon while trampling fried onion
rings into a rented carpet can lead to some beautiful contracts.
    Just outside, the sober little fishes are getting the same great
air show the sharks are watching with plastic highballs in their
hands. First the factory fly-bys, then the freelance aerobatics and
the moan of engines and the flash of *lomcováks.* And don't try to
fly in from midafternoon till after six, because the field is closed
while the military demo teams rip open the sky and use it up from
hill to thundering hill.
    The Editor bared his teeth one day and told me to go out and
find somebody from the Aerobatic Club of America to interview,
because it looked like they were going to have to pass the hat
again to raise enough money to go fly at the International Cham-
pionships in France in 1972—flying homemade airplanes with
nickle-and-dime donations against the Government-subsidized
Communist Bloc nations. Ah, America.
    Dawson Ransome, who heads up the ACA, was out somewhere
hissing around in his Pitts, but I found Art Scholl, who had just
arrived in his Chipmunk and was out on the grass by himself
throwing a ton of suitcases and tools out of that cave in front of
his cockpit. I tried to interview him, but he asked me to load all
the stuff in his rented car. Then I tried again and he asked me to

help him crank up—literally—the Chipmunk and follow him while he taxied across the field. I tried to interview him some more while he took off the propeller, and then the cowling. When he asked me if I knew anything about carburetors, I wandered off, and that's when I saw the Sopwith Camel.

A Sopwith Camel, rearing up there in a field of parked Pipers: It was spotless, with RFC markings, a Bentley rotary engine, wire wheels, twin Vickers machine guns and not a soul in sight. It was sort of eerie. I stayed out there with the Camel for a long time, rubbing up against it, talking to it. I snuck into the cockpit, and we remembered when we were shot down in France. Later, I brought all the fellows from the Ziff-Davis chalet to see it, but it was gone.

I went over and asked the old Reading pilots who were sitting on the hookworm bench, and they shifted around a little and told me it was in the hangar, so I got all the New York Office people to peer into the locked-up hangar through the dusty windows. I could see it sitting proudly in there, in the dark, but they all laughed and scoffed and said they couldn't see a thing.

The next day, they sent me out to fly the French Rallye Minerva and got me all nerved up to fly this fantastic picnic of an airplane by describing the cute little blonde who was going to be my check pilot. I worked through the crowd to a tough-looking chap who seemed to be in charge of the Minerva stand. Said I was looking for a cute little hot-pants doll name of Penny Couch, who was supposed to (snort) go fly with me. The tough-looking guy said, "She's not here just now, but I'll take you. I'm her husband." You think that wasn't a ride to remember? It was supposed to be STOL: He could have taken off in his fireplace and flown it up the chimney.

The day after that, Dick Collins found me outside the exhibit hangar lying in the grass with my head under a rose bush, looking green. He asked what was the matter. Collins, who always looks as though he is about to get his picture taken, would never be found lying in the grass. I told him I had just been blitzed in the Messerschmitt-Bölkow 209—that I couldn't communicate to its crazy ex-Luftwaffe pilot, Werner Blasel, that I had had enough snap rolls and loopsivaks. Then I got sick. Then he let me have the stick, and I had to do a few more to prove something for America, and got lost and couldn't find the airport, and why did they keep sending me out in all these weird, upside-down airplanes, and making me play the humiliating scene with Jim Bede all over again, while guys like Tom Block were riding around in air-conditioned Merlins and turboprop DC-3s? Why me, who gets airsick, always drawing the bareback bronc rides? I mean, I just shook hands with Bob Hoover and he busted out laughing, remembering my ride in his Shrike—and that was two years ago.

Well, it was a wonderful show, and I even saw the Sopwith two or three more times; once, I swear it, in a hotel room. Reading might be the Paris Air Show of America, but I don't think they realize it yet. It's still unposed, unsophisticated, just like when it began 23 years ago, when a bunch of Dutchmen from the Reading Air Service said, "Business is good. Let's throw a beer party and thank everybody."

I hope the Sopwith is at Reading again this year, I have to get this thing settled once and for all. And I hope you're there, too.

Maybe Next Year . . .

The whole week of the 1970 Reading Show, I waited—by the flight line, in the booth, in the trailer, on the grass, watching the sky for the BD-4. I was going to get to fly the Bede! They were going to let me fly the Bede, free! But the Bede never came.

I went home to Texas and thought about it all year. A year later, there was good old Jim, sweating in the booth, laughing, shaking hands, having his picture taken. People love Jim Bede. I said, "Bede, it's me, I'm back. I'm still assigned to fly the BD-4. How 'bout it, Jim?" Good old Jim Bede forgave me for waiting a year. He put his arm right around my shoulder, yessir, I was going to fly the Bede, and no waiting, but right this minute, on the fly-by with famous aerobat Gene Soucy manning the controls.

I got in with Soucy, who was awful busy. That's probably why he didn't have anything to say. The door pull came off in my hand, but I decided not to say anything about that, I was so grateful, so

I hid it under the seat. (That's where it is, Jim.)

Gee, it was great to fly the low-level high-speed pass with Gene Soucy at the controls. How I would have loved to touch them, maybe just a teeny bit. Good old Gene laid it in over Reading at 220 mph. I kept looking at the redline at 200 and wondering how they would write it up in the hometown paper. On the second pass, he hit 225.

It's a very fast airplane, and Gene didn't do any of those steep banks or pull-ups that make a guy so jumpy. He was very careful. They said I could fly it the very next day, at nine in the morning.

Well, it was different from the year before. At least the airplane was there, and I stood around it a long time waiting for good old Jim and all those great guys. Finally, I had to go fly the Minerva. When I came back, Jim said, "Where were ya?"

We decided to fly it as soon as we could find the key. Soucy had the key. Jim went off trotting—honest, trotting, he was so glad I was finally going to get to fly his airplane. Then we saw Soucy's little Pitts taking off. I said it was okay, I'd just wait right there under the wing till we got it all together. It was nice out there, sitting in the grass.

Then it was time for the fly-bys again, and Bede and I came up with the idea that maybe Gene would let me fly it by. I bet I could have got 220 mph out of it, too. I began to think about me and the famous Gene Soucy ripping by all the girls on the ground. Boy! I'd really hold it right down in there. I sure was getting excited. Jim and I hauled the airplane out to the flight line. Soucy came up and said, "I'm flying it by myself."

I went off into the hangar and cried awhile, then I decided that everybody really meant well and there was no use getting emotional about this. So I went back out to the airplane, but I couldn't find it again. Maybe next year, eh, Jim? Next time, you call me.— G. B.

I came away from Reading all warm and happy again from being with the people who make the magazine and ready to start the new series, "Life at Little Airports," or "Lala," as it soon came to be known in the acronymic language of publishing. Such verbal expediency had also produced something as grotesque as calling our spin-and-nearly-crash morality stories "I LAFFT," from "I Learned About Flying From That."

The story was as random in its unfolding as anything you could hope for. A lady had been writing me to come to their little town and see her daddy's restored yellow J-3 Cub. Just as I got there, it was wrecked.

Life at Little Airports—Caldwell, Texas

I said, "Linda honey, does your Dad's airport have a big yellow wind.tee set off in a grove of trees?" She said it didn't. So I banked over and circled the other way to give her a look, "Then if that isn't a wind tee, I believe somebody has put your Dad's Cub into the trees."

"Oh, lordy," she cried, "I knew there was some reason why you came here today, and I changed my plans and came with you. I'm needed. It was meant this way. See, there's Dad's truck, and the hangar's empty and there's not a soul in sight down there. Oh, he needs me. Daddy may be hurt!"

Linda had been nagging me for a year to come to Caldwell, Texas, and see her Daddy's Cub and then go over to Hearne and meet Old Man West. Old Man West is 76 years old and has flown in the wars and with wild animals over Africa, and is writing a book on sex, or flying, or both, and he's got this old cabin Waco biplane and messes around with gliders and sky divers, and somebody really ought to do a story on Old Man West.

On their first anniversary, I had given Linda's husband, Chester, the gift she most wanted him to have: his first airplane ride. That was 14 years ago, and now the whole family flies, her Daddy, Hubert C. Faust, is a TV repairman and the airport manager at Caldwell.

It's a nice-looking airport, too—a crisply paved, lighted strip of 3,700 feet—and they hope to start selling gas as soon as they can get some oil company interested in putting in a pump. They have two striped metal buildings, and there is a pretty circle of orange

and white boxes around the wind sock, and on this day, a bright
yellow Cub in the trees by the meadow.

Well, Daddy was hurt all right, but not like she thought. He was
not in the Cub when it went in. Nobody was. Mr. Faust came up
with a look of great grief in his face. "It was all my fault, I guess.
I checked everything but the throttle, and it was wide open. I had
her chocked good, but she just come to life. Swarmed me. I ought
to know better than to prop a plane alone, long as I been flying
[since 1946, off and on]. I grabbed at her, but she just circled me
and went off yonder, just missed that Swift and the Mooney, cut
the fence like butter and circled out there in the pasture, then
here she come again.

"Had her tail up, wanting to fly. I figured coming through that
fence the second time would stop her, but she just zipped
through, crossed the runway, sort of turned herself into the wind
like 'Lookee here, I can do it by myself!' Got her feet up, rarin' to
go. She was real pretty out there. Going good when she went into
the trees."

Linda was standing in the hot sun with her arms around her
Daddy. "Oh Daddy! Lord have mercy!" She was crying. Mr. Faust
explained that the Cub was like another baby in the family. Folks
flew in from miles around just to look at it.

We trudged over to the trees, followed the path through a third
cutting of a five-strand barbed-wire fence, and there was the tail
sticking up with that little original Cub decal on it smiling at us.
I smelled the sweet, pungent odor of fresh-cut bark and crushed
foliage and turned earth. It had just happened.

It really was an immaculate Cub—all original instruments, the
fabric new and waxed and rubbed. The family had rebuilt it at
home. We stood around sort of helpless. The Cub didn't cry out,
and she had dealt stoutly with the scrub oaks. There was not a
wrinkle to tell of a broken spar or bent tubing. Only one fat wheel
curled up uncomfortably under her belly, and her fresh snout sort
of bent down into the earth.

"Lookee there," said Hubert softly, pointing to the guilty throttle, still open. "I let that highway patrolman that lives in the house
trailer fly it last, and he left it like that. Not his fault, though. I
should have checked." The Cub lay silent, strutted wings spread-

ing the trees apart. A yellow-breasted field lark was singing in the heat somewhere.

We turned and left, Linda and her Daddy stopping to pull at the barbed wire, trying to get the ends to meet and entwine once more.

We decided to go on over to Hearne anyway and find Old Man West. "It's 15 minutes north," said Hubert by way of directions. It was.

On the way, I reported to nearby College Station Radio to clear traffic, and the controller asked me, "What's the cloud base on all that cumulo stuff?" I told him just a minute and I'd go up and look. It was 3,500, and he thanked me. Sort of neighborly, like borrowing a cup of sugar.

Hearne has one of the finest runways in Texas—7,000 feet of broad, endless white cement. Not hardly any airport, but they have one hell of a runway. It was a "war base" back in 1942. Now it's a huddle of sungrayed tin buildings and the bleaching bones of two Normandy-invasion Waco gliders. Linda thought they were old house trailers. I explained that those things, full of men, were towed by C-47s and cut loose to glide down in the dark behind enemy lines. One trip, one way, and the survivors had to come out shooting. Linda looked a long time at the gaunt skeletons, the wind blowing her coppery hair. "They were very brave, weren't they?" And the long-forgotten ghosts lined up on rusted piperack seats grinned and clacked their appreciation.

I went into the airport shack, where a sweating, frustrated man was on the phone trying to get the party line. He held the phone out so I could hear the cackling going on. I got the feeling that there's no use being in a hurry at Hearne.

Finally, a screen door slammed and a feisty little Mammy Yokum lady came out of an old house and through some shade trees past the empty hull of a spent Cessna 150 and wanted to know what we all wanted, and yes, she knew somebody was trying to use the phone, but she was talking to her kids.

Well, Dr. William Windborn and his party out of San Antonio wanted gas. That meant another trip back to the house for the key, and then another trip to get the power turned on for the pump, and didn't we know that her dinner was on the stove and burning to a crisp?

Dr. Windborn found a ladder and filled his tanks. He offered credit cards and was told he'd have to fill out the receipt himself. "I don't know nothin' about all that," snapped the lady, who turned out to be Mrs. West, and no, the old man wasn't there. He was off to Georgetown again with that old Waco, foolin' around with those glider people.

Meanwhile, Linda's Daddy had showed up in his like-new Cessna 150 with his wife, Elva, and they had brought their camera, a little old Hasselblad. Hubert said he was sorry we had missed Old Man West. I told him that Old Lady West was plenty fine enough. The old sprite threw me a flinty look and said if I wanted gas too, it would be cash, and she didn't have any change. I could almost smell the cornbread burning.

Calvin Woods arrived next. All he wanted was to get started for El Paso in his elderly Luscombe. He had 700 miles to go, and it was already past noon. Ma West clipped him a dollar for leaving his plane under the tool shed and reminded him that "using our car ought to be worth something." Calvin grinned up another dollar and spurred off in his shiny Silvaire.

A steady stream of airplanes kept interrupting Mrs. West's dinner, and she was getting madder than a wet banty hen. Kept locking up the building and the pumps and having to unlock them again while the new arrivals took a "no offense" meekness and worked out a system of parking and fueling the planes, carefully staying out of Mrs. West's way.

Hubert said that since I'd missed the Old Man, I ought to at least go look in one of the hangars. It was just like opening a time capsule. There was a beautiful Cessna 170, a Schweizer 2-22B sailplane, most of a Mooney, an Ercoupe, some kind of pregnant Cub that had three seats, a Mercedes-Benz with the engine out and a Curtiss pusher made in 1967 by John D. Pruett. You just can't hardly find a hangar like that anymore these days. I was beginning to be really sorry we had missed Old Man West.

I went and got Mrs. West, who reminded me of my Indian grandma, to come pose in the pusher. She got up in that nest of wires and fussed around with her skirt and told me not to get so close and she didn't want her picture in no dang magazine anyway. I told her little chance, hand-held at one-eighth of a second.

With the Fausts, we enjoyed the beauty of flying the two Cessna 150s side by side back to Caldwell. Faust would make Cessna proud they invented that airplane. "Sure it's expensive, but it means so much to all of us, and we find so many ways to use it. I guess it's one of the finest things a man can get for his labor and his money."

Back at Caldwell, we found the Massey brothers and their wives. Ray was just leaving in his Mooney to go back to Oklahoma City, where he works for the FAA. Brother Melvin apologized for driving. "My Cherokee 180 is back in Baytown with a sick carburetor." They had come to Caldwell for a reunion—"to get some ticks and redbugs and some of Mamma's cooking."

They were all anxious that I should realize what a good town Caldwell is and how proud they are of having a modern airport. Mayor Hubert Willis and the council really got behind it. They used a lot of state and Federal money, but the whole town pitched in to help. Caldwell only has 2,000 people, but it's the county seat. Made Faust the manager because he was out there all the time anyhow, and they got a lot of traffic, too, since the town got the new coat-hanger factory. Had a feller in from Mississippi just the other day. They scanned the skies, as if to conjure up some more traffic and prove the point, and a Cherokee Six snouted in with Russell Nance bringing a charter out of Shreveport—some kids to stay at Camp Wagon Wheels. "See there? We get 'em all the time."

A windmill turned in the fresh, clean, country air—the highest obstruction around the airport—and at the cafe, I looked back anxiously at the cameras in the car. Hubert said, "It's okay, we never lock up anything around here."

I stood and had my picture taken with Linda and her Dad, and promised to come back when the Cub was fixed. "Well, I'm gonna fix her this winter," said Faust, "but it's sure gonna run up the price of teevee repairs around here for a while."

I left them in their clean little city of trees and friends and flew across rich farmlands toward that gray pall of pollution full of scything jets that marked distant Houston.

Flying liked the story so much that they gave me a blurb on the cover and my family had to go out and buy eleven-foot poles to reach me with. And as subsequently happened on all my Lala stories, friendships sprang up between me and the people I came to know. Nothing tight, just the kind of easy "keep-in-touch" friends that you send Christmas cards to. The follow-up on this story was that fixing up and restoring Linda's daddy's Cub became a town pride-project. Mrs. West still isn't speaking to me, but if I'm ever lonesome or low on coffee near Hearne, Texas, I got a home.

This would be as good a time as any to pause and do a re-cap on the picture war that has been going on as long as I have been with *Flying*. The opening guns back in '70 were memos telling me never to send in Kodacolor prints. Most of my requirements would be in black and white, and if they ever needed color they would ask for it. And never, absolutely never, to use anything but transparencies. OK?

After getting my first batch of black and whites, shot at Oshkosh, Stephan wrote in January of '71:

May I speak to you strongly about your photography? The stuff you're doing just isn't right for us, for two reasons—one easy to solve, the other more difficult. The first is that whoever is doing your developing and printing (I sent them to Kodak), has mastered the technique of taking sophisticated modern film and turning it into early 1930s positives. . . . send us the undeveloped film, let us have it professionally developed and then select relevant prints to a usable 11 × 14. . . . but we just can't work from the glossy, utterly un-contrasty, developer stained, lint spotted small prints you send us. There's only one way a Nikon F with Nikkor lens can take pictures as washed-out as the ones you send us, and your processor has discovered it, whatever it is.

As if that wasn't rude enough of me, now I'm going to carp about *your* technique, which is the harder to solve of the two photographic problems. If you look objectively at your EAA photos, for example, you'll see countless examples of spinners cut off, props cropped, a pair of legs growing out of the bottom of the cowling, pickup trucks in the background, people bending over in the foreground, rubber traffic cones, bare shoulders, elbows, sticking into the pictures. . . . we try to work for a clean, unconfusing, even sometimes artificial style. I know there are a lot of people standing around picking their noses at EAA fly-ins, but it makes a better picture if you get the airplane at dawn, when there isn't a lady in harlequin glasses and pedal pushers in the background.

I have taken the liberty of screwing up a number of your pictures by marking them to show you what I mean. I hope we are still friends.

I mounted them into an album. The funniest collection you may ever see. Red marker pen circles around the offending parts of my grey toned pictures. "Where did it go?" at a missing prop tip, "Who dat?" at spectator peering. "Out, Out!" "Omi God!" and so on. They are classic.

Stephan swept on:

"Another technique problem is that all your shots are from five feet nine inches above ground level. . . . flop down, belly up, shoot up, waving strands of wheat, anything. You overdo the walk right up and fire away technique. . . . now, if we are still friends . . ."

We are, but a year later a memo from Stephan indicated no progress in my photography: "Keep sending us those photos that the drugstore developed and we'll keep having to pay an artist to illustrate your stories. . . . but what the hell . . ."

Later I got this from editor George C. Larson in New York: "Bud Loader explodes whenever he sees color prints. Wow, are you lucky you weren't around to witness the wrath of that man when we got your last batch."

The pictures were of Linda and her dad and Ole Man West and the Wrecked Cub. After Lars sent them back with the above memo I got an immediate follow-up: "There's going to be some real neat-O art stuff to go with that first grass roots piece, see, and in order to give the artist something to go on, we need those outstanding Bax Kodacolors that you sent and I sent back."

Out, out, brief camera!
For me, these shots were full of sound and fury . . .

. . . for the Wilkinsword,
they strutted and fretted
—but signified nothing.

A boy and his Stearman—about to leap upward,
there to write Glory in the sky.

Here is my memo that accompanied the Kodacolors:

So we are sending Kodacolor to *Flying?* (Guffaw!) Does SW know about this? (oh haw haw haw), Have you unloaded Loader? (Snort, chuckle). You caught me just in the nick of time. I had just given my Nikon to a wino and canceled my account at the drugstore where they do my developing. (hee hee, haw, snort, choke, guffaw!)"

Another continuing go-round with Stephan was about people asking me for copies of the photos I took of them, and my wanting to give them a set and asking Stephan if I could get copies.

I remember what he said when he put a stop to this once and for all. Something about the pictures being done by custom commercial developers and processed for the magazine in a separate plant. The roll of film is dropped down an iron-jawed slot, which must be unlocked with great rusty chains, and the roll of film falls through subterranean passages and ends up in a secret cave, deep in the bowels of Bald Mountain from which nothing ever comes back. And don't ever ask again.

Actually I am not all that bad a photographer and have photo illustrated eight of my previous books with my own work, one of them an essay about combat Marines in Vietnam. I use the Nikon to produce some fairly artsy local tv commercials, and I love to take airplane pictures more than anything, but Bud Loader works to such high standards—the photos in *Flying* are final selections from mountains of pictures—that I am only now learning to get a few squeaked through.

Another part of my education about photography has been a few assignments with Russell Munson, who not only did the seagulls for Dick Bach in *Jonathan Livingston Seagull* but is a gentle genius to work with. Russ carries his equipment in an old cotton sack and will shoot up an entire cassette of 36 frames on just one angle of one subject. He brackets all exposures, constantly shifts, high, low angles, different lenses. Russ on a job says very little but his shutter sounds like a rattlesnake. I mentioned this to him once and he said, "Bax, getting me here from

New York for this day involved a lot of expense. Film is the cheapest thing I have."

He says that any man who can get the picture he wants in one shot should please take one of himself walking on water. Also, if you do not get the airplane picture two hours after sunrise or two hours before sunset, wait until tomorrow. Flat-lighted, high-noon pictures of airplanes are worthless. And if you can look at a picture and tell it was shot with a wide-angle lens, then you are not using the lens right.

Another advantage Russ has is that photography is all he concentrates on. Sometimes I have felt like a one-man band when working alone, or as Stephan once said, "Your present problem seems to be that you can't fly with one hand and set the shutter with the other. Also, your hand shakes when you photograph tits."

The worst photographic indignity came when I offered to let my wife Diane take the photos, mostly as a lure to get her to go with me on assignments. I figured they could throw out her pictures as readily as they do mine. Of the two stories she photographed, the magazine used her stuff for both.

But wait. Flying was not aware that Diane was using the camera, and they listed the photo credits to me in the magazine. The only thing worse than Diane having the gall to write a letter of complaint to "Flying Mail" was their printing it.

From "Flying Mail," August 1976:

Helpmate

At the risk of sounding picky, I must point out an error in the photographic credits in the September Bax Seat "Whisper Cat." The picture of the Turbo-Cat on page 130 was not taken by Gordon Baxter. It was taken by Diane Tittle Baxter. I realize that Mr. Baxter needs all the help he can get. As his room-mate, however, so do I.

Diane Tittle Baxter
Village Creek
Silsbee, Texas

On the second publication of Diane's photography they ran her a photo credit. Didn't pay her but ran a photo credit.

And to wrap up this mini-feature on the F-stop business at *F-ng,* during the brief period when we ran fold-out covers and all our cover planes had to be facing west, Stephan solicited his editorial forces for ideas and originality, as New York always does. His all-hands memo was an idea hard to top. "We need cover photo ideas with some sort of a little surprise for when the reader turns the fold-out, like a couple fornicating on the wing."

This opened up the concept of a whole new magazine in my mind. A combination of the publishing empires of Bill Ziff and Hugh Hefner: We'd call it *Fly-Boy,* the ultimate enthusiast magazine.

One thing the current management of *Flying* has no enthusiasm for is war. You may not have noticed, but we have no current "military" section and seldom run anything about airplanes that were designed to kill people. This has produced an almost schizophrenic relationship between *Flying* and the Confederate Air Force. A few examples of the crossed lines of transaction are such feelings as: These are machines of war, but they are classically beautiful; the Texas Aggie-and-cottonfields background of the old Colonels seems pretty far to the right of the Harvard, Yale and Princeton background that has prevailed at *Flying*—but—one of the things that *Flying* must not do is let such private value judgments color the publication.

To sum it up in simpler language, those old 1942, Alamo-mentality Colonels seem about half crazy to our "effete" Eastern editors. Yet, they did do much to win the war, and the public loves them and their flying museum. They deserve honest coverage if for no other reason than that some of it sells magazines.

Of course the war was not won exclusively by Southerners. We just seem to have had more fun at it. An example of *Flying's* attempt at fair coverage of the CAF was the recent expedition and feature story of Bob Parke going down to Rebel Field and flying their B-17. Parke was a real combat pilot, flew many missions in -17s, and, like many men who may have seen too much, will never be gotten into bar talk about flying in the war. The closest I ever came to it was one night, just the staff after a hard day's work, relaxing over good 12-year-old Scotch. Parke said, "Madness. It was all madness. You know the real reason we flew such tight formations? It was to keep you from splitting out of there and running for your life as any sane man would do." But Parke went down there and soldiered through flying the B-17, he really tried, but his writing about his reunion with the old bomber was, well, laid back.

My own feelings about the War Birds are wildly romantic. I guess I didn't get shot at enough. Some, but not enough. What I was trying to say here, in the story on the CAF that we ran in December, is that for some of those old guys, flying in the war was the most exciting thing that ever happened in their lives, and what they have done is to prolong those few exciting hours of their youth for 30 years.

Ghost Squadron

They are all Colonels in the Confederate Air Force, that aging collection of men and of the warplanes that saved the world in the summer of '42. A loosely knit bunch, made up mostly of professional Texans, they travel over the country with their priceless flying relics like MacNamara's Band, "playing at wakes and weddings and every fancy ball." They are self-supporting but always broke, passing the Stetson through the crowd "to keep them old birds flyin'." But they are one of the best air-show attractions in the world, swooping down upon the tiny, upturned faces with that chilling sound that once filled the air over Normandy's beaches.

I watched them before the great crowd at Galveston with mixed emotions. Hungry to hear those Allison supercharged V-12s moan their song just once more. Touched by the deep rumble of the distant B-17, that proud queen that killed so many of us so young. Delighted in the folksy way they taxied up and parked them in a row of war paint and let the ropes down so all of us could press forward to touch, to smell, to see. Not the museum's dusted varnish, but the hot mink smell of a twin-row radial engine, still slick in its own slung oil.

Little boys with wonderous eyes were hoisted up on the shoulders of granddads: ". . . we had a Dilbert lootinant that flew one of these Wildcats into five parked planes . . . sent him home as a Jap ace . . . har har har . . ." A Colonel with gray hair and bourbon-blossom nose was sitting on the wing now in his gray cowboy outfit signing the little boy's autograph book.

Do I wish they would take themselves more seriously? If England could afford a group like this, they would call themselves the Royal Academy for the Preservation of etc., etc., and be wearing club ties and velvet vests. The manners and morals of this group are strictly America, love it or leave it, backyard beer and barbecue. But is this bad? I don't know.

Then the shark-mouthed P-40 zig-zagged smartly into its ramp space, crossing between me and the reddening sun. For an instant, every bold rivet stood highlighted in molten gold. The hawk-faced pilot was a black cutout, the sun behind his Stetson touching the gaunt cheeks. It was like I was seeing all the P-40s at once, in all their flaming battles, and all the men who flew them to glory —seeing all of them at one instant.

These men call themselves the "Ghost Squadron"; they are still 18-year-olds, who have remembrances of things long past with these flying fragments of the mightiest armada that ever swept clean the skies. But do they have the right to do this? To fly these things instead of letting them sleep safe like sculpture in museums? One by one, they will go in. Fifty-year-old reflexes, and high-strung machines built for a few hours in battle, now fatigued with 30 years' age. One by one, they'll stop time forever. Wonderfully. Gloriously. But should they? I don't know.

I came home, put on my old flying suit, my helmet and goggles —the new ones that fit over bifocals. I climbed into the cockpit of that 25-year-old PT-13D Stearman and ripped off and wrote "Glory" in the sky. Flew it until the cage of wires sang its song, and thought of what terrible secrets are hidden in those ancient wooden wing spars. Flew it until the prop blast made my head clear and 18 years old again, as it always does. Then I decided: Those old boys are as crazy as bessie bugs.

4.

Too Many Engines, Too Much Dixie

In the autumn of '72 Stephan wrote, "We feel that 'Bax Seat' is worth an incalculable amount, but since we can't convince the accounting department of that . . . we are giving you a tiny raise."

You would be amused and astonished if you knew what most national magazines pay their middle-cut writers. I would rather fly and write about it than eat, which is about what it would have amounted to if the broadcast business were not supporting me in those days. I once compared my trip expenses to what I was being paid for my stories and told Stephan that "editorially I am cheaper than innkeepers, car renters and vassals hired to drive huge public aircraft."

But I never complained about it much because in my mind's eye I could see a long line of writers outside the door at One Park Avenue all wanting to write for *Flying*, all of them better than me, and all of them willing to work cheap.

My arrangement with *Flying* has always been surprisingly casual and loose. At times even haphazard. In the fall of '72 we discovered that we had lost track of what stories I had been paid for. A flurry of memos ended with Stephan saying, "By now you should have been paid for all that stuff, and we've decided that we still love you. SW."

I told him that "I give up on trying to keep the money

straight with y'all, just send me a little whenever you think of it. I'm only in this for the glory and because I was weaned too young."

The end of 1972 also marked the end of what Stephan sometimes called "Baxter, boy aviator," or what I thought of myself, a pasture pilot. There was no grand scheme to this, but the magazine began to push me into upgrading my ratings. The process began in September of '72 and the effects of it began to thread through all the following year. It started with a multiengine rating, went through commercial, gliders, and seaplanes and ended in the chaos of getting instrument rated. It's not an uncommon thing at *Flying*. New hands, even office girls, all are encouraged to learn how to fly and then to take it onward and upwards as far as it will go. Sometimes we get a classic out of it, such as Norbert Siepyan's "I, a Pilot," about turning a scholar into an aviator. But always the experience is harvested into new copy that comes along at just about the right pace to match the new readers and new students, who can relate to what is happening to us and take heart.

I went for my multiengine rating first because it was easiest. As you read the story you will come to a mysteriously veiled incident in which the FAA check rider said, "If you ever write about this, I will personally write to Oke City and have your certificate withdrawn!" Well, I think the story is old enough and funny enough by now to go on and tell it.

I did a supercomplete preflight, including full flaps down to see if the hinges were still there. And of course, we headed down the runway without me, the Fed, or my instructor riding shotgun in the back ever noticing the flaps were still full down. About halfway down the runway the FAA examiner pulled one engine. I promptly pulled the other one and began to brake, at which time the Fed restored full power to both. At about 50 knots the 310 leapt off tail first and tried to climb nose down. I'd never felt anything like it and thought the check pilot had done something rotten with the trim tab. I was very busy as we ran out of airport and skimmed the fence. We all discovered the full flaps about the same time and the sweat I left on that handle corroded it forever. It was an outstanding example of flap milking. With the first breath he could let out my examiner said, "You know that would have been an automatic bust, don't you?" And the only reason it wasn't was because he was a fair guy and the student, the CFI and the FAA had all made the same mistake and we all knew it.

A Fistful of Throttles

Picking up your multi-engine rating is like buying a new suit: Spend a few hours and a few bucks, and you come out looking very impressive. None of the glass hill to climb like the maddening business of the instrument exam.

Two things lured me away from little bug-smashing airplanes and gave me the hots for a fistful of throttles. First, the Cessna 310 has always turned me on. That flying razor blade—so scary-looking on landing, those little bird legs reaching out for the deck like a carrier fighter all tip tanks and pointy nose. Second, speed, man, *speed.* That's what serious flying is all about. A thousand-mile trip in a 172 and I'm staring down at checkpoints like I'm flying in glue. I found my magic number is 200 mph. Ruined me, flying right-seat guest in a 310. The words kept forming in my mind: "time machine!"

Then a Cessna 310G came to live with us out at the grass airport last summer. Pappy called her Gee-Gee. "Go whisper in her nose, and she'll take you anywhere." Now, a G might be an old airplane in some parts of the country, but to call Gee-Gee old would be like criticizing Hedy Lamarr because she's over 35. Sure, she had a few spur marks on her and not all the stuff ever worked on any given day, but there was lots of stuff to choose from.

There was always some CFI current in 310s who would be passing through with an hour to spare, and I pasted up nine hours. Three of them learning how to get the door shut. (May I suggest the general-aviation industry skip one model year and spend the time perfecting a system for dealing with all the body openings in their products?)

Then three hours listening to sure-fire but conflicting accounts of how to hot-start a fuel-injected engine. The only guy I know who has unquestionably mastered this secret is Bob Hoover, who hot-starts both of them from a stall at 500 feet over the air show. If Hoover doesn't have it down pat, you'll read about it in the papers.

Then three hours of differing ideas about how the Cessna 310 should be flown. The 310G, however, has its own very strong ideas about how it is to be flown, and you will not get away with anything else for very long.

It took some time to get used to the idea of approaching our stubby runway faster than most of my airplane friends cruise. And don't ever get those wing tanks to oscillating on final, or it will be ha ha ha all the way home.

Looking back on my mongrelized instruction, I only wish they had taken me up to 5,000 feet and shown me what Vmc means during the first hour instead of the last. The 310 is such a big, solid, honest flying machine, and no one could have ever told me that at Vmc with one engine roaring and the other at zero thrust, this magnificent thing would twist irresistibly out of my grip to roll over on her back and die. If they had taken me to that edge of the world first, everything else we did would have made plenty of sense.

Maybe it's best I didn't know, because I had one of the old-school, sink-or-swim instructors who had me fly the runway at 75 feet, gear down, dirty, with full tanks, five souls on board and one engine chopped. All he ever said was, "Don't get slower than 110." Then I got the airplane cleaned up and it still wouldn't climb and I didn't dare try to turn, he asked what I was going to do now. I told him I guessed I would just carry on until we came to a two-story farmhouse, and then we'd hit it.

Actually, flying the twin was not a hard transition, but my hours were nothing but engines yanked on takeoff, engines yanked on landing, single-engine go-arounds—a whole lifetime of all the terrors a twin pilot could ever dream up. The success of each hour's instruction was gauged by whether or not I had any dry places left in my clothes.

Don't bother to write outraged letters to the editor about all this; it's the state of the art out in the boonies. And anyway, I've already had Judgment Day with the FAA. Oh, I was ready. I could draw you a picture of the panel from memory, and knew most of the pilot's manual by heart. All but the parts he asked about. If he asks you to scratch-build the fuel system, you better have brought your tools.

With a heart full of love for the 310G and nine hours in the saddle, I did present myself before this formidable man designated by God and the FAA. He gazed upon me without a trace of enthusiasm and muttered something about: "Who comes now seeking permission from his Government to ascend into the skies with an engine on each wing . . ."

We will mercifully draw the curtain of privacy around what happened during the next hour, for that man said to me: "If you ever write or speak of me and what has just transpired in this aircraft, I will personally write Oklahoma City and have your rating summarily withdrawn."

Only let me say that I crept away at the end of that day a humbled man, convinced that the FAA does not take lightly their one and only chance to determine who shall get the coveted "multi-engine land" tacked onto their license. The last gotcha was from ole Pappy. "Hell no, you can't solo it. All you got is a permit to learn. Come back when you got 30 hours dual."

Right now, what I wish I had is a 172 that would go 200 miles an hour.

My correspondence with *Flying* about a choice of schools and the long task of learning to fly instruments accumulated. An appropriate excerpt, from Stephan: "Bax, if you are going to learn to fly gauges, you gotta learn to spell gauges, not guages."

A letter from Jim Leahy found me. It was an invitation to the first annual Stearman Fly-in, at Galesburg, Illinois, a grassy pasture in the Indian summer of mid-America. There were 30 Stearman biplanes and the men and women who love them. I was in hog heaven. The Stearman that carried off most of the trophies was the cream-and-yellow 450 that Ronnie Langlois built up for Jeff Jenkins, the one I flew for the story "Graduation Day." Ag pilot Munsey Pierce, who lives in a 450 Stearman, made N450RL do things that no weekender could have dreamed of. For example, he won the short-takeoff contest in 190 feet.

The Day the Stearmans Came Back

O prairie mother, I am one of your boys. I have loved the prairie as a man with a heart shot full of pain over love. Here I know I will hanker after nothing so much as one more sunrise or a sky moon of fire doubles to a river moon of water . . .
    —Carl Sandburg, "The Cornhuskers"

Carl Sandburg caught the prairie mood for all time, and if one is flying over this great sea of land, let there be respect for what is being reflected up to the wings. If the pilot's pennant is only a Stearman biplane, one of the last fluttering vestiges of the cloth of Old Glory that once lay across this land, then ask what is a Stearman? "It is an oil-burning, gas-eating, stack-winged biplane, flown by an idiot." That's what Jim Leahy said, and Jim loves the Stearman, and flying, and it was out of his head that the idea came to have all the Stearmans in the land come streaming in one day and gather at Galesburg, Illinois just for the fun of it.

Leahy and Sandburg are both from Galesburg. There must be something in the ceaseless, prowling prairie wind that brings dreams to life in the hearts of such men. Jim runs an electrical shop, born too late to be what he should have been—a P-51 pilot. Lester B. Lundry, that quiet birdman who has taught so many prairie boys since the 1930s, taught Leahy to fly. Lundry watched the boy reaching for aerobatics, said, "Son, you need to get yourself a Stearman. Nobody's ever took one apart in the air." Leahy found one—Cliff Du Charme's, but Cliff debated whether Leahy was worthy to own it.

One year at the Ottumwa antique airplane convention, Leahy met Tom Lowe. Tom has the military look—close-cropped head, sunburnt beak; you could lose him in the marching ranks at Parris

Island. He flies for United, but even with a head full of numbers, Lowe too had found and loved that old wire cage, the Stearman. Together, Leahy and Lowe flew wing and wing into the autumn, and the idea began to bubble: "Wouldn't it be something if we could invite all the Stearman guys here someday and . . ."

Around the kitchen table, their wives licked and mailed out 2,000 invitations to the First National Stearman Fly-in. That's how many of the original 10,000 of these wood-and-cloth airplanes the FAA shows as being intact, somewhere. Many of the letters came back: "no such person," or "left no forwarding address"—a character trait of Stearman pilots.

Thirty airplanes did come, and that's a long row of Stearmans parked wing to wing. They came mostly from the Midwest, curving in on their steep, rounded approaches. Most landed high, rough and with much rudder-fanning. A few hours of mind- and muscle-battering in that open cockpit numbs the delicate touch of even the best. When Dick Reade, builder of the slick custom MCMDs, arrived from Hayti, Missouri, I thought I recognized his sunburst orange and cream.

"Who's that?" I asked as he skittered along from wheel to wheel.

"Can't say," squinted a veteran Stearman pilot. "He ain't through yet."

There wasn't much of a program or "planned play" out at that windswept airport. Mostly, it was a matter of just watching the planes come in. Larry Palmer-Ball led a formation of four from the Louisville, Kentucky area. Larry is a polishing nut. At first, we thought he had a chrome-plated Stearman, but it was just that every aluminum part was polished blinding bright. The group he infected flew Army blue and yellow and are referred to by their widows as the Palmer-Ball Air Force.

Then a glossy black-and-gold MCMD custom streaked in, slick from cowled engine and wheel pants back to faired rudder and headrest. Out of its cockpit there arose a most unlikely figure, like Faust coming up from Hell. First a great, red nose framed in white whiskers, and then the bulk of a magnificent paunch heaved upward. All of this balanced on the cockpit rim to unsheath a pink, bald pate, and then it dropped to earth with surprising agility, like some giant Santa Claus, and was swept away by a throng of admirers.

"For God's sake, what was that?" I asked the little Italian chef with the Kaiser mustache who got out of the front hole.

"That was Red Irwin. He flies for Gulf Oil."

"Flies what for Gulf Oil?"

"All of it; he's their chief corporate pilot, and you are standing beside a $48,000 Stearman. Look inside, but be careful."

There, packed like jewels in black leather, was a full IFR panel. Instruments from crotch to chin, two of everything. When Stearman 811 Golf calls Chicago Center and squawks ident, wouldn't you love to be there?

The wonderful day of surprise packages wore on. A garden-variety yellow one taxied up smartly and drew gasps as the pilot began to unbundle. This Stearman had 11 jugs. The pilot was unmistakably a girl. Pat Friedman, who stood laughing as her husband attempted to follow her in with only one brake working on his open-cockpit Ryan STM. At the banquet that night, Bob Friedman won the Ace Trophy for five confirmed kills of runway lights.

Actually, neither Friedman nor anyone else so much as grazed a wing tip, although the day was livened by winds gusting up to 35 mph, and the judges of the formation contest failing to judge the fly-by, mistaking it, they said, for aerobatics.

Galesburg is a lovely town. Clean is the only word for one of the only such places left in this land. The airport is inviting—a criss-cross of long, paved runways next to the traditional cemetery, ideally served by no control tower, two hustling FBOs and Ozark Airlines. Ozark sends in two whistling swan Fairchild F-27s two times a day, ready or not.

Wherever man builds his Eden, however, the worm is in the fruit. Beneath the green sod of this fine, sleepy airport there run hard ridges of contention between men.

Of the two fixed-base operators, one is the new boy, one is the old-timer. Harrel Timmons, the new boy, runs Galesburg Aviation. He was once a civil engineer, but the fox was under his shirt for flying. Defying his own fine sense of logic, he abandoned his career and followed his heart. In 1968, he gathered some backers and bid in as the Galesburg Cessna dealer. "Galesburg is a big small town, conservative in ideas, politics, everything. We have to prove to them that the airplane is here to stay. By working all day, seven days a week, we broke even last year," he says with a triumphant grin.

Lester Lundry, of Lundry Flying Service, just across the ramp, saw his first airplane in 1912. In 1918, he saw another. In 1928, he went to Barney's School of Aeronautics, at Peoria, but he was still the cautious farmer. "If they ever make an airplane I can sit down in and take off my hat, I'll get in the game." When the Taylorcraft appeared, Lester Lundry sat down and took off his hat. He has been a Piper dealer and flight instructor since the mid-1930s.

Lundry talked to me on a day when he had 30 Stearmans roaring around outside and 500 people inside his hangar, had given an hour of dual and two FAA written exams, and had rented all his cars. "And if taxes and insurance rates don't stop going up, all of us in this industry are simply going to have to raise our rates." Deliberate words from a serious Midwesterner who has taught hundreds to fly, logged over 20,000 hours and never had an accident.

Harrel Timmons and Lester Lundry. Different men with a common goal, living and working side by side, and yet the word is that they seldom speak.

Then there was the airport manager, a political appointee, reportedly in the plumbing trade. We were told that this worthy was unsettled by the uproar at his fiefdom. All those prehistoric relics waddling and snorting around out there across his greens. Nobody slow-rolled the runway, and the formation takeoffs were in well-spaced single file, but he was threatening to report us to the FAA. Would have been a simple matter: The FAA was there, sanctioning and happily enjoying the show. The affair was solved by a phone call to the city manager. The exact words used were: "Get him out of here or I'm going to deck him." The airport manager was not present for the trophy ceremonies.

How strange that the borning of a national event always lacks the support of the townsfolk at first. We knew about the Stearman fly-in in Texas before they knew about it in downtown Galesburg.

The local press started with a slug on the sports page, but after 5,000 people turned out to see the biggest swarm of World War II aircraft in the same sky since 1945, the story quickly hit page one. The local telly and radio woke up, too, but the story never reached beyond the cornfield borders of the county line.

Now, there could not be such an exotic collection of antic machines and of men so emotionally involved with them without having at least one good poke in the ribs. In fact, a pitiful little trophy was made up for just such an event, with crooked engraving and a bent wing. Let me tell how you-know-who won the Hard Luck Award.

At the last minute, George Mitchell and I scrubbed our plans to fly up in his two-holer and one of M&M's beautiful ag planes. We had front and back trouble: a cold front and a yellow streak down our backs. And what was the first plane I saw float into Galesburg? November 450RL, with Mitchell's dear friends and worst competitors, from Jenkins Aerial, at Winnie, Texas: Ronnie Langlois and Munsey Pierce, bronzed and grinning after flying nearly a thousand miles in two days.

"How was the weather, fellas?"

"Aw, nuthin' that wouldn't bother a couple of little ole ladies." Snicker. Guffaw.

From then on, every time I saw that white spinner on the nose of the 450, it was poking its way in for another trophy. Munsey won the short-field takeoff event from a three-point attitude in 190 feet. The surprised judges had to walk back to where they had blasted off. And they won the first arrival trophy and the Sore Butt Award for having come the most distance—eight trophies in all, more than any other plane. Every time Langlois came up to collect another trophy, I owed him another round. It was awful.

Leahy and Lowe had promised there would be no "Best Stearman" award, in hopes of bringing in working airplanes; but only one ag-plane showed. Dusters and Sprayers Supply, of Chickasha, Oklahoma, sent a best-airplane trophy anyhow, but it was too big to carry home in a Stearman. The matter of who to give it to was checked to Ken Wilson, of Evansville, Indiana—the guru of Stearman restoration—and Galesburg's own Roger Smith, another military-aircraft buff. The trophy was unloaded on Richard W.

Hanson, of Batavia, Illinois, whose Army-marked bird had stars and bars and every original stencil in place—everything except a gas-rationing card stuck on the windshield. Hanson sleeps with this aircraft under his bed. His wife is comfortably hangared, of course.

At last, saturated with the sights and sounds of Stearman biplanes, and the promise of "same time, same place next year" (September 28–30), and the hope, maybe, of Lloyd Stearman himself attending, I was killing time between Ozark and Braniff at O'Hare. I told the barmaid, "It was only a bunch of silly old men in silly old airplanes, living in their yesterdays."

Barmaids are more tender to truth than that, and she replied sweetly, "They're not living in yesterday, they're only keeping a good memory alive."

So let us accept this more generous offering from the bosom of the barmaid. Fifty men of otherwise good sense and tidy lives did cluster their aged wings at Galesburg, beating the earth with the roar of 30 round engines. As they did, invisible flags flew once more over Kelly, Randolph, Pensacola and Willow Grove. They filled the blue skies over Galesburg, the land of Lincoln and Sandburg, and I thought of the simple line on the rough rock at Sandburg's grave: "For it could be a time to remember."

An invitation to come over to Clover Field at Houston and get rated in gliders fitted among my rating hunting ambitions, but the actual experience far transcended just getting another ticket to write about. I came close to catching the feeling of it in the story, but closer in a memo to Stephan, which we did not print because the magazine isn't ready for this kind of stuff yet. I suggested that the ultimate trip would be to soar a Blanik, stoned and naked, with a beautiful nude girl strapped into the other seat, Moody Blues music piped in and the cockpit filled to the sills with warm whipped cream and go slow roll it. Anyway soaring does come close to the ultimate experience of the beauty of flying.

Find Your Boy Self Again

What happens after you have flown all the airplanes, made all the money, fought the good fight, and suddenly the golden Septembers are rushing past your wings? Can you ever go back and find your boyish self again? Of simple times and sunny fields when laughter came easily? C. C. Holt and Dick Taylor did. They went back to Lilienthal—to gliders and the beginnings of flight. They became the patrons of soaring at Houston.

Clover Field lies just south of Houston's sprawl—soon, but not yet, to be choked to death by smog and suburbia. It is an airport of miscellaneous turf runways, as though each previous tenant had beaten a takeoff path in his own favorite direction. The clover is shared with some grazing horses, a snorting circuit of mini-bikes, a Smith biplane, a Luscombe, some Ercoupes, a Piper Clipper, an abandoned Convair airliner and a black-and-white nanny goat. You can use the goat as a windsock; she feeds upwind. Land upgoat.

The gliders lie tipped in the center of the field in a cluster of automobiles. Lush Marsha, the F-102 jock's wife, will schedule you for a ride or offer a jam sandwich. It is a quiet gathering. They lie upon the grass or rap to Moody Blues coming from the tape deck of the MG, and they gaze upon the Schweizers and Blanik phantoms circling in the blue haze. The sailplanes come droop-snooting in over the oil-rig tower, spoilers tweaking, and stop like blade-winged footballs on the tee, balancing.

The neat little Japanese doctor is getting his rating this weekend. The Korean and the tall Chinese are his friends. The leathery old ex-B-17 pilot in the scuffed Wellingtons didn't tell anybody he was high-time; he let his touch tell the story and soloed quickly and stalked off tall, looking like he had found it at last. The full-blown blonde left her husband and baby at the car and bought a wring-out ride in the Blanik and climbed out after the loops and spins all damp. She led her husband off by the hand with a peculiar glint in her eye. Glider freaks all.

When I sat down in the gaunt-framed Schweizer 2–33 and they

closed the lid, I've never felt more like I belonged. Good vibes flowed between us. Thinking back now, I never missed the engine, except that my left hand had nothing to do. One engine is reason enough for anxiety, two engines make me wary as a cat. No engine seemed as it should be.

Being snatched aloft by the sweaty little Super Cub is a necessary humiliation. The pitch-up, the wild veering and scuffling of being dragged like a box lasts only a moment. Then there is life. Superior life, and one must hold low until the Cub finishes its dusty business on the ground and gets airborne itself.

Towing was the most demanding. George Metts's voice came from the rear bassinet: "Just center Jim's rudder on his bald spot and you're in perfect tow." Of all of aviation's needle-and-ball-chasing games, this one is the most diabolical. There is a control lag in the movement of such a long span; it's like straddling a seesaw at the pivot point and trying to keep the board level in shifting winds. There is a bright orange bit of yarn blowing back from the pitot tube. It tells you how years of gentle Cessnas and docile Pipers have withered away your rudder feet. I was stirring the stick like mixing a thick chocolate cake when Metts muttered, "It would be better with about half as much of that."

At 2,000 feet, the last sound is the bang of release, and the nylon snarls off after the Cub. After that, you can faintly hear sounds drifting up from earthlings. Ah, then it becomes all that flight was ever supposed to be. Wings sprouted from my shoulders. I wheeled with the silent hawks. The up wing raced against the sky, the down wing seemed to run backward. So much adverse yaw that the novice needs a touch of opposite just to hold the circle. A bubble of lift and I was stealing from God, wanting to laugh, to sing. After three and solo, I would have to slap my mind and say, "Remember, man, this thing also descendeth, and you will be, you *must* be, perfect in the slot lest you hang among the pears in yonder orchard."

The Schweizer would whisper and strum and make little soft, fluttery sounds, and I lay with my head against her canopy, caught in the trance. But the check ride untranced me. Now that Dick Taylor was in his mean-man FAA suit, I soared too high on tow and got above the Cub, lost him. The rule is release. I asked him if he wanted to see the rest of it. "No."

A miserable wait on the ground, avoiding eyes. I always bust check rides. Then a second chance, and now a precious word on my sparsely printed ticket—"glider."

Have you ever, in dreams, flown free? It was like that.

"The Old Barge" and "Hawk Lips" were mood pieces, paintings set in cameo. Not going anywhere, not saying anything, except "ain't it lovely?" They were attempts to capture the thoughts and feelings that creep in and fill up the soul of a solo pilot and then evaporate too quickly after he is back in the noisy ground-world again.

The Old Barge

It is time to go out and do battle with the Trinity River bottoms again. Beaumont is VFR, Houston is at minimums and you know what that means: The devil himself will be waiting in the Trinity River bottoms above Anahuac, sitting cross-legged with the ceiling down around his hairy ears, curling tendrils of fog up out of those scraggy hardwoods. Ask the pipeline pilot who just came in, stamping life back into his feet as he goes for coffee. "Aw, it ain't bad." Give a pipeline pilot 50 feet and he's VFR. Ask the Metro pilot with his new gold cuffs, he don't know, he'll be butting his Twin Otter along on top. You're gonna walk this lonesome valley all by yourself.

There it is, that wet wall of gray where the rice fields end and the woods begin. Must be the evil of all that happened down there. Savage ghosts of murdered Indians clawing; conquistadors in bright armor sinking in the mire, beard-ringed mouths shouting; the pirate Lafitte up from Galveston with new chests and corpses to slip into the muck. They all come writhing up from the gray woods, and rain spatters the windshield. The world becomes opaque, the Lycoming goes to auto rough and my hair rises stiff and weird.

If it gets worse, I'll make for Harmon's strip and have coffee with his good-looking secretary. And there's always the Interstate; they didn't build any towers behind those taillights. The radio goes to garbage. It's all right. I'm like a man feeling his way across his own living room. Approach comes on friendly and mentions that the San Jacinto Monument is on my course line and slightly higher. I tell them I have been thinking the same thing. Wouldn't that be a grand entry into Texas history?

"Hey, what ever happened to your old man, the one that used to fly and write?"

"Oh, he flew into the San Jacinto Monument one day. You can still see the mark."

Soon, I'll have my instrument ticket, if I survive the going back and forth to the flight school in Houston to get it. Then I'll fly along on top of this place and dump my ashtray on all these dark groanings down here. Oh, the insufferable contempt of aviators unbound.

Some days, though, there is sunlight. I sit bathed in a golden reverie, one fingertip on the yoke, all the needles on the instruments painted in place. I turn slowly and look at the slender joint of wing and strut, the beauty of the shape of the airfoil, dimpled aluminum and rivets in stark light, the unseen phenomenon of lift. The Trinity comes out of the trees below Liberty and opens her skein across marshlands, gathering little serpent bayous and looping, spreading, puddling lakes, until like the veins of an aged hand, she clutches the top of Trinity Bay and pours into the sea.

I see this beauty with a hawk's eye from the cabin of my airplane. Houston lies ahead, shadowed towers shouldered together, gasping for air. The distant shroud is filled with the voices of many airplanes unseen. Soon I will be busy, but for now, I can linger over these patterns. The ageless story of a river coming to the raveled edge of a continent. My eye picks out mud lakes dotted with reed duck blinds, Interstate 10 arching its spine across the waters, the lonely sentinel of an oil rig on an island with one round, rusted tank.

And one day when the low sun had tinged the marshes gold, and given bold outlines of long purple shadows, I saw the barge. Weathered, it blended into the grass like a crouching bird. A barge, alone and dry, a domino resting on an open palm of land.

What godawful things must have happened on that day! The peaceful land below darkened with a hurricane's fury. Shoutings lost in the wind, hawsers parting, flung back writhing in the white spray as this old turtle of a barge took wings and flew away in madness and glee. The waters covered the land, winds roared openmouthed from the sea, the ghosts of sunken galleons groaned and stirred in their graves of sand.

When it had all passed, the old barge sat there in golden sunlight and calm, pressing its weight on the grass among the peeping rabbits.

I drooped my flaps and throttled back, swooped down to look. Hidden waterfowl rose up at the rush of my shadow—white herons, bulleting ducks. Alarmed to the very hollows of their flight bones, they circled about the hulk like spilled pearls.

A rush, a glimpse of rotting timbers, caves of shadow, rusting iron. How I'd love to come here, to feel its roughness, smell its dankness, to sit in the sun on the curled decking and listen to the whispering.

Hawk Lips

"Alan," I said, "let's take the kids and go see what's happening at the airport." We collected little Chris, Eric, Matthew and Gordon IV and ended up in a motherly old Cessna 172. Man, it looked like a barn loft full of owls. When I looked back over my shoulder, I couldn't see anything but big, round eyes everywhere.

"You little punks really want to fly with Grandpa?" I asked.

"Yeah, yeah, let's go! Take off!"

So we went up and bumped around for a while and it got very quiet; they were strapped down so deep they couldn't see out. What difference will it make, I thought, if we have a few kids floating around in the cabin? We unstrapped them and let them stand up. "Now don't play with the door handle. That first step is a long one."

"Hey, just like little model cars down there. Hey, look at that

little-bitty train! Gollee, ain't it purty?" We got to see eight para-
chutists come out of two jump planes, and we got to see the glider
cut loose from the towplane, and we watched all this high color
floating and gliding down through the student traffic.

After we landed, I parked the car out near the runway overrun,
where they launch and land the glider. It was a wonderful place
to park the kids, who were pretending they were sky divers and
were practicing bailing out of the Buick. They put on sunglasses
and undid the shoulder harnesses and shouted commands. Peri-
odically, all four of them would fly out the windows.

It got to be my turn to fly the glider, and Alan made all the kids
come over and kiss Grandpa good-bye and get a last look at the
old man. The towplane hauled me up to 2,000 feet and I cut loose.

I had noticed this hawk circling over our corner of the field. A
hawk is always hunting a thermal, especially a thermal that might
be over mice, and I think he figured the grandkids were mice and
was planning on carrying one off with him. Anyway, I shouldered
into the thermal with the hawk and circled at about 40 mph in
zero sink. He had his wings spread all the way out, glorious and
free, and his pinions out on the ends were trembling, like the
glider's wing tips. He was right out there, looking me over like he
had pulled up alongside and was going to write me a ticket.

Well, the hawk and I started to play. He could turn faster than
I could, but I could ease in on him. It was so beautiful to look out
there and see that big bird so close. If I got too near, he would
duck under and come up on the other side. I dropped the nose
a little and picked up speed, began to whistle at about 60—which,
for a glider, is moving along—and I looked out there and the hawk
was still with me. He had sort of hunched up his wings, and the
slipstream was just tearing at his feathers. He looked at me with
hooded eyes, and that hawk had a savage little grin on his mouth,
the wind blowing his lips back over his teeth, and his eyes sparkling. I could see glints of red and gold as he flashed in the sun.
I swear he was enjoying himself.

Then it dawned on me that we were gliding farther and farther
from the airport. I remembered a story about a sailplane pilot on
the West Coast who had followed a seagull, riding a wave of lift,
and when they got way out to sea, the gull sort of laughed, turned

around toward land and started flapping his wings. Ain't no way you can flap your wings in a glider. So I let the hawk win our game and eased on back to the landing slot. I was a little low, and I'm sorry about getting bark on the wing of the glider, but they ought to do something about that tree at the end of the runway. Actually, it's more like a bush.

We were driving back to the hangar when I got to thinking what it would sound like if a transient pilot who had never seen the grass airport before were to call in, "Ahhh, this is Piper 34 Xray, give me your airport advisory. . . ."

I can hear our line man come on and say, "Well, we got three students in the pattern on touch and go, we have two jump planes at 10,000 feet, there are eight jumpers free-falling, a glider has just been released at 2,000 feet over the active runway, radio-controlled models are aloft over the ramp, six Japanese kites at 1,500 on the downwind leg, we have a hawk on short final for a mouse, a '73 Buick on the active with four kids just bailing out of it, the active runway is 12 and look out for the tree. Actually, it's more of a small bush."

The guy would think he had called up the zoo, and he'd go off and land somewhere else and have his radio worked on. It was a beautiful day at the little grass airport. As long as I live, I'll remember looking out at that hawk right beside me, feathers rippling, tears streaming out of his eyes and a big grin on his face. That's kind of hard for a hawk to do, because a hawk has real stiff lips.

Stephan said he laughed out loud when he got the copy for "I Abort This Exam" at the idea of someone declaring a missed approach on an FAA written. Well, hell, it made sense to me. You declare a missed approach to avoid crashing, don't you? I was only trying to make a clean getaway rather than have them tell me what I already knew—that I had flunked. It didn't work.

Not mentioned in here, but should have been, is a primary reason to go for your commercial ticket, even if you never in all your life intend to fly for pay. The commercial pilot's requirements do more than any other thing to put a fine polish

on your flying techniques. I had always thought I was a pretty
good stick and rudder man, having grown up with such tender
airplanes as the Luscombe and the Stearman. In short order
instructor Ken McGill had shown me how little I knew about
flying, even in a muley old Cessna.

You can prove it for yourself. Take a good, tame Cessna 172
out and try to fly it in a 360-degree turn at anything beyond a
45-degree bank. It's easy if you know where to put your hands
and feet, and it's like paddling a canoe through a whirlpool if
you don't. After the required hours of me and "Mustache"
McGill shouting at each other in the sweat fumed cabin, I went
for my check ride with local FAA designee, Jerry Griffin.

Griffin was the little blonde-haired kid at the airport fence,
Glenn Parker taught him how to fly, and that's the purest
lineage for a pilot in the Beaumont-Port Arthur area. He never
left the airport. Today he is a hustling FBO—a Piper dealer—
and carries all the honors the FAA can bestow. Jerry and I are
lifelong friends. I have used his planes often, but he had never
said what he thought of me as a pilot. Apparently that is a social
taboo among aviators. You might always wonder how good or
bad you are, but one of the few places you can find out is in the
official framework of a checkride. Jerry gave me a grin and
thumbs up and said, "Now you are flying like you should
have." I asked for more. "You always had a good feel and touch
for airplanes, Bax, but you were the sloppiest pilot I ever flew
with. Even the cows coming home at night tracked a better path
than you did."

So thanks, Ken "Mustache" McGill, wherever you are.

"I Abort This Exam"

Blew my commercial written exam, I did. Went right into the FSS
and Pffft! Oh, I thought I was ready, really ready. Ask me anything.
Sit close to me and let me whisper FARs in your EAR. My mind
was overstacked, like a haywagon to be gotten to market before
it all blows away.

Not that I need a commercial ticket, understand. I was like

Lucifer plunging from the heavens, powered only by flames of pride. I had been a private pilot since most of you were still wearing sleepers with feet in them. Private was enough to fly for fun. But private has lost a lot of its swagger. Private: as in piddle, Piper, puddles and put put put. Ah, but to lean, the subject of the awed whisper, on the Coke machine, "He's a commercial pilot!"

They have a little side room for exams at the flight service station in Lake Charles, but there was a guy already in there, so they gave me the corner desk in the big room, the room with the radio, the radar and all those hanging sheaves of weather. The FAA men in white shirts were cordial and all that. There was a "good luck," and then we touched gloves and went to our corners to wait for the bell. The moment arrived and I became an Applicant for Written Exam on Government Soil.

With the confidence of the pure of heart, I unfolded my issued Phoenix Sectional and my 60 fourple-choice questionnaire. I hit the outer defenses running lightly on the balls of my mind. I knew the stuff alright, although the guy who phrased these questions didn't seem to have much of a grasp of it. He kept giving me a choice of answers two of which were sheer folly and two utterly unworkable. I found myself wanting to help him along. I wanted to write in marginal comments, little essays of explanation to clear his head, but I would remember that no human would grade this sheet. It would be grazed over by a computer, curious only about whether my soft-lead pencil marks were in the proper parking slots. Defiantly, using body English, I tried to put meaning into each mark.

Then I discovered that I had left my plotter at home. I did have my Jepp chart PV-2 plotter, bristling with mileage scales, but if any of them fit on a sectional chart I never found out. Griped about this glitch, I rummaged up a Government envelope (penalty for private use, $300), hastily found a scale on the sectional and got 30 miles worth of pencil ticks across the top edge of the $300 envelope. But from there, nothing went right. Time-distance problems, fuel problems, none matched the choice of answers. In a light sweat, I reworked them, allowing for my boll weevil plotter, as the clock swallowed up another of the precious four allotted hours.

I began to feel a damp, rising sense of panic. Background noises filtered in. I could hear every pilot from Lafayette to Lake Charles, from Beaumont to Houston. It was a spanking clear day, and the FSS crew were evaluating the wits of each passing pilot by the number of gulps and gasps and fumbling sounds that came over the speakers. "A day like this and nobody needs us." All but some yo-yo out there who must have been beating his way westward at all of 60 knots. He went on forever, calling up each flight station, giving his life history and requesting a complete weather briefing every 50 miles. "He wants us to fly his plane for him." As a nonperson, I was overhearing the FSS in real life, like a man accidentally hidden in the ladies' rest room and listening to the girls compare dates. Some things, a man is a lot better off never hearing.

I grasped the horns of the test questions, leaving all the time and distance problems in the wreckage of my path. Visions of a 98 score became taunting yesterdays. Now, even the easy ones were wadding up in my mind. Everyone knows the cardinal altitudes for VFR flight, but look how they worded this: measured from above ground level or above sea level? Okay, good for you, but according to magnetic heading or magnetic course? Treachery, I tell you, these questions are loaded with treachery.

All that exams of this type prove is that some men can comprehend an insurance policy. To learn by rote is to educate a fool. Why not let us sit at the feet of some good gray examiner who could probe our minds, who could draw forth and examine our store of knowledge? But then what would they do with the computer? I have a suggestion about what to do with the computer.

Things were deteriorating fast in my corner: Less than an hour to go and I was running out of time, out of confidence, out of tobacco. Then a school bus pulled up and unloaded 40 children and four brass-mouthed teachers. A tour!

"Oh, lookee the big green tee vee screen!"

"Where do you keep the airplanes?"

"Why is the old man over in the corner crying? Why is his head in the ashtray?"

They left. I still had 20 questions and only 20 minutes to go. No way. I quit.

"Sir, I abort this exam."

Shocked silence.

"Well, Bax, you can't just abort. It ain't like a missed approach. You either pass or fail."

"Then I fail."

In sympathetic silence, he gathered up my papers. I explained about no plotter and nothing coming out right and showed him where I had copied the scale. As gently as possible, my friend explained that I had copied the scale of the Phoenix area inset, and that the real scale is at the bottom of the chart. And if I had only asked for it, there was a Weems plotter right in that middle drawer.

Out in the sparkling sunshine, I wanted to go right up to that Cessna and kick it in the side. Tear up my license. Catch a bus. Or a social disease.

I sulked a week. Wouldn't even go out to the airport. Went down to the depot and watched the trains come in. Engineers don't have to navigate; you ever think of that? For me, they should put flanges on airplane tires.

Later, I went to mean ol' Bob Marsh's flying school at Houston Hobby Field. I crawled in, enduring their scoffs and jeers while they strapped the books to my back and shackled me to a desk. Three days later, Bob signed off my 40 grade and I pulled a 78 in the Houston exam office. Ain't much, but it beats 69.

All this stuff is just alibis. Truth is, I wasn't ready.

1973 was building into a special year for me and the magazine. Along with backing me for my ratings, they sent me out to Aspen for a story on mountain flying, gathered me in with the flock again at the Reading Show and let me go to Oshkosh for the big EAA party. I'm saving the Oshkosh story for later, it was of another year, but there are a couple of quotes out of this one worth lifting. My companion on that trip was Alan Rayne, of "Cross City" fame. Alan *thinks.* Abstractly. I asked him why no doors were locked at Oshkosh, how they could leave all that valuable camping stuff and all those tools lying around and he said, "They perceive themselves as a tribe. The tribe does not steal from itself."

Walking among the Classics of the '30—the Fairchild 24s, the Wacos, the Travel Air and Fleet biplanes—I mused, "I wonder why I have such a strong emotional reaction to these airplanes, why they are so appealing to me." Professor Rayne replied, "Because that is how airplanes looked when you first fell in love with airplanes."

Homeward bound out of Oshkosh, Alan pointed out that by bending our course line only 10 degrees we could arrive at Naked City, USA, just in time for the Miss Nude America contest.

This resulted in the shortest "Life At Little Airports" story I ever sent to *Flying*. It was one paragraph long, and it is reprinted here in its entirety:

August 8, 1973
LIFE AT LITTLE AIRPORTS
Naked City, Indiana
Gordon Baxter

Naked City Airport, (Chicago Sectional). Turf strip overrun with parked cars of a crowd of 7,000 who came to view 50 naked girls vying for title of Miss Nude America, and four naked parachute jumpers (three male, one female) from a Cessna 182. Unable to obtain other data, notebook was with my clothes.

Bax.

Among the vintage aspects of 1973 was that I got the title of Associate Editor. There was a shifting at the top, and a drawing up from the bottom. I was offered a permanent staff job as Senior Editor that fall. Whenever possible, ZD promotes from the inside. I put on my Going to New York Suit and made the journey to meet with Parke and Wilkinson and discuss the new job. In one of the most difficult decisions of my life I let the opportunity pass, and this was accepted with good grace and understanding. I can't claim the clear thinking behind that decision; it came from my wife, Diane. Pillow talk. She acknowledged my kid-dream of having always wanted to be an aviation writer, but pointed out that I was already that, working out of Texas. There was little to be gained in more fame and approbation, but much to be lost in moving into more regimented and disciplined work for the magazine, leaving our wilderness home deep in the forest on Village Creek and becoming a city cliff dweller or commuter. "You would last about a week in the city."

I still sometimes regret not being closer to the magazine people, but my nearest neighbor here is a quarter mile through the woods, and sometimes that gets me to feeling hemmed in.

The upcoming bit of nonsense has a mistake in it. Not a typo, but a whole word used wrong. This rarely happens at *Flying,* where each manuscript is handed round a circle of editors made of some very impressive academic and engineering backgrounds. I think it may have been that this was an uncommon word. We sometimes get a little in-house confusion from the generation gap. I once wrote that I had settled down to fly "the old Espee line," and I got a call from one of our sharpest, but young, office girls asking, "What is the Espee line?" It was the slang name for the Southern Pacific Railroad, but railroading terms, once a part of household language, are now little needed and have died out. If you already know what it means you are probably over 50 and live south of the Smith & Wesson line.

Flying also gets its share of things they would like to forget. Stephan Wilkinson reached literary fame by being quoted in *Time* as the editor who told Dick Bach that *Jonathan Livingston Seagull* was "just not our cup of tea" and sent him packing.

Another was a story the magazine ran in '73 on flying in icing conditions. A well-known Alaskan bush pilot shared his years of experience by saying, "Playing with ice is like playing with the Devil: Fun, but don't play if you can't cheat. If you are sneaky, smart and careful you can fly 350 days a year and disregard 99 percent of the bullshit you hear about icing." His very last words were, "Be brave. Defensively." Up in Alaska, they are still looking for him.

This story is not all that grim, but the wrong word is still in it. Only one person found it, and we printed his "gotcha!" letter. I ain't gonna' tell you. But I do owe a tip of the hat to Justin Wilson, famed teller of Cajun stories.

Cajuns

Out at the Grass airport, we were discussing the perversity of sky divers. Mustache Ken McGill, the pilot of Old Blind Barnabas the Second, the jump plane, pointed to the Cessna 190: "Just look at that thing. Look at where they put the wheels, way out there on the end of those big long springs. My God! No wonder they prefer to leap out and come home on their own devices." Old Blind Barnabas the First was lost to us last year when its pilot encountered a secret ditch. All there was to walk away from were the hard iron parts, the big, round engine and those wheels way out there on the ends of long springs.

But McGill says the jump troopers are a special pain. Big, smelly, bare-armed and hairy, they make crude jokes and obscene gestures and put their boots all over the cabin. Worst of all, you have to stay alert for the "last man out" caper. If he can, one of them will lunge for the keys, switch off your engine, and fall out the door waving your keys and mouthing something unintelligible into the slipstream.

It's no problem, of course. You're right over the airport at 10,000 feet, and all you have to do is make one good landing. It's just the humiliation of the thing.

Then A.J. Judice, the crazy Cajun, spoke up on the special problems of skydiving crawfish. Cajun is one of several nicknames given to the Arcadians who were cast out of France and then Canada as a public service several hundred years ago and who overpopulated the low-lying and swampy areas of Louisiana and Texas. They are noted for their zest for life, love, boudin sausage and crawfish. The less you know about boudin, the better you will like it.

The Cajun culture here is typified by Landry and LeBlanc, Cessna 180 floatplane pilots out of Lafayette, Louisiana. LeBlanc was once standing on a float propping the engine for Landry when the propeller caught in his suspenders, whirled him around five times and cast him up on a shrimp-boat dock a limp heap of rags.

Landry shut the engine down, rushed up to LeBlanc and cried out, "Speak to me!"

To which LeBlanc replied, "Why should I speak to you? I pass you five times a minute ago and you don't speak to me."

Judice specializes in breeding and racing crawfish. He told us of a recent attempt to import a stud crawfish from Rome. He had the stud and his bride safely but illegally under his beret during the flight to Shannon, Ireland, keeping them alive by pouring Martinis onto his beret.

He had a few bad moments with Italian customs before leaving Rome. His beret kept squirming, and the sensation on his scalp was indescribable. Upon arriving in Ireland, he found both craw fish dead. Dead but smiling. He figures that they bred themselves to death. Next time, separate berets.

But about how he gets them to bail out of an airplane: He has a radio-controlled, five-foot-span model of a Stearman. He smears the area around the cockpit with boudin; the crawfish works his way out of the cockpit for a nip, and whisk! The wind snaps the chute open. His backup system for balked jumps is a timer that slides back a cover on the cockpit floor, revealing a lifelike photograph of a hungry Cajun. He claims the crawfish always gives a scream and vaults right out.

Unfortunately, the Stearman was lost to us for further verification and photographing. It went out of control during the Diamond Jubilee celebration at Port Arthur, buzzing and awakening the crew of a racing sailboat and then, upon landing on the ceremonial grounds, colliding with a metal keg of tap beer in a brave effort to avoid a crowd of thousands.

5.

Without Looking out
the Window

If 1973 was a golden year for my relationship with the
magazine, 1974 was the backside of the curve. What was
wrong with the rest I don't know and wish I could define. I had
choice assignments, including a trip to Tullahoma, Tennessee
to see a sky full of beautiful Staggerwing Beechcraft and a
chance to spend time with one of my all-time hillbilly music
favorites, Roy Clark. I watched him grease in a landing with
his MU-2. Roy turned and whooped with glee. "Only landing
you'll ever see me do, Bax, and until the day you die you will
believe I am that good a pilot!" *Flying* printed all that, but it
was just flatfooted writing. Again, I seemed to have lost my taw.

Phrases like that, "lost my taw," began to gall my editors.
Now any good ole bare knuckles marble shootin' boy would
know what I mean by that, and the use of it falls readily and
naturally to hand. The staff formed a review board, passed my
work around, flat-out rejected or rewrote my stories, and finally
let me have both barrels for talking country.

With Stephan Wilkinson as their spokesman, the group,
made up of George Larson and Norbert Slepyan, said, "Should
be edited carefully as a 'professional' piece of journalism, taking
out all of Gordon's good ol' boy mannerisms and affected illiter-
acies."

"Ahm gittin a bit tarred uv all that sheeit ennahoo, and I think it's about time we edited Bax so he reads like a writer, not an Okie."

"Edit to tighten. Baxter has a brilliant eye as an observer but sometimes a completely unselective head as a journalist quoting an interviewee.

"A Baxter who is funny and sorta cute but not quite seeming to realize it is terrific. A Baxter who is trying to be cute and super friendly and full of enthusiasm is a teeth-aching drag . . . and occasional lapses into localisms or away from Goode Englishe are fine, but Bax is starting to sound as if he is trying to *prove* he is the country boy he already appears as. Maybe a gentle warning to him about the too-positive, too-cute, and too-accepting direction he has taken would be timely."

I could only signal agreement by sending them a quote by Paul Crume, from his comment on my writing that he made seven years ago on page one of the *Dallas Morning News:*

Mr. Baxter is at times the best writer in Texas, though the literati have not discovered this yet. . . . Very often his column in the *Kountze News* is trash, but sometimes the words in it have been a song that you do not hear very much anymore . . . sometimes a feeling comes up from Baxter's prose that is like the bluest smoke from a rich pipe of tobacco. It happens when he isn't watching.

I also corrected them about "sheeit." In Texas that's "shee-yut."

Don't think, though, that their criticisms were just outpourings of Eastern Establishment Effetism. Those guys aren't like that. Take Larson, who was so "tarred uv all that sheeit ennahoo." George is one of those twice-blessed people who can write and photograph equally well. Until recently, he was Senior Editor of the magazine West of the Rockies. Before that, he was Managing Editor. He is a Harvard grad, but you can't tell it. He looks like John Denver—you know, healthy, rosy cheeks, merry blue eyes. He loves to cook Chinese and after the meal can get out his flattop guitar. He knows the words to all the songs Roy Acuff ever wrote.

I do not know if quality control is a problem to other writers, but it still rides with me. Nobody ever said it better than my agent, Connie Clausen, when she called to tell me I had been admitted to her small circle of excellent authors. "You are raw genius, and sometimes you write pure bullshit, and I am convinced that you do not know the difference."

Lucky for this raw writer that some of the New York office were more editor than pilot. In a magazine full of pilots learning to write, Norbert Slepyan was a writer who learned to fly. Slepyan's literary credentials dwarf his pilot's license on the wall: UCLA, Princeton, teaching at Queen's College, Trade Editor at Harper and Row and then at Scribners. Unlike the memo-firing Wilkinson, Slepyan used the phone to Texas:

"Bax, you have a line here where you say, 'He's in a fix and you're a-fixin' to fix his wagon.' Could we perhaps put a fix on that?"

Slepyan was Managing Editor at *Flying,* where his literary skills eclipsed He, the Pilot, so they hauled him upstairs to help launch ZD's new Books Division. He and his wife, Mary, became family friends. Diane says that one word describes the big, bearded man: gentle.

New York was having little luck with me as a pasture writer but shoved me into getting my instrument rating, which forever ended my days as a pasture pilot.

Me and My Rating

Instrument flying, I had concluded, is an unnatural act, probably punishable by God. Even if it isn't, the whole idea of flying an airplane when you can't see out the window seems self-defeating.

I knew a few instrument pilots. Technicians. The type who would read the marriage manual on their wedding night, or sip Coca-Cola at a party when everyone else was being thrown into the pool. I have a friend—a doctor, a little steel-rimmed guy with bald pate and the strongest, coldest fingers, like forceps. He flies his Mooney just exactly like in the book. His approaches leave a crisp dotted line in the clouds. He bugs me.

I respected instrument pilots, understand. Awed by them and their sudden popping out of the lead belly of a cloud and taxiing up to where we stood, huddled like fluffed-up birds under the dripping eaves. Getting out with their little secret chart books. Who is this Jeppesen, anyway? I peeked at those flimsy little chicken-track charts. No rivers, no railroads, no drive-in theaters, all written in Egyptian. No rosy colors to tingle a pilot's imagination.

I put aside any idea of my ever flying instruments. I'm going to be a low-time pilot all my life. Flying since 1957, yet the total hours stay below the magic thousand. A very sparse ticket, lots of white space around those words, "private—SEL." That's for SELdom. I had heard that instrument flying was such a demanding skill that unless a pilot went out and flew in the clouds often enough, his rating would turn to ashes in his wallet. Why should I be an instrument pilot? Would you trust a part-time brain surgeon?

Anyway, being a VFR pilot kept things exciting. Residents of small Texas towns still wonder about that madman circling their water tanks in rainstorms. Or the guy who flew a Champ down Main Street to read the name on the post office. (Had to. All it said on the school bus was School Bus.) Come to think of it, the IH (interstate highway) approach system has never been openly credited. Think of its merits: You are too low to be hit by other airplanes, too high for the cars; no TV towers grow in the middle of the interstate; and if you stay with it, it's bound to take you *some*where.

Flying VFR all these thrilling years has kept me in touch with America's heartland. The farmer on his tractor, shaking his fist. The big, shiny roaches in the No-Tell Motel during unexpected little overnight stays. The thrill of eventually finding my way home again and that phone call to my widow—I mean wife—"Cheated death again!"

I admit it: I was nervous about some things. Like being around the Feds, for instance; and omni navigation. Remember now, those gadgets crept into airplanes long after I started flying. (I always meant to ask why one day you fly toward the needle, other days away from it.) But with a good pipeline right-of-way underneath me, I could usually get it sorted out after a while.

I really hated going into big, busy airports. All those chaps snapping at each other in strange languages; and something about approach frequencies, which I decided not to fool with. I'd just fly up low, real close to the tower and say, friendly like, "Hi, this is ol' Cessna Two-Niner Betsy, can I land with y'all?" I don't know why that seemed to get everybody's noses out of joint.

Well, as you have no doubt noticed, instrument pilots are evangelistic. "Bax, you really ought to get your ticket."

"Yeah, sure. I already got one." And I'd whip out my blue card with the hole in it, and hold it up against the sky and read what it says on it: "When color of card matches color of sky, fly." I believed in that. Like Pappy Sheffield always said to his students out at our little grass airport, "Keep one wing in the sunshine and keep smiling."

That's true, too. You look at the face of a pilot who has both wings in the cloud. He looks positively gloomy.

Finally, one of those evangelists got to me. Jerry Griffin; runs a Piper outfit over at the cement airport. Calls it Professional Aviation. They wear coats and ties, shave every day, and keep those little stubby airplanes waxed so slick that a fly landing on one would break a leg. I respect and admire Jerry. He's the blue-eyed, blonde-haired, all-American kid who grew up at the airport fence. His operation is his dream come true.

Jerry is a "nonstress" instructor, as Bob Blodget used to say. After I got used to the funny way the Pipers ran down the cement and popped into the air, I began to look forward to the hours under the hood beside him. He purred, blending with the purr of the low-winger. I remember the enchantment of those first hours with Jerry. He gave me the confidence that I could defy all the senses that all my ancestors had developed since they came down out of the trees and began to walk on their hind legs. I was fascinated with the little science-fiction world that grew in the green-and-white glow of the needles and numbers. I had my own horizon, my own gravity. We flew into the sunset, into the nights, into the clouds. It made no difference, for I had my own little universe swimming before my eyes.

Gradually, the instruments came to translate into attitudes of flight; they became an intellectualized extension of my own senses. Drunk with professionalism, I went right out and bought a black attaché case and some bifocals. It was the first time I had ever needed a place to keep papers while flying or needed to know what all those little close-together marks on the dials meant.

Somewhere along in here, Jerry sent my license off to Oklahoma City and it came back with a blue seal upon it. Now, at least, I would not be an automatic dead man in 120 seconds if I flew into a cloud.

Griffin said the instrument flight test would come easy enough, in time, but we were both worried about that glass mountain ahead: the written exam. In real life, I am the morning mouth on local radio. On a disc jockey's schedule, that meant early to bed, early to rise, attend a night school and look more dead than alive. So Jerry did a noble thing; he referred me to the Bob Marsh Aviation School, on Houston Hobby Field. After that, I'd pass the written in a matter of days, I was assured.

My first thought was that Marsh operated a diploma mill. His school teaches the FAA exams, and I never heard of anybody failing to pass a written when Bob Marsh sent them reeling off to the Fed's exam room nearby. I went to Marsh expecting three days of cram, wham, bam, thank you ma'am, but I was staggered by the mass of knowledge needed and the relentless digging into a massive pile of Government publications to get to it.

Marsh gives the student a dummy exam, the student researches his answers, wrong ones are circled on the graded paper and the student has to display a complete working knowledge of every subject missed during a *mano a mano* oral review with an instructor. The process simply goes on and on until the student has learned this new vocabulary and all its attendant rules and can snap out the correct answer to every squiggly blur on a weather-depiction map and every bird footprint on a Jepp chart.

Marsh says he builds his study course around the FAA written-exam format so that the student will be familiar with it when he sees the real thing. He has mastered a workable technique of imprinting "Government-speak" upon the clay of a student's mind.

After three days of this, all I wanted was out. I kept gazing off toward distant blue skies, longing to find a place not boxed in, so I could lay the Stearman over on its back and shout "Ya-a-a-ah!"

I was never born to fly with a bunch of books in my lap. Marsh, who learned to fly from Moses, and had retired as chief pilot for Howard Hughes, shook his fine silver head and looked wonderfully sad. "There's only one learning obstacle I cannot overcome in a student—lack of motivation." We parted with regrets, but as friends.

A few years rolled by. FLYING published its *Guide for Instrument Flying 1973*. The demand exceeded the supply, and the magazine soon became a collector's item. Plans were made for a sequel. The New York office searched its roster of far-flung editor-writers. "Who is our most hard-case VFR pilot?"

"How about Bax? He doesn't even like to sit indoors in a cabin . . . He's nearly 50, a part-time flyer, set in his ways . . . if he can get a ticket, anybody can."

"We can really make a case for instrument flying . . ." And so the Word went forth.

I kicked. I screamed. Bled real blood. Offered to fly around the world in a Champ with one hand tied behind my back. Said I'd grow a moustache and write about a talking seagull. Anything but this. Didn't they realize it would be the ruination of one of America's last unspoiled pasture pilots? Anyway, I never got a chance to read *Guide for Instrument Flying.* They never got as far as the grass airport in Texas.

New York sent a copy. I read it, and it like to have scared me to death. All this nonchalant tossing off of such phrases as: "Of course, anyone can keep the airplane right side up." Hell, I couldn't.

But if this cup cannot be passed, then let us drink the most bitter portion first. In November of 1972, I once more appeared before Bob Marsh, hat in hand, asking for a go at the written exam. His only comment was a bear hug, and that he had been expecting me.

We mounted an all-out campaign, and this I recommend to any busy man. Get your affairs in order; take about a week off; and present yourself to a reputable, well-organized ground school and concentrate on dat ol' debbil, the written exam. The flying part of it will make more sense to you later.

In order for me to live with this ground-school monster for a week, a most strange business alliance was worked out, involving the publishers of FLYING, the owners of Radio KLVI and a 19-year-old Houston bride. We moved the radio station from Beaumont, Texas to Houston and installed it in the front bedroom of my newly wedded daughter's home, which is just blocks from Marsh's school on Hobby Field.

The housewives listening to my morning show got music, news and witty recitations of FAR Part 91. I was totally saturated with this new world of words; I couldn't shut it off. I went to sleep at night dreaming that I had my hands around the throat of whichever Government lawyer had written all that stuff. It couldn't have been written by a human pilot. It obviously was never intended to support an airplane in flight, only its own bulk in court.

I who had known the freedom of the hawk became a studying automaton. A sponge of the assorted knowledge that a man must arm himself with to fly without outside eyes . . . true course is magnetic course, plus or minus variation . . . magnetic heading plus or minus deviation equals compass heading . . . the following documents must be displayed inside the aircraft . . . Zulu minus six equals Central . . . pressure altitude . . . density altitude . . . indicated airspeed . . . calibrated airspeed . . . true airspeed . . . the hemoglobin absorbs carbon monoxide 200 times faster than oxygen . . . My mind staggered. It reeled. It separated and rolled up into little balls. I had slit open the belly of the body of aviation and was swishing around in the innards, and I began to wish I'd never seen them. If it was going to take all of this just to fly by instruments, then ATRs must be gods. They should be allowed to ascend the flight deck adorned in silken garments, with private pilots as acolytes bearing candles.

For me, there was no way. I felt like a savage brought out of the jungle to be taught the whole body of civilization in one week. By the third day, I was silly, numb. My head felt as though it had been injected through the ear with numbered putty. Bob unchained me and sent me home. "Look at your handwriting. It's gone all to pieces. Go home, fix a drink, go to bed. Tomorrow will be worse."

On the last day before the exam, they heaped me with books. *AIM,* FAR, ZAP—all the stuff I needed to know, and all of it scattered through a million subparagraphs. If a lawyer had to go through this many slithering books and back-flopping pages to research a case, nothing would ever get to the courtroom. They would settle it out on the lawn with short-barreled pistols. Why doesn't somebody codify all this junk? I rebelled. I told Bob the hell with all this, teach me with words. Let me sit at your feet, tell it to me in real words as the ancient masters did. No man can read an FAR.

But inside me, the growling glow had begun. I was ready, and I knew it. I was stiff with it. For a week now, I felt as though I had been shackled with chains inside a wooden box only four feet high and four feet wide, new Government documents and a pan of water being shoved in through the trap door. After seven days and seven nights, I was ready. I sprang out into the daylight, all covered with hair, howling and gnashing to get to that real exam.

That FAA exam room was a place Hitler could have loved. Rectangular, white-walled, sterile, windowless except for the one-way-mirrored door. The matron, in a seersucker uniform with black name tag, ran her Geiger counter over my lunch bag. (Man, it's a six-hour exam.) The Geiger counter found my little transistorized calculator and shrilled its alarm.

Feds in dark coats with narrow ties came running softly. I explained that ever since the fourth grade, I had flunked anything to do with math, and what a shame to blow questions on weight and balance and time and distance just because the towers of figures toppled for me. A hurried conference over the exam rules found nothing that said such a device could not be used, "So long as it does not have a memory circuit," they warned. It didn't, and that little handful of transistors saved me about an hour and at least a half dozen wrong answers.

I entered into the stark chamber, my footfalls crashing among the earlier inmates, who looked up, glaring, until I had rattled around and built my nest. From that time, the only sound was an occasional deep sigh—more like a drawn-out sob. Once some guy's stomach rumbled and I almost bolted and fled; thought the building was caving in.

Marsh had commanded, "Use those Mickey Mouse things I showed you. Place a strip of paper over the question and read it line for line. Move your lips if you have to. I've watched you read, you gulp a whole paragraph. Do that in there and you'll swallow the hook that's buried in the question for smart guys."

I drew up two columns on a scratch pad, headed "possible" and "out." Bob had said that every question would have four answers. "Two will be dogs, one will be the 'deceiver,' one is the correct answer. Put the dog numbers in the 'out' column, then you just have two answers to consider. Then think, man, because if you don't have a full knowledge of the intent of the question, the deceiver will appear to be the most believable answer."

A part of Bob's Last Rites and Benediction ceremony is to challenge the applicant to predict his score and write it down in secret. Bob does the same, and a two-bit bet is made on the outcome. I gave myself a four-point spread; 68 to 72. Bob had written down 78. When that ominous letter arrived from Oklahoma City, my final score was exactly what that crafty, mean old man had predicted. He insisted on payment by check.

Rejoicing, I started for the door, free at last to go fly the airplane, the easy part. But another manacle had been slipped over my cuff. This time, the chain led to what you had better not call a Link Trainer, for it is in truth a Cessna 172 Flight Simulator— a one-of-a-kind modification of the Link. It will do anything a 172 will do, and some of it much more suddenly.

Had I but known what the next 19.2 hours in the green box would bring, I would have given up on the rating and put in for pit crew at *Car and Driver.* "The airplane," said Professor Marsh, "is a very poor classroom. And if you cannot do the required stuff in the simulator, then you will have plenty of problems out there." So I climbed in and they shut the coffin lid.

If I said "Ahhh" or "This is . . ." then I had to start over. Me, with 28 years of broadcast radio—I began to get mike fright. They badgered me, and how I longed to get one of those instructors into my control room for just a day and make an ass out of him. But soon I was using this new-found skill with the radio as I commuted into Hobby by Cessna each day. Some hillbilly, like I used to be last week, would call up with 17 planes on the frequency and say, "Hobby Tower, Hobby Tower, this is Cessna November 1234 Alfa, and ahhh, we are . . . about . . . over downtown, ah, and we plan to land at Hobby, ah, what's y'all's active runway? Over."

Gritting my teeth like the rest during this soliloquy, I would wait for a breath of silence in the chatter and hit them with my carefully rehearsed "Hobby, Cessna 8529 Bravo, Fry Intersection with Juliet." And like magic came, "Two-Niner Bravo, report right base 30." Just like that. In seven seconds, each of us knew all we needed to know about the other. I felt pretty smug, although it had taken me a week to find Fry Intersection.

But the confines of that little green box were paced off by Satan himself, and his footprints are called holding patterns. Paul Carrington taught me how to find my way into those little private cells of airspace. Direct entry, parallel entry or teardrop; what a delicious name for it: teardrop. Also sweatdrop. It got so bad that each day, I used a different brand of antiperspirant. And each day, I surfaced from the box dripping like a fish. The laundry began to reject my shirts.

Big Brother's metallic voice became inescapable: "You are flying through your fix . . . you are 100 feet above assigned altitude . . . what is the reciprocal of 134? C'mon, c'mon!" And more nagging about radio technique: "Six-One Xray, say altitude."

"Twenty-two hundred."

"Never heard of it."

"Two thousand two hundred."

"That's better."

Time stopped in the green box. No yesterday, no tomorrow, just those walls closing in. Bunched up, I tried to cheat. I muttered, cursed, got vertigo, spun, crashed and burned on the VOR approach to Galveston. Once, I even stalled and crashed on takeoff. When that thing shuddered and broke and those needles started unwinding, I felt a shock of real fear in my chest. Slammed in power, dived for airspeed, actually died when the altimeter hit field elevation. Only the raucous laughter and beating on the box from outside, and the fact that my smoking hole was now 400 feet below sea level, brought my senses back. Still, no one will ever make me believe that thing is just bolted to the floor.

I, an airplane pilot, was suffering the indignity of having to jiggle this internal bungee-cord-and-bellows box into level flight and keep it there among slithering needles. My red tracings on the plastic overlay outside looked like the homeward route of a drunk boll weevil. I alibied that the mechanical phoniness of the thing was impossible—that I could fly a *real* airplane. Then the immaculate Tony Koenninger stepped up on the running board, reached in with one hand and flew a perfect approach. For that, I could hate him. "The trouble with you, Bax, is that you have never flown a real airplane like we are asking you to here. Going home tonight in that 172, see if you can fly within five degrees of heading and 20 feet of altitude."

This was the beginning of the next great turnaround in my thinking about flying. I discovered what a sloppy pilot I had always been. I had been wandering along like a strutted cow coming in at milking time. I began to really try to nail those numbers. Soon it got to be a habit, and a second bud of pride—of wanting to be professional in flying—broke through the thick bark.

But it was still slow going in the box. I regressed for a time, and they put me back to basics. Depression led to savagery. I slammed it around, rejoicing as the bellows hissed and groaned. New clearances to copy piled upon corrections not yet made. In my great fury, I would have leaped out of that thing and punched my instructor, except that the years Tom Adams had spent in that flying trapeze called a helicopter had developed his biceps powerfully. Always, his voice would come in: "You can fight it, but you can never win. Make it come to you."

The urge to kill born in the simulator was not just mine. Tommy Reedy, a high-time ag pilot and part owner of Reedy-West Air Service, in Angleton, Texas, was going through the same torture an hour ahead of me. Tommy was in the school because "It's getting so you can't go anywhere VFR anymore." The quiet, taciturn Reedy once sprang from the infernal box and made Marsh a cash offer for the thing so he could take it home and chop it up with an ax.

Lorene Holmes, who was going the IFR route so she could be as good as her Beechcraft, could sometimes be heard softly weeping inside the infernal device. She suggested that a drain plug be installed in the cockpit floor so that a finished student could be poured out into a pan and set in the window to cool.

An hour or two in the box would dissolve me into utter stupidity. Once when turning right again instead of left for a teardrop entry, a ghostly voice whispered through the fuselage, "Left. Turn left." I later learned that there is a hidden peephole in the thing, so they can see how white your knuckles are, but I never found out who my prompting angel of mercy was.

Later, in the real airplane, I was being eaten up alive on a back-course approach into Hobby. I had forgotten about reverse sensing. Approach radar couldn't even tell whether I was heading for Hobby, Andrau or Ellington. A shaking cup of coffee in my hand, I told my instructor at debriefing that I didn't see how I had botched it up so badly; all the other times had been right down the slot. He gently reminded me that this had been my first one; all the "other times" had been in the simulator. That's how real the experience had seemed to me.

The campaign to get the instrument ticket had begun in early November. It was now approaching New Year's and the winter gunk had moved in over the Gulf Coast. I soon learned that if Hobby and Beaumont, my home base, were reporting VFR minimums, the clouds would be hugging the ground between the two, over the spooky Trinity River bottomlands over which I crept and cheated along Interstate 10. During this time, a Cherokee Six pilot trying the same stuff at Baytown got vertigo and slow-rolled in at the threshold of Humphrey Field, dispatching himself and his passengers.

There was only one tall obstruction along this course—the 570-foot-tall obelisk of the San Jacinto Battlefield Monument. My game was to find the white stone shaft in the haze and mist without hitting it. In wilder moments, I thought of what a fine way to go this would be:

"Say, whatever happened to your old man—the one who used to fly and write about it?"

"Oh, he hit the San Jacinto Monument in the fog one day. You can still see the mark, about halfway up to the star."

Tour guides would add this event to their spiel. A niche in Texas history. Oh, how I longed for that instrument rating, and how I hoped to live long enough to get it.

And now it was 1973, early January, and we were walking out to the real airplane for the first time. Bob Marsh's instrument trainer is a Cessna 172 bristling with antennas for almost every navaid except radar and inertial. It sat crushed low on its spats with its burden of electronics and long-range fuel tanks.

Each day began with one of those preflights that everyone ought to do but nobody does unless under the eye of the Feds or a flight instructor. As I inspected those little cotter keys that hold the aileron pins in place, as I have done on every Cessna for the last 15 years, I got to wondering where this custom started. Has there ever been a report of the ailerons falling off a Cessna? Does Dwane Wallace ever worry about those little bent wires? Later, in the course of 31.5 hours in that thing with Jim Shelton threatening to tape my hands if I didn't stop wigwagging those ailerons and zooming my turns all over the sky, I began to consider that while the cotter keys may never drop out, it did seem likely that I might *wear* them out.

Shelton and I droned through January together in the growing understanding and friendship that develops between men who fly side by side for long hours. The flight syllabus was a repetition of the pattern learned in the simulator. Radar vectors to a holding pattern, then to Galveston VOR, another hold, then the Galveston VOR approach, missed approach and back to Hobby for whatever instrument landing was in use. About two hours under the hood, with the worst saved for last, as it would be for real.

With the elastic headband of the hood slowly squeezing off the blood supply to my brain, I entertained Mr. Shelton with such comedy as attempting 180-degree intercepts to a radial, and getting lost over the Galveston VOR. I was mildly surprised to learn that actual flight was even more demanding than those dark hours in the womb of the simulator. I say mildly, for by this time, I didn't really expect anything to be easy or turn out right. Shelton helped: He turned all the radios up to full blare to get me used to this new element of chaos. During the first few hours, he worked all communications; I had my hands full just keeping us right side up.

"Scan, man, don't stare at any one instrument . . . take little bites at that radial intercept, then center those needles with the rudders . . . hold that heading; in this business, flying a heading is everything . . . pay attention . . . concentrate . . . this is an exercise in self-discipline . . . quit flopping those ailerons; you want a five-degree correction, so skid into it."

And more: "I let you get lost over that VOR. Everybody does it sooner or later. You must keep a mental image of where you are relative to what those needles are telling you. If you ever lose the mental picture, you are *really* lost. There's two attitudes—yours and the airplane's . . . relax, man, your legs are like iron on those rudders . . . relax . . . don't fight it . . . make the airplane come to you . . ."

Holding at a VOR was the worst for me. As the needles became more fidgety, I would cramp in more and more rudder until I was unwittingly holding reverse aileron. "Jim," I said, "this is a crooked airplane. It's kinked up somewhere and will not fly straight."

"Turn it loose a minute." I did, and it jumped sideways so far I missed the whole VOR again. Shelton laughed out aloud.

Missed approaches were not too bad, except for my fatal fixation on heading to the detriment of altitude. I was also still plagued by occasional vertigo. Once on an approach to Galveston, Scholes Field did a slow roll right inside my head. Jim had said, "If I ever yell 'I got it!' I mean I got it. I'm not interested in finding out which of us is the strongest." He stopped the barrel roll and said, "If you ever get disoriented on approach, declare a missed approach and get the hell out. That other will kill you. A missed approach is for re-orientation. Never be too proud to go around."

I'll probably remember Shelton's ILS technique forever. "Your road is narrowing down to two and a half degrees on either side. Say those limits out loud to yourself if it helps, but leave those ailerons alone. Use rudders. Pedal it like a bicycle. And that glide slope is just like sliding down a slanted wire. If you're too low, level out and gently fly into it again; if you're high, ease off a little power and let her sink a little."

I'd come down that chute babbling to myself, sweat trickling cold down my ribs, "two left, just two, that's all you get, wait for it, and you're low, hold level, and there it comes . . . centers at 36 . . . hold 36 . . . and now you're high . . ." When the hair started to crawl on the back of my neck as the altimeter went below 250, Jim would flip up the hood and there it all lay, right where it was supposed to be, like the pathway to the Pearly Gates.

At this instant of transition to contact flying, Jim would lean forward, peer into my face and ask, "You alright?" I don't know what he was looking for, but I felt great. He varied between being a most gentle and sensitive instructor and the most infuriating stress teacher, but a word of praise from him was worth the Medal of Honor to me. Once he flipped the hood and I found us in a bucketing crosswind. I painted one on and made the first intersection turnoff. He may have smiled, and I thought I heard him mutter, "Ain't no hill for a stepper."

After other flights, we would taxi to the ramp in sullen silence, and once he said, "You were so bad today I don't even want to talk to you about it." I regressed badly at about the two-thirds point, as I had in the simulator. The blowup came on an ILS approach when I reached for the mike to report "outer marker, inbound." While I reached and talked, I swerved right, pegging the needle. Jim shouted, "Now what the hell did you do that for?"

Furious with myself as well as him, I yelled back, "Because I'm just a gahdamn student, that's why!" I overheard him telling this to Marsh later; both of them whooped a laugh.

These regressions brought another pride-crushing back-to-basics session. We flew the course without the hood, "So you can see what you have been visualizing." Then without a word, Jim took over the controls and began the most astonishing demonstration of routine flight that I have ever seen. The sly old master unwrapped his hidden stock of tricks and opened up my eyes to why professional pilots seem to be doing so little at the controls. He painted the needles in the center with almost imperceptible rudder movements. Went from approach speed to cruise speed and through altitude changes apparently using only the throttle. The last thing he ever touched was the trim wheel, and that just once. "Now you do it."

I copied his techniques and felt the tingle of having broken through to a subtle management of the airplane that I never knew was possible.

"Jim, why in hell didn't you show me all this from the beginning?"

"You weren't ready for it. Not deep enough into instrument flying to know that you needed it until now."

"Yessir."

It's funny; I always call him Jim on the ground, but calling him sir in the airplane seemed natural, too. Now I understood why. One of the unexpected dividends awaiting you when you finally decide to don the plastic hood and find out what *all* the knobs on the panel are for is that you will enter into a level of flying proficiency that most VFR pilots don't even know exist.

January dissolved into February, and now I was so anxious to get it that I was overtrying. "Bax, you are worrying this airplane to death. Relax, man; you got a lot of bad habits to unlearn. I can force you to fly that panel with your eyes, but you are still listening VFR. You're flying partial panel. And quit ducking down to pick up those charts in a turn or one of these days you'll go snap-roll vertigo doing that . . . and think ahead, man. Plan. Always consider your alternatives; so the VOR just flipped from 'to' to 'from' and the needle never centered? Well, what are you going to do now? Listen carefully, Baxter: When you are sitting up here in the gunk all by yourself, if you don't have a cold, deadly reason for doing something—then don't do nothin'."

Fatigue, frustration and humiliation began to move in on me. Even if I ever learned to fly the insane perfection that these guys wanted, would I have the cods to actually bicycle down that beam someday, alone and blind, scared witless, knowing that the altimeter was going through 400 and there was solid earth down there in one minute more of this? Would I have it to go on down to the published 250? That one I still don't know, though I did it every day under the hood. I was pretty discouraged. Fed up, in fact.

A particularly shaggy approach at Galveston and the start of the long, butt-weary flight back to Hobby, concentrating on those slippery needles. Jim could sense how it was. Lit a cigarette and stuck it up under the hood on my lip. I slipped off my boots, wiggled my toes, unclamped my hands and decided he was probably the greatest guy in the world. The airplane flew better, too. But as for me, I was probably unteachable past a certain point we had already reached some time back.

Then one day I heard a chilling exchange over Houston Approach that wiped out any lingering doubts I may have had over the loss of "freedom of the skies" and my own sinking motivation.

A Braniff captain on the ILS into Hobby reported in resigned tones, "There's a 150 playing around just under the clouds out here."

But for the random chance of a few seconds either way, that Boeing would have popped out of the cloud base on gauges and speared that happy VFR pilot in his little tin fish. The hell of it was they were both legal. The VFR pilot was clear of clouds and all that, but nothing required him to have an approach plate that would show him that he was playing in the middle of the busiest street in Houston, or be tuned to the approach frequency or even have his radio on.

I realized then that flying may be a great game, but it can only be survived by everybody knowing and playing by the same rules. Yet eight out of ten of the players are required to know only about one-fourth of the rules. Freedom of the skies be damned; this is madness.

I may become insufferable about this, like a reformed drunk busting into saloons and slapping the drinks out of everybody's hands, but for the first time in my life, I don't feel too guilty about calling myself a pilot in front of other pilots. With the ink still wet on my ticket, I'm no instrument pilot. (They said, "Here—now you have a license to go out and kill yourself.") But I'm working at it. And I have never worked so hard for, or been so proud of, anything in my life.

Getting there took from November 10, 1972 to February 10, 1973, and it didn't finish with any flourish of trumpets or garland of roses. At the low point of the sullen rides with Shelton, I was smitten with pneumonia. Two weeks of skulking around wondering if I was well or sick, and then I presented myself to Marsh's on a Saturday. I wasn't well, wasn't still sick, but any flying would be better than no flying. It seemed natural that the Old Man himself came gruffing out to ride with me; Saturday was Shelton's day off. "I don't like to shout in airplanes," was Marsh's only comment as we set sail to go crashing around the course.

On the home leg, he stirred himself out of his corner to pester me with a lot of irrelevant questions about what I'd do if this or that happened. He only stiffened up once when I almost pegged the needle on the localizer coming home. As I bicycled out of that one, I heard us both emit a long, shaky sigh.

Taxiing back to the ramp, he asked: "How do you think you did?"

"No better, no worse than usual, sir."

"Well, you just passed the check ride."

An instrument rating is truly a line of demarcation in flying. Once a pilot has crossed it, his innocence is gone, and looking way back now, I think maybe a lot of the fun too. I really think that single-engine, single-pilot instrument approaches are one of the most dangerous legal sports in America, but it is a controlled danger. Unlike the sunshine pilot whose role in weather is sometimes one of passive terror, with him as the unwitting victim, an instrument pilot can always coolly evaluate the level of his own skill against that of his chosen adversary and decide whether he wants to draw down on him or not. He can also call it quits and go someplace else if he discovers he is outgunned and is pretty sure this game will end with a smoking hole in the ground. He has options on his danger not open to a vertigo-spinning VFR pilot. But I still think a solo low approach is the most exciting controlled close call you can find to play while wearing a dress shirt, tie and jacket and looking perfectly sane.

As usual, like any ham with any newly learned trick, I kept coming back on stage and doing it over and over, not aware until Stephan gently memoed me that while the "there I was, flat on my back at 10,000 feet, nothing on the clock but the maker's name" stories were good, he was almost beginning to wish I would go out and find a Stearman again. The first instrument story was "Forty More to Yarb."

As a footnote to history, let me assure you that this high-altitude transition point, Yarb, is still found only on the Dallas STAR arrival plate called Blue Ridge Five and is viewed mostly by line pilots. They named Yarb for Ed Yarbrough, out of admiration and affection for this big, gruff, retired Air Force Colonel who became American Airlines Director of Traffic Control and who helped to set up the Fort Worth approaches.

But since an intersection may not be named for a real person, they can never admit it. They just smile if asked.

Forty More to Yarb

It was the first time I had ever air-filed IFR, and it was easier than I thought. McAlester Flight Service Station took my case history, then handed me off to Fort Worth Center for final diagnosis. Ft. Worth came right back with a cheerful "cleared as filed," and I climbed to the requested 4,000 and entered a weird world of clouds: white clouds, gray clouds, blue clouds, and much pitching and heaving.

The first problem arose when an eastbound Aztec called Ft. Worth for a lower altitude out of five and for some zigging around "the buildups at McAlester." Knew this would involve me; was already holding the mike when Center called and asked for an ETA to McAlester VOR. Regretted having made initial filing from a wild-ass guess but estimated McAlester in 15 minutes. An old aviator once told me, "Always tell 'em 15 minutes. It's believable."

I was still pulling maps off the ceiling and fishing for a cross-bearing from Ardmore VOR and listening to that Aztec crying in the chapel when Center rang me up again. Estimated McAlester VOR three minutes this time, knowing it was a bad move. Sure enough, Center was back in three minutes. Told him I was still north of VOR, hunting it—a poor choice of words. Center suggested I verify tuning and try cross-bearing from Ardmore and was I really at 4,000 feet?

Had the leans by this time. Gauges were all on straight, but head wasn't. Very possible altimeter was stuck at 4,000. Tapped it. Looked out the window to see if I was still tied down to chocks. Got glimpse of McAlester runway. Made triumphant report and heard them call a clearance to the straining Aztec. Aztec had encountered bad buildups over McAlester, and I wasn't exactly in a feather bed myself. Noted that white clouds lifted me 500 feet and left warm moisture on windshield; blue clouds dropped me

500 feet, left cold moisture on person. Made a mental note to write something definitive about this someday.

Aztec whistled by unseen. Suddenly realized that none of us was on radar, that Center was dealing but not betting.

Ahead stretched 98 nm of Victor 63 to Blue Ridge VOR and approaches to Dallas. Had good cross-bearing from Ardmore but no indication of movement. Tapped VOR glass in friendly way. Leans getting worse. Now steering with left-side pedals and right-side yoke. Tried to work time-distance on computer. Got ground speed of 35 knots. Could hear Center working five P.M. Jetstream inbound to Dallas. At about 10-second intervals, the 727s reported Blue Ridge at 16,000, Shiloh at 7,000 and handed off to final approach. Been three days for me, and my VOR not showing "from" McAlester yet. Decided all instruments correct, aircraft stuck on radial. Think cool thoughts. What would Kung Fu Caine do at a time like this?

Center asks me to report Yarb Intersection. Look on en-route chart. No Yarb. Check Dallas plates. No luck. Look in Webster's —already leaning all the way over into suitcase anyway. No Yarb. Search memory for folklore. A yarb is a root herb, akin to the sweet potato . . . no, a female member of the Marine officer corps? I inform Center I will report Ravenna.

Flight lasts through several shift changes at Ft. Worth Center. Voices seem to get younger. Think I hear retirement party for original controller. (They give him a gold watch; I hear laughter.) Becomes a tradition to call up that ol' Cessna stuck out on Victor 63 and see where he is.

Lashed back at them once. Asked for winds aloft at four. Told me southerly at 10 with the sun setting in clear skies over Dallas. Whippersnappers. Little do they know what we pilots are going through out here in distant cloud castles.

I report Ravenna. Word goes around Center that the 172 has made Ravenna. Beautiful word, Ravenna. Named after a raven-haired Southern beauty whose loved one went off to fight at Blue Ridge and Shiloh and never returned. Several of the guys at Center call to offer congratulations. Meanwhile, jets that only recently departed JFK are reporting Blue Ridge, thousands of passengers are deplaning at Love, reuniting with their loved ones, going on with orderly lives. New union contracts are being negotiated. A Braniff pilot has gone to the apartment of a stewardess he has gone with for five years and broken up with her and returned to his wife and cocker spaniel.

In a choked voice, I report Blue Ridge, ready to copy the lightning-swift sequencing to Shiloh and approach.

Center clears me to land.

"But I'm still 40 miles out."

"We know. It's okay; they've all gone home."

The magazine printed a lot of typing from me until August when J.K. West came to town in his B-25 to visit his brother, Earl, the chief pilot for George Mitchell out at M&M Air Service. They casually called and asked if I would like to come ride in their bomber.

JK's B-25

Ol' Man West had two sons, and he taught them how to fly. Oh lordy, did he teach them how to fly! Out of the cloudbursts of the war and into clear skies they flew, and still do, strapped into round-engine dusters, sitting up there bronzing in the sun.

One day, J.K. swapped a run-out Stearman for a B-25. Swapped even, he did. Now what kind of man would keep a B-25 for a pet? Brought it over to the grass airport and it sat there hangar high, and J.K. and his brother, Earl Junior, gave me a call: "Hey, you wanna come ride the B-25?"

It sits out there all olive drab. The West boys are hunkering in the shade of a yellow-nosed nacelle plucking new grass. "C'mon, boy." I follow under the shade of the long, narrow belly to where it lets down its bib and climb up onto the flight deck and look down on the world. "Sit in the right seat, boy." Right in the tiger's mouth.

"You let me know when you see gas drippin' out of that one."

"It's drippin'."

First a slow milling of the prop, then the blur and the shuddering cowl all wreathed in smoke.

"Don't see no flames either."

" 'at's always a good sign."

We poise, tail out over the wire fence almost to the railroad tracks, with them little Cessnas cringing against their chains. J.K. does the run-up, twiddling mag switches from a '31 Packard dashboard, with its engine instruments all clustered in the middle like they were installed with a shotgun, and an artificial horizon big as a dinner plate. Right out of the Smithsonian.

"This thing working?"

"All them things is working."

My window slides shut easy, greasy and (click) locks. Right then is when I decide to go on and trust those 28-year-old engines. If a man keeps a window track clean, you just know he takes care of the engines.

"I'll do this takeoff. The field is kind of short."

That's when it dawns on me that he's gonna let me . . . oh, lordy. Then he's pouring on the cobs and the seat back is crowding me. This twin island of rushing sound and all that tonnage is over the fence now, rattling kitchens below, and J.K. raises both paws off the wheel and smiles me my invitation. Just like that. I'm flying the Army Air Corps B-25 bomber, medium, twin-row Wright, 1,700 horsepower, tra la la.

Take that, Army Air Corps. You were wrong about me, see? You washed me out in '43. I would have died for this, truly, but you gave me latrines to clean and garbage cans to dive, and the sandy, dusty stockade, and rides in the six-by truck with the chicken wire over the back and floppy fatigues to wear while those other finks wore pinks and wings and little cookie-duster moustaches and 50-mission caps. Oh, were you ever wrong about me! I laugh, thinking of all the tons of manuals they had to read to do this and here's ol' Colonel West giving it to me in the sweet essence—

"Hold 110 on approach . . . approach flaps coming now . . . gear coming down . . . I got a wheel . . ."

"I got a wheel."

I reel in some cable, and she turns sweetly onto final. A refinery slides by in the canted windshield. Another mood steals in: Men died in planes just like this one, turning low over refineries. Metal opened, all jagged and shrieking wind. Turrets hammered, and hot, spent .50-caliber brass rolled thick in new blood.

I look down at the flight-deck floor where cigarette butts roll thick in seed rice. The West boys smoke a lot and always have rice left over in their cuffs.

"Full flaps coming in now . . . hold 100."

You know all the pitch changes are moderate? Gear, flaps—all of it J.K.'s heavy leg is pressed against the trim wheel, and I don't want to bother him so I just muscle it. No worse than a Cessna 182. Lining it up, I walk those tandem rudders—they're alive. Droop a wing for a little crosswind. She just stays wherever you put her; North American built stable airplanes. No wonder the Army hung onto its B-25s long after the other mediums had gone to aluminum pots. This great thing is four-by-four honest!

"Flies just like an airplane."

"What'd you expect?"

I flare a tad high, but she forgives me, settling in easier than a 310 would have. Then we try a few touch-and-goes, my teeth drying out because I can't quit grinning. Then it is brother Earl's turn, and I get up to move aft.

"Why you sweating so much, ace?"

"I was sitting in the sun."

The Brothers West flying together: The cockpit is just two Wests wide, and the harmony between them fairly sings. Earl has it easy—one hand—and I notice he pokes J.K.'s leg out of the way and flies the trim all the time. You watch, all the really good pilots do that. Earl makes a Stearman-size pattern, gets a squeaker.

"You wanna do another?"

"I wanna quit on that one."

The brothers laugh, light up and leave the hammer in on take-off, gee-whizzing at the 30-foot-a-minute climb, and then go streaking off across rice fields, back to the grass airport.

"Hey, ain't that ol' Murph down there?"

"Yeah, that's his truck all right . . ."

Ol' Murph is farming rice, riding high on a combine, sitting on almost every ticket the FAA ever issued and thousands of hours

of dusting with the West boys. And you just know what's gonna
happen to ol' Murph next, don't you?

He never saw it coming nor heard it over the roar of the combine. It streaked between two harvesting machines umbrella high.
Up, up into a duster turn, and down, tilting over the rice paddies.
This is how it must have looked through Doolittle's windshield.
Murph is out on the running board of the combine now, jumping
up and down on his hat. It's Murph all right. He's a redhead. We
go by again, pointing and waving out the side windows.

"Lookee ol' Murph! Haw haw, hee hee hee."

We wave out the window at about 200 knots. Going away, I
think I see ol' Murph is trying to spell a four-letter word in the rice
with his combine. We left a good swath harvested our own selves.

The Wests, giants at play at what they do for a living, were full
of joy now. They left me off at the grass airport dancing with glee
as the sweet harmony built up to a roar and the B-25 sucked up
its gear, assumed its low, lethal silhouette, and bulleted for Angleton. What kind of men keep a B-25 for a pet? Some men putter
it off at golf with stingy little balls. Some men live grandly.

February of '74 found us in the indecisions of the first fuel
crisis, with *Flying* flinching as the price of Barons bottomed. It
was as quickly as we ever reacted, almost news-magazine style.
My part of the fuel war was to go out and see what the little
guys were thinking. I circled the Southwest, got varied replies
about the threat of a 50-percent fuel cut for general aviation
including "I of course we only fly for business reasons . . ." But
the guy who cut closest to the bone said, "Ay-rab blackmail,
that's all it is. You gonna have to choose one, your Bonanza or
Israel. What we ought to do is land the Marines at Cairo and
drag that Sheik Ahmed Yamani down the street behind a Har-
ley-Davidson until he can talk some sense."

By March, I was sending Stephan stuff from deep in the
clouds again.

Little White Buttons

I was a freshly rated instrument pilot but had never flown alone in clouds—a student matador who had yet to feel the brush of the horns. How would I be in the Moment of Truth, that prolonged narrow escape called "the instrument approach"?

I could hardly wait for an IFR day so I could go out and get de-flowered. Then came "ceiling 800, visibility 10, tops at three"; just right, with room to chicken out at either end. I entered the stuff and noted two things at once: It was awfully quiet in there, and according to the instruments, the airplane was standing on edge and falling.

Upon reentering the cloud base, I had some trouble acquiring the localizer, due to a 35-knot wind from somewhere, but I could hit it momentarily going either east or west. After some of this, approach control asked me for an ETA to the outer marker, and I heard them park a Delta DC-9 in the holding pattern behind me.

I really felt rotten—all those nice folks getting late, jouncing around in a circle. I tried to get approach to just let the jet in and I'd go on home, but I was locked into the system. They kept repeating. "You are cleared for the approach."

It was hard to reply. The mike kept standing out from the panel on its cord at odd angles. "May I be excused, sir?" Naw, that ain't it. What *is* the thing I say to get me out of this? I remembered it two nights later, sat straight up in bed and shouted, "Missed approach!"

Meanwhile, I just cashed in my 800-foot altitude insurance policy and sank out of the game. They cleared the DC-9 out of holding and I whispered, "Sorry, Delta." Father Frog whispered back, "S'alright."

I tried a few more passes on subsequent days, proving only that I have a good knack for recovery from odd attitudes. So I went to confession to Old Hairy Ears, who flies offshore helicopters in the fog with one hand while scratching himself with the other. I told him IFR scared me.

"It should. All you got right now is a permit to go out and kill yourself. What you are good for now is punching out of here on low days, getting there on top in the sunshine and approaches to not less than 600 feet. Wade out a little at a time. Get experience. File IFR even if you're just going to the men's room. Get used to the system."

So it came to pass that I was weathered in at Addison, an airport that lies well within the Dallas ring of terror: Two days of sigmets and then the FSS said, "You can go if you leave now. The tornadoes are not due for another hour, and the thunderstorms have not yet formed a solid line."

I looked up at the fleeting gray scud swallowing 727s at 600 feet and thought, "Who, me? Fly my own plane?" The Moment of Truth had arrived. Real horns.

Ft. Worth Center was playing "let's thread the little fellow through the jet stream." Course changes, idents, altitude shifts and frequency switches flew at my head. It was like sitting in the grandstand at a Harlem Globetrotters game and having them toss me the ball to come down for one free shot with three seconds left to play, the score tied and me in street shoes.

At that moment, two little white buttons on the instrument panel were worth all my earthly treasure. One button agreed to hold the wings level, the other was willing to hunt for and lock onto whatever course I gave it. I would like to publicly thank Mr. Mitchell for having built this almost-autopilot, and Mr. Piper for making it available on small craft, and Mr. Jerry Griffin for wisely ordering this device on the airplanes that his Professional Aviation rents to us sometimes instrument pilots. You are all wonderful people.

A 300-mile track home and I never saw the sweet brown mother earth except for the runway at each end. The sky was a vast aquarium of blue—white cloud floor below, dark ocean above. The omni whiskers of my little Piper fish twitched to distant signals and assured me that I was actually tracking a straight line to somewhere.

A little breath of confidence wafted into me. Hell, this was going to be all right! I leaned back and enjoyed a sinfully good cigar. A feeling of quiet pride: no longer a low-flying fugitive making pylon turns around water tanks in the rain. I was flying by the rules, and it was easier. True, I had to dismantle all my life-learned habits as an earth creature and newly install all these senses in the tidy universe of the instrument panel, but this was pure flight, unbound by remembered horizons.

"Beaumont Approach, Cherokee 53 Tango is with you at seven." Even that slippery eel, the localizer, lay still to my hand and land emerged about where expected. At the ramp, laughter bubbled up in my throat: I realized that for the first time since I had become a pilot, I had taken the car keys with me. How do they phrase that in the FAA publications? "A competent performance . . . is one in which . . . the successful completion of the maneuver is never seriously in doubt."

Contact with Earl West brought us to Stearmans again. Earl had checked me out in Stearman biplanes many years before and has always been a sort of hero to me. He is not much known to throw words around needlessly. He checked me out in six words: "Let's go." he said as we got into it, and, as I was trying to decide what the handles did, "Fly it," he said over his shoulder from the front cockpit as the first landing attempt bounced us hangar high. "Land it" was his decision on the next bounce which left us low and slow. The way I could tell he was ready for me to solo was that he climbed out and walked away.

This story, like all the rest in this book, is true.

Nosedragger

Alan and I went out to fly the Stearman. Neither of us wanted to, but he was about to marry my flaming-blonde daughter and figured there were certain tribal rituals expected of him.

It was waiting for us out in the weeds, rearing up like a rib-stitched praying mantis. It was dinnertime, and all of the regular crew was at the long table tending to baloney sandwiches spread out on paper sacks. What we should have done was go in and watch the duster pilots eat. It would have been a better show.

There was just Alan and me to light the fuse on this thing, and he'd never seen one before. I showed him how to climb up the canvas sides and not put a foot through the wing; then I leaned in and told him what he'd be doing while I was out front, heaving the propeller over to try to get it started.

I told him all the good stuff like switch on and switch off. I showed him the throttle quadrant and how to stand on the brakes. I only forgot to mention two little bitty old things: that you can just about open that engine up with the first inch or so of throttle and that everybody holds the stick all the way back. That's what keeps the tail planted on the ground, no matter what else may happen.

Now, anyone who has ever messed around with Stearman airplanes knows they are full of surprises. The first surprise this time was that the engine fired on the first pull of the prop. The second surprise was that the throttle was about wide open. The old Lycoming gave a few astonished smoky explosions and then got the bit in her teeth. "This," I thought, leaping nimbly through the air, "is going to be one of those great moments."

"Brakes!" I screamed at Alan as I rounded the wing tip, but I could see him already standing on them. Stiff as a pool cue he was. The big biplane was roaring and quivering. It crow-hopped a few times, its locked wheels wrinkling up the turf like a cheap rug. Then the tail started to rise. Oh, Lordy, he wasn't holding the stick back, and the prop blast deflecting off those down-pointing flippers was elevating him. I tried to find some shoutable phrase, but Alan was down in the cockpit now, trying to switch off everything he'd switched on.

Then he was up, rising majestically skyward. Alan wore a full beard in those days and was a great, dignified-looking chap. He turned and gave me one last look of resignation and despair, as he rose like Moses ascending to the heavens. The prop dug into the earth just as the engine died.

In the silence, which was broken only by the sounds of fresh-flung clods thudding off the hangar roof and of gasoline starting to fry on the hot exhaust, Alan said, "What do I do now?" "Get down," I screamed. I was still at the screaming stage. Alan unclasped the seat belt and shot out of sight. There were dull thuds and groans from deep in the belly of the old airplane. He reappeared and teetered about on the sharp edges of wings and wires.

"Pops," he softly said, "there ain't no way. It's like trying to crawl through a harp."

Then all the crew showed up, bailing out of the pickup truck. They've got this quick reflex out there on the duster strip: Anytime an engine revs up and then there's a sudden silence, they know somebody is into something. They sized us up, and then the laughing started, with them rolling over and over in the grass clutching their fat sides, tobacco juice spurting everywhere, wanting to hear us say in words how we did it. One got a rope, lassooed the tailwheel and tied it to the truck. The others caught the tail in their arms as it dropped.

We all went around to the front to gawk. Where the prop came out of the earth, there was a fresh hole big enough to bury a hog in. But oddly enough, the propeller blades seemed unbent. One mechanic got a stick and started to measure the distance from the prop blades to the engine, to see if they still tracked. Another shoved him away: "What kind of a mechanic are you? Using a stick! Heah, gimme that." And he whipped out a slick, shiny steel tape. "Boy, you gotta use precision instruments around aircraft." He laid the tape in place and squinted at it. "Thutty-one and three little marks. Okay, swing down the other blade."

Then they fired it up and eyeballed the blade path. Sure enough, the blades were slashing the same track of air. Almost.

"Well, let's test-hop her and see if she slings a blade, or the engine jumps off."

"Golly, who's gonna do that," I asked, round-eyed.

"You are, you idiot. You don't think one of us would go up in it, do you? And keep it over the strip, so we won't have to go lookin' all over for it if she comes apart."

The story about the 200-mph Cessna 172 is more of my permanently fixed complaint about the frozen state of the art of general aviation aircraft design. The magazine was willing to run my adverse opinions but balked at my identifying the scene as the Reading Show and the comments as coming from our own people. The rationale was simple, and Stephan's comments were pithy:

Dear Gordon,

We are sending this one back to you to try again . . . the problem is that
taking the reader behind the scenes of a magazine always comes off sort of
childish and annoying; look at all the *Air Progress* shots of its editors at play
. . . at *Car & Driver's* constant in-jokes about what the staff did over at the
editor's house last night. The reader doesn't give a shit. He paid his dollar
for the magazine and that's what he's buying, not the editor's jokes, or
Wilkinson's Ivy League education. Nor does he want to hear what a har, easy,
fun time it is putting it together.

Therefore take us out of it. As Slepyan said, "How many times in how
many ways can we say to our readers, 'Look at us, how brilliant, sociable and
even musical we are,' and get away with it?" Larson also pointed out that it
is a little embarrassing to have *Flying's* editors yelling loudly about what can't
be done.

Set the scene in an anonymous hangar, and don't do too much of it, because
the really interesting part about your manuscript is the part about the 172,
not the people.

Your Lake piece is really nice [I had just gotten seaplane rated and had
submitted a we-fly-the-Lake-Amphibian story.—G.B.], though Collins has
used his huge red BULLSHIT stamp on the page wherein you said it was a
150-mph airplane. [Collins was right. I could still be snowed by a guy who
was nice enough to let us go play with his airplane.—G.B.]

Also have your St. Cloud story at hand. Fell asleep reading it. I'll have
more nasty but meaningful things to say after everybody else gets through
reading it.

Best,
Stephan Wilkinson

St. Cloud had a sedative effect on the others and was quietly
put away.

I invite you to play "guess who" as you read the disguised
200-mph Cessna story. I think Stephan was right and still feel
sort of creepy over taking you behind the scenes now, but that
is part of what this book is about.

The 200-mph 172

"What this world needs is a good 200-mile-per-hour Cessna 172," I said, and they laughed. I was serious. A good everyman's 200-mph airplane. Bede might be about to do it, Cessna ought to. Why not a 200-mph Cessna 172? Two hundred miles per hour —the magic number that would put the little guy from Middle America out to either Coast in an easy day's flight. They scoffed. They jeered.

We were in that ancient and honorable pilot's pastime of lallygagging under the shade of a wing, watching the exotic fly-bys at the Reading Air Show. I had been half asleep, watching the sleek airplanes fly sleekly, the chunky airplanes chunkily, and dreaming dreams of a great airplane that could do it all.

What really surprised me was that every man among us was a pilot and every one of them took up the cudgels against the probability of my ultimate airplane. There was Prescott, the aeronautical-design consultant, with his background of engineering and computerspeak. There was smiling Jason, fair-haired young executive of a Midwest corporation, and Steve Nicely, distributor of children's books and high-time twin-Cessna owner and user, and Happy Harry, the hang-glider idiot from San Something, California, sitting there with his leg in a cast, trying to coax a teenie-bopper into adding her autograph to the mess already there. All of them proved to be stodgier than the most time-worn airplane builder in all of Wichita. Negative thinkers. With speed and precision they wrecked my ducted-fan pusher model, poohpoohed my turboprop and laughed uproariously at my everyman's pure jet. "It just can't be done, Bax." Well, by golly, I always thought that airplane design was still the art of the possible.

Steadily falling back and regrouping, I called out, "How about those externally braced, fixed-gear, high-wing monoplanes built way back in the mid-1930s? Every one of them would outperform today's 172. And how about the original Cessna Airmaster? Even Cessna once built a better monoplane than it built today—clean, lean, no struts!"

More guffaws from the loungers. "You ever fly one of those old fabric Airmasters? What a truck. Cessna knew what it was doing when it went into the 170/172 series."

"Well, all right then, how about the *Spirit of St. Louis?* There was a high-wing cabin monoplane that flew 120 miles an hour and was utterly reliable. We going back to 1927? Did the progress of design end with Lindbergh and Ryan?"

Prescott, who is in on design and testing, countered with, "How about the Cardinal RG?" He said that Cessna was quickly developing it into what it always should have been, that its Edsel image would vanish forever, and that the real action in light-aircraft design was a study of spoilers as an advancement over ailerons, but that the Cessna 172, that four-door Chevy six of the airways, would go on forever at 130 or so mph.

Then Jason, who spends more time in a cockpit each month than I do in a year, struck the foulest blow of all: "Suppose you did have a 200-mph 172. You would have gotten here from Texas in about five hours. What would you do with the time you saved?" Almost four hours saved? Mr. Jason, that's time enough to do an interview and get beautifully dinnered, but most of all, it means not being stuck out there forever waiting for the needle to move on some omni.

Jason, who could pretty well have his pick of the singles or light twins, but who is currently flying a beautifully equipped, full-IFR Cessna 172, replied, "It's safe, it's roomy and it's quiet, and besides, I like to look at the countryside." But Jason, don't you ever feel its slowness? Don't you ever feel like getting out and beating it on the sides? Nicely chimed in, "Bax, you came to Reading in a 600-mph Boeing 727. What was your total travel time?" Well, let's see, we got up at four A.M., drove an hour and a half to Houston, flew into Philadelphia, rented a car and drove to Reading . . . "About 10 hours I guess."

"You could have made better time than that in the 172, and look at all the fun you missed."

I went over and collared some guys from Cessna. "Why can't you guys build a 200-mph 172?"

"Whaaaat?" Looks of disbelief. Who is this madman, anyway? Then the negative answers began to flow: "Why, in effect, we have. It's the Reims Rocket, built by our associate in France." But a quick consultation revealed that the Rocket, for all its six cylinders, 210 horsepower and constant-speed prop, gets a top end of only 156 mph.

Then came the justification of the 172 as it stands today. "More than 20,000 of them, the most widely sold airplane in the world . . . the essence of the 172 is a delicate balance of speed and economy . . . the best balance there is in an airplane of that category . . . put in a bigger engine, you carry more gas, soon you have a very fast airplane with room for one guy inside . . ." Then somebody remembered the Cardinal RG: "We're getting 171 mph out of that with only 200 horsepower." Then back to the 172 as it stands today. "We've done a little cleanup, we're getting 144 calibrated on the new 172; have you flown it yet?" But nobody wanted to think about the 200-mph dream.

I pushed them some, got them to talking about a laminar-flow wing, big engine, turboprop, but they kept sliding out from under me. "We have people who like to go fast and people who don't. Hell, we have 52 different models now." And then came the clincher, with some logic that I leave to you to ponder. "If we did make a 200-mph Cessna 172, we might lose, in the process, what the 172 really is. There is a certain essence to any successful airplane and if you tipped the balance of things, it wouldn't be a 172 anymore."

I always thought that the only excuse for an airplane was speed. I always thought that airmen believed in the art of the possible. Let it be recorded that we peaked out in 1974.

6.

Why Pilots Sweat
in the Winter

By 1975 Stephan had been given his own magazine and had moved down the hall at One Park Avenue to become Editor of *Car & Driver.* My loose connection with *Flying* became even more random, and as one of my memos said to a passing editor, "I miss the iron hand of SW." Another in January, seeking the whereabouts of the last seven stories I had sent in, said, "I almost dread asking the status of this stuff, fearing you will say the cleaning lady threw them out with the trash. But knowing can't be any worse than sending them off into the void."

I got plenty of correspondence on my attempted "We Fly," about the Geronimo conversion of the Piper Apache. First there was doubt that anybody in Seguin, Texas had thought of anything that Piper hadn't already tried out. With 20–20 hindsight I can see that was true. Piper's Geronimo, a conversion of the old Apache, is called Aztec.

My first try at the story brought out Richard L. Collins' big red BULLSHIT stamp across the pages. Ex-Navy pilot and Geronimo Builder, Walt Lackorn, had demonstrated to me that he could get it off or land it in a measured 300 feet. There were four of us aboard, but we were below gross weight. That and the subsequent re-fly are in the Geronimo story, but I fudged a little on the altitude we did the spin from. It was actually 800 feet over downtown Seguin. We raised it to 1,000 for the magazine, to hide some of the folly.

Collins thought none of this was funny. In fact, he was blazing mad. "You know what I would have done if some guy spun me 400 feet out of 800 in a twin with one engine out? I would have told him to land at once, gone to a phone, called the sheriff and had him arrested and then written him up for the Feds! One of these days some over-enthusiastic demo pilot will kill one of us. I always ask the guy what his level of experience is and get a clear understanding about what we are going to do or not do on the flight before I will get into his airplane."

Collins is right about all that. Once at Reading I was riding low and slow over the green hills of Pennsylvania in the late McCulloch gyrocopter, and the happy sales-pilot was going on and on about how safe this whirley was and how easy to dead stick it in with auto-rotation, when he ran out of gas in one tank. I just leaned back and enjoyed the anticipation of coasting down into a farmer's field, but you should have seen that pilot sweat and play the fastest four-handed game I ever saw, switching tanks, priming and getting a re-start. I asked him why all the hustle if this thing was as safe as a big downy thistle, and he wouldn't even talk to me. Couldn't maybe. His swaller knot looked awful tight.

That Dick Collins was up in arms about this matter was no small thing. As *Flying's* Professor of Technique and Safety, he has had a strong influence on the magazine and on thousands of pilots. His own preparatory university was in the lap of his dad, Leighton Collins, at the controls of an Aeronca C3 in 1934. Leighton published *Air Facts* magazine into the 1970s. Bob Parke says of him, "He showed us the way." Son Richard grew up to be Managing Editor of *Air Facts,* came to *Flying* as Senior Editor-Little Rock in 1968 and became Editor in 1977. Collins can devastate an offered manuscript with two pencil strokes, like a quick rasp across a polished piano top. Eagle Scout Collins is totally trusted by the aviation manufacturers and is one of the most knowledgeable writers about airplanes and how to fly them. And you can trust him with the women and the money.

Anyway, I came away from Seguin thinking Walt Lackorn was one helluva pilot, still do, and I liked the Geronimo so much I bought into it. And that is why I wanted to call the story here "The Thousand Dollar Set of Keys." One of my two partners crashed it before I ever got to fly it, and my part of the settlement was one thousand dollars. For a set of airplane keys I never got to use.

Geronimo

It's only fair to tell you at the outset that this has been one of our most difficult pilot reports. After test-flying the Geronimo conversion of the Piper PA-23, I liked it so much that I bought one. First airplane I ever owned, and one of the loveliest, best-equipped and best-performing airplanes I ever flew. One week after acquiring this machine, with my set of ignition keys still buzz-edged and brand-new and never once in the lock, one of my partners and a close friend flew the machine into the trees and utterly destroyed it. My share of the after-crash clean-up costs came to about $1,000, and that's why I call these pieces of virgin brass my Thousand Dollar Set of Keys.

But let us begin at the beginning. In 1954, Piper opened the market for light twins with the introduction of its PA-23 Apache, powered with twin 150-hp engines. With its fat wing and rotund shape, this epic aircraft soon earned names of affectionate under-standing, names like: "The Twin Cub" and "Bug Smasher." The Apache is notoriously stable and forgiving—and also notoriously slow.

In almost 10 years of production, Piper produced about 4,000 Apaches before doing a fix on it by introducing the PA-23-250 Aztec. The present Aztec is a direct outgrowth of the Apache root line; it was, and is, a solid aircraft design.

In San Antonio, Texas, in 1963, the year that Piper closed down the Apache assembly line, an era was also ending at the shops of

Dee Howard. The brisk business of converting light bombers and military cargo craft to luxurious executive-transport planes had about played out, and Fred Burger, one of Howard's associates, decided to branch out for himself with a cleanup of the poor, but plentiful, Apache. He decided to use the 180-hp Lycomings because they fit, and type certification came quickly.

Burger did the obvious things to slick up the Apache and give it a clean, contemporary look: he added the pointed nose, square rudder with fin extension, Hoerner wing tips and clamshell doors to enclose all three previously windswept tires. With testbed tufting, he found the messy areas around the nacelle and wing junctions and designed fairings to ease the passage of air. Burger's mainstay in the mechanics of all of this was the gifted Ed Ondrej, who is still an officer and chief engineer of the firm today.

After all the snipping and smoothing, they named their sleek bird Geronimo, after the chief of the Apaches, and word spread through back hangars of the pine-tree South, where men want to believe such things, that the Geronimo was capable of nearly 190 knots. It's not and never was, but it will hit 175 flat on the deck, balls to the wall, on a cool day. Geronimo owners are quite content to plan their trips for 165 knots and smile off the extra as advertising.

Mr. L. B. Pete, a sort of conglomerate businessman in Crossville, Tennessee heard of the Geronimo in 1965 and set out to acquire one for running his traps. At last report, he still has it, complete with the optional Rajay turbocharger. He also has the company. Pete arrived at the factory just in time to learn of Burger's untimely death from natural causes, bought the assets, retained Ondrej and moved the plant into the old Navion factory at nearby Seguin, Texas, where he also gained ex-Navy pilot and former Navion man, Walt Lackorn, as general manager. With things set in order, Pete went back to Tennessee. Lackorn and Ondrej, with 33 real craftsmen, began trying to catch up on the orders. They are still at it today, with 25 factory Geronimo conversions completed in 1973, 15 done in the third quarter of 1974, and the demand for mail-order, field-mod kits dominating the output.

There are about 300 aircraft today that can get a "say again?"

from the tower by calling in as a Geronimo, but a lot of them are state of mind. The distinctive rudder, nose and streamlining are not too expensive and can be bolted on by Joe's Flight Service, giving your lowly Apache much prestige and eking out an extra knot or two of speed. But Lackorn says a true Geronimo (about 100 exist) carries a serial number from the factory at Seguin and starts out as bare, sand-blasted tubing. Factory-made aircraft have many out-of-sight goodies not STCed for field-kit work, such as the new Lycoming 180s with constant-speed, full-feathering props, the square-topped instrument panel with modern T layout, soundproofing, an optional sixth seat and kick-out window, and the major airframe inspection and overhaul that bring the basic frame back to factory-new tolerances. Factory Geronimos also get a new interior and are completely stripped and painted to the customer's order. The final touch is a rams-horn yoke that says this airplane is custom-made for you.

There is room for about six aircraft at a time inside the Geronimo works, of which an average of five will belong to their original owners, the sixth being made up on speculation. The factory works at an average of about two planes per month—not on an assembly-line basis, but work a man could sign his name to—under the watchful eye of Ed Ondrej.

Ondrej told me the Geronimo will fly along at 145 knots, giving about 10 nautical miles per gallon, longer than you can stand it. Optional tip tanks raise fuel capacity from 108 gallons to 156 gallons, and at economy cruise of 65-percent power at 6,000 feet, I began to get figures like 1,650 nautical miles and 10 hours' duration and gave up. Let's just say it would get you home on a Sunday.

We also found that with standard tanks full and four aboard, we had to put 97 pounds of sandbags in the back to bring the Geronimo up to its gross weight of 4,000 pounds. So what we are hearing about is a roomy airplane that will either go very fast or cruise all day, that costs about half as much as an all-new airplane with similar performance. So why is the sky not filled with Geronimos?

Because, as a grass-airport sage might put it, "Who me, pay $43,750 for a 15-year-old airplane, plus instruments? I can get a good used 310 for half that and still come out ahead." Thus are learned the bitter lessons of airplane economics, although there are many 30-year-old DC-3s and Stearman biplanes that are still factory-fresh looking and earning a living every day. Good airplanes with good maintenance age very slowly.

There is a certain prevailing aura of doubt about the claims made by converters of airplanes as to what their machines will do. If you add up all of the Geronimo speed-increase claims for each separate mod item, you get a total of 41 knots over the original Apache top speed, which just isn't there. As though speaking to a child, Lackorn explained to me that the speed increases were figured for each item if it were alone added to a stock Apache. A 10-knot gain for the wheel enclosures?

The people at Seguin are painfully aware of these attitudes and are equally suspicious of blown-up factory figures. "They take a perfect airplane on a perfect day and can spend as much staff time as needed to get their published figures. You come down here on short notice, take whatever plane we can spare, and we have to live with whatever gets printed. Either way, it hurts. One writer got overenthusiastic about the Geronimo and said it did 190 knots. I'm still trying to live that down."

My own experience was this: I arrived, along with a prospective buyer, with only a weekend to spare. The only airplane available was a year-old trade-in with 1,100 hours on the engines and no time to change the plugs. The figures that follow are based on that airplane; it's also the one I bought. Of course, it no longer exists, though if you'd like, we can get out those photos and grieve together a little.

With four of us aboard, Lackorn got it off the ground in 300 feet and landed it in the same distance without setting the tires on fire. At 7,500 feet, he windmilled one engine and held altitude while making turns into the dead engine, then climbed at 380 fpm on one engine. With much burbling and shaking, we did some dirty stalls, power off, breaking clean at 47 knots IAS. Back on the ground, Lackorn bet me a bottle of bourbon that I could not hold it under 78 knots on takeoff. I won the bet, but at an uncomfortable climb of 2,000 fpm initially. Then he moved a customer into the left seat and had him try it, all of us being in a boisterous mood by now, turned on by the Geronimo's remarkable low-end control. The Geronimo has a single-engine minimum-control speed of 62 knots windmilling, 64 feathered, and Lackorn chose to demonstrate this and a lot of other stuff by instructing the prospect to horse back on the yoke until our climb speed was below Vmc at about 61 knots. Then, at 1,000 feet and without warning, he pulled the left engine.

The Geronimo snapped left and under. The customer, who had never seen a spin before, followed Lackorn's calm instructions to throttle the right engine off, and we recovered in a half turn. "See? All that, and we only lost 400 feet," said Lackorn. I got instantly airsick, but the customer made up his mind to buy the airplane.

After a decent interval, I contacted Lackorn about trying again, this time, my way.

"Go ahead and fly it again, I guess I'll have to live with your slaughterhouse figures," growled Lackorn as he loaded 97.4 pounds of sand in the back after weighing us and the cameras and topping up the tanks.

On the second try, I came up with the same figures as before, with the exception of adding clearance of a 50-foot obstacle at gross weight for minimum-runway requirements. That stretched the 300 feet to a measured 447-foot takeoff and a 555-foot landing, field elevation 560 feet, temperature 68° F. with the wind on the nose at eight knots. Dual disc brakes are part of the Geronimo conversion. I bought the airplane.

Bought *into* it, anyway, with two doctors, all of us multiengine and instrument rated. We formed a corporation with bylaws spelling out what we expected of each other. One doctor drew the short straw to be first to fly it. The night before the crash, he said, "This is about the happiest day of my life. It's my day off; I'm going bass fishing up at the lake, and instead of a two-hour drive, I'll just have a short hop in our beautiful new ship."

The doc, who is as precise and meticulous with his instrument flying as he is with his surgical instruments, got caught in one of the oldest and least-known IFR traps. Looking down on the uncontrolled, lakeside, paved strip, he could see the lights clearly. It was an hour before dawn, and the local forecast made no mention of the very thin layer of ground fog hovering just over the lake; nor could he detect the fog by looking straight down through it.

The doc used standard IFR approach figures and first became aware of the fog when the landing light blinded him on round out. A less conservative man would have just dropped on in and made it. An airplane with a higher wing loading might have sunk on in, ready or not. But the doc elected to clean up and go around, using standard instrument procedures. He went into the tall pines at the end of the strip doing 78 knots and climbing 500 fpm.

"I looked up when I felt the first thud and saw black shapes; more thuds and I felt us going down. I really was thinking it was just a hard landing, maybe in brush off the end of the runway, and I must be denting the plane up pretty bad. Then I sort of came to and was standing outside, and I saw the size of the trees we had cut down and that the wings and engines were gone." The doc and his fishing buddy walked out to the highway. One of the things that Lackorn had mentioned in his sales pitch to us was the strength of that old steel-tube truss fuselage.

I touched base with Lackorn at Seguin again recently and he's still selling all he can make. I called a number of Geronimo owners, and all of them are happy and proud of their aircraft. I phoned the president of Piper to see how Lock Haven was holding up under the impact of all this, and he said, "Gosh, I wasn't even aware of it, but I have been out of the office a few days."

Flying was still getting a lot of "grey of cloud and dark of night" stories from me in my newfound bravado of being a serious and professional instrument pilot, but in my own mind I was still a cherry. I had done some overcast punching and lots of sunshine on-top flying, but most of the approaches were into 800 feet and over a mile situations. The Feds had vectored me through one medium grade thunderstorm and I got to see what lightning looks like from inside a cloud. They had lost or forgotten me once on an IFR flight, and I had attained a healthy suspicion about Big Mothah Radar, relearning who *flies* the airplane, even when you can't see out the windows.

To make an approach to low minimums—two hundred feet, rain and fog, visibility one-quarter: I knew I could never be a real matador until I had faced my own bull and gone in cleanly over the horns. Instead of being grateful for missing it, I was longing for the experience. Part of what you get for reading too much Papa Hemingway when you are still young and impressionable.

I finally got it, and it was scary as hell. But I still feel good about it.

The Big Sweat

I need to share this one with you while the hair, hide and hooves are still on it. While the sweat of it is not yet washed off and precludes, through our covenant, the reckless lying of survivors, the bravado of tomorrow. I have just made my first really low approach: "300 feet, one-quarter mile and fog, sky obscured, runway visibility range 4,000 feet. . . . Did you copy the weather, Niner-Six-Zero?" Do you want to drink of this cup? Are you aware? Are you sure this is what you want to enter into? Oh, gentle tower man. Later, after you had held me like a mother holds a tiny babe in arms and crooned to me, and I was rolling and alive on cement, you did tell me that at the moment of my touchdown, the sky had lowered still more and what we really had was 200 feet, and the lowest decision height that I can find on the plate for Beaumont-Port Arthur, Jefferson County is 216 feet (200). Oh, lordy.

Understand, I did not overtly bargain for this. My personal decision height is 800 feet and one mile, because I am green and an amateur at this, and until this day there were many important things yet unresolved in my mind. But overriding it all was the simple fact that low approaches really scare hell out of me. And, until I contacted Beaumont Approach at Honey Intersection, still on top in the dying brightness of the sun, I was expecting 800 and four. I got it in writing, from the FSS at my departure point, just two hours ago at Love, Dallas.

There was that business of Houston ATC, who was one of those garglers who sat too close to the mike and ripped off all his lingo like we were all Delta captains with Collins flight directors to pave the way and one good man with nothing more to do than listen close on a high-powered radio and try to make English out of what he was spouting. This Houston ATC got peeved with me because the Cessna was slow and rented and I was not high-keyed to the fact that Niner-Six-Zero was me. How could he know that what I was doing was putting on my buckler and my shield and preparing to do battle when my moment of truth would come in that white ice cream below? My mind was often far away. And once, when he got churlish with me, I got churlish with him; in my most easy Texican, I asked, "Hew-ston, cain't you talk like thi-yus?" It was chancy, but it cooled his machine gun some. When he handed me off to Beaumont Approach, we were both thinking good riddance.

And when Beaumont let me down into the stuff, I decided this was not the time for false pride and to take this man to my warm side and tell him how it really is. "Beaumont, take me slow. This will be the lowest approach I ever made." And that's when I felt the humanness of the man in the cement tower peering into his green scope at the man in the fragile aluminum who was about to bet his old arse and all of its fixtures. He took me slow. Let me tell you now and tell all the high honchos of the FAA who this man is. He is Glen Martinka. I never met him, never pressed the flesh, but for a while tonight, we were brothers.

Glen took me down to 2,500 and then down to 1,500, and in my mind's eye, I could see all the refineries and their tall stacks superimposed on the opaque grayness ahead. Glen kept calling out targets to me—yes, there was other traffic. An Air Force Herky bird was over here sharpening the blade of skill against the stone of danger. And unbelievably, there was some klutz out in a Grumman Traveler shooting approaches. Jerry's Aviation. Whoever it was, they must have cods to carry in a wheelbarrow to go play on a day like this. "Beaumont, thanks for the traffic reports, but I can't even see my own wing tips." And Metro went barrelling out for Houston, ho hum, just another day. Pros, those guys, peapatch pros, the great captains of tomorrow, but man, for me, I was at the cinema, watching in disbelief this own flesh and blood going to descend to 200 feet in fog. Part of my mind leaned back, munching popcorn, enjoying the show. Part of it was trying to hem up the localizer, and sweat was running free, between 110 and 140 degrees.

And Glen came in with "You are at the localizer and cleared to land," and I realized that he had done all he could for me, and the moment of truth was at hand. Hear me, I'm no kamikaze; I had heard them tell the Herky bird that Ellington was 700. I had a Plan Two; a missed approach and a night in some plastic motel in Houston. But I was committed, too. I must see the Bull. At last, now, after all these months of imagined terror, I must call him out. Toro! Toro!

Oh, why 'n hell can't I hold a good localizer course? It's a learned skill, that's why, and I have gotten rusty to its subtle tones. Sinking into grayness, I made it academic. I was back at Bob Marsh Aviation in the simulator. It is all academic. If I don't make it, I can just flick off the switches and get out and face the sneers. Also, I was thinking, this will be sudden and not hurt much. Also thinking, in the next 20 seconds I am going to find out something I need very much to know. And so I descended, splitting my mind between the wandering needles of glide slope, localizer and all that. Reasoning, rationalizing with myself and betting nothing less than life, sweet life.

Do you know that the earth greens the obscurity when you are near her? A dark, dank greenness of Earth. I knew. I was aware of her closeness; playing fortissimo with the rudders. Oh, gentle Cessna, mother of all aircraft, gentle, broad-winged bird, forgive us our trespasses. Earth was nigh. And then the lights. The crucifix of lights. Not all the candles burning yellow in St. Peter's could be more holy than this. "I got the lights." Hell, I could have landed on a postage stamp from there. What matter 4,000 feet range? What matter that I could not see across the field in the fog? Stearmans, Cubs, Airknockers, I can land short. And I was still holding Glen's hand. I had asked him not to make me change to tower at the marker for that is the most crucial time, and no time to be playing with the radio. Glen Martinka carried me to the ramp, like a father holding up his newborn son.

I am curious. Even to death, always curious about life and all its processes. I took my pulse. One hundred and sixteen over a normal Southern-boy 72. Not bad; they don't call in the astronauts until the pulse reaches 155. I was well below the screaming point. But the hands shook. The line man laughed, "I don't think you are ready to repair any watches." Right.

"To put your life in danger from time to time, breeds a saneness in dealing with day-to-day trivialities." My personal minimums are still 800 and one mile, but the terror factor is gone.

"The Flying Goofball" is a thinly disguised autobiographical account about nearly running out of fuel while other options were still open. The good part of the story is at the front, then it goes pawing around like a cat on a concrete sidewalk, trying to find some way to excuse or cover up what it has done.

I found no answer but some consolation in astronaut Walt Cunningham's recent book, *The All-American Boys*. He tells about astronauts in training, shuttling their T-38s between Houston and Los Angeles and racing. Hot fueling at El Paso to gain five minutes. Coming in second at LAX and trying to land short and turn off at the first intersection in those twin jet supersonic birds to beat the other guy to the ramp. And blowing out all the tires. I have done that. My wife introduces me to other pilots as "Ace here, he lands short, turns off at the first intersection . . . and rides up to the ramp on the firetruck."

Diane tells of the early days when she flew with Braniff. They had Convairs similar to those of Texas International. Where there were sometimes parallel schedules you would be treated to the rare sight of two Convairs, bright in company colors, flat-out racing down on the deck across the West Texas plains. And I know of yet another pilot, no longer with TI, who slow rolled a brand new DC-9 on a ferry trip.

Cunningham admits to catching the jet stream and making it nonstop from LAX to Houston and landing in fog with one engine shut down and the T-38 taking on more fuel than the book says the tanks will hold. He talks about the challenge. The tingle. So do I.

In his book, *Slide Rule,* Nevil Shute speaks of it too. "To put your life in danger from time to time . . . breeds a saneness in dealing with day-to-day trivialities."

To that I would add, *controlled* danger. With a Plan Two.

Any way you look at this event, it remains what it is: an unsupportable folly.

The Flying Goofball

The pilot was of middling years and instrument rated, and so was his rented Cessna 172. What he did was to almost run it out of gas in the middle of an IFR night over the wooded swamplands of southwest Louisiana. Had he run it dry, he would have been memorialized in one of those endless reports that say, "Almost one out of five accidents resulting from engine failure is caused by fuel starvation." Among other things lost in the wreckage would have been the record of what was going on inside his head during his last minutes.

He arrived at home plate safely, though shaken by the experience, and, in the cold light of dawn, felt compelled to share with me his innermost thoughts, dwelling not so much on what had happened but why. He seemed dismayed by the awareness of something within himself that was both alien and deadly and recognized that his experience with peril had been almost planned and that the telling of it was a part of the payoff. His choice of words, his body language and shining eyes confirmed it. Beneath the light dusting of contrition there was an "Oh wow, look at me!" He was aware of that, too, as he told of how he passed up opportunities to reduce or eliminate the danger until, at last, his escape opportunities and his chances of making it had both diminished to a point of equal nothingness. At this time, he began to experience some total emotion, a natural high, of which only a part was fear and a sense of his own frail mortality.

"I want to tell you this while I'm still pringling over it," he said and told how his jaded navcom set would either nav or com but would not do both at the same time and how he could have avoided all this anyway from the outset by buying gas. "They told me the gas man had gone home for supper, but there was an emergency number if I needed him. Who wants to call an 'emergency' when he's used only an hour and a half out of four hours' worth of fuel. So I broke one of my own rules: never miss a chance to gas up."

He described his parting from the small circle of friends at the airport. "We all felt the mood at the dark and spooky airport—the cold metal of the plane, the night utterly black—but only one of the guys' dates felt it enough to say it. 'Y'all be careful, hear?' she said. 'I'm always careful hon,' said I. 'These things scare me to death.' "

He said his first concern was getting settled down for the transition to instrument flight. Then he found an airways intersection that afforded a good check point for working a time-and-distance problem. He was bucking a 30-knot headwind but never realized it until he worked out the actual groundspeed for himself. Seventy knots! He worked it again, and it came out the same. Until then, the gas gauges weren't even on the instrument panel; now they loomed big as watermelons.

He worked out a time-and-distance problem to home. It matched exactly his fuel on board—no reserve. Just 20 minutes away, but well to the left of his course line, lay a large metropolitan airport, but he held his heading for home, thinking, "Jesus, I've never done a fool thing like this before."

Fifty miles from home, and with both gauges sunken into their final quadrant (they seemed to rush there), he contacted ATC and was advised that he was 15 minutes late on his flight plan, that the weather was good there, but the gas sellers were gone for the night. "I pictured the hassle of trying to get a rental car, a room or driving home and back. But you know, I really wanted to try it, to tough it out. Get home-itus? Partly. Deadly game of wits? Yes, some."

As he left this last lighted airport behind, he learned that surface winds were only seven knots and variable, so he asked for minimum low altitude. He was cleared for 1,500 feet, but knowing the terrain was empty, he descended to 1,000—and became a third-degree open-freestyle player at the wits game. "I throttled back to 2,200 and leaned that Lycoming down so far that it occasionally reached back and banged on the firewall with its fist. But those gas gauges froze. They ceased to move. I decided I must have figured out a way to refine and manufacture fuel in flight. Then I got the cold collywobbles, real ones: one thousand feet in the mists, over the trees and alligators. This was no game; I could really get killed doing this. I felt humble."

He figured he had a total of four hours' endurance in the Cessna 172. By the time he had been in the air three hours and 50 minutes, home plate radar contacted him, and he learned he was 11 minutes from the threshold. He advised them of the situation and flew the remaining miles enjoying their undivided and most solicitous attention, while letting his mind leap through broken cloud from one forced-landing site to the next in the city below.

When he topped off the tanks upon arrival, he learned that he had 4.5 gallons usable on board when he reached the ramp. He had learned that one can use low power settings to trade speed for endurance, but now he wanted to find out why he had done it. "This is how people run out of gas, but why me?"

Because I suspect that this sort of behavior is more common than any of us would like to admit, I called the Civil Aeromedical Institute of the FAA offices in Oklahoma City for a most revealing conversation with one of the flight surgeons there. I told him the story.

"What you say is not surprising. We have solid figures that one third of the fatalities in general aviation accidents originate from irresponsible acts. Flying under bridges, chasing coyotes, buzzing beaches, landing on the road for a beer, flying through the arch at St. Louis—suicidal stuff. These are problems dealing with human psychological makeup, and we have no psychiatrist on our staff. In fact, there are only nine health conditions that we can refuse a medical certificate for, and that amazes aviation people from other countries. We know there are behavior patterns that can reveal this sort of individual, and we have considered asking the DOT to let us use a person's traffic-safety records for early-screening purposes; but that smacks of Big Brother watching you, a sort of invasion of privacy."

The FAA medic then mentioned that a computer cross-check is made on reported accidents and that repeaters may get a friendly visit from the local accident-prevention counselors, but the nature of the visit can only be advisory. He spoke wistfully of having flight instructors act as an early screen to weed out the immature or emotionally unstable students, but there is no plan to do that. The FAA does get a rich input of data on the application for any airman's medical certificate, if you volunteer your background of dizziness, nervous trouble, drug or narcotic habit, excessive drinking, attempted suicide, your traffic convictions or other brushes with the law. The local medical examiner is asked to note any "personality deviation." My FAA spokesman made no mention of what, if any, use is made of this information. He did say, however, that they are aware of the use of the airplane for suicide, real no-note suicides, that get chalked up with the accident statistics. The FAA seems to be aware of, but powerless to deal with, the flying goofball.

This is not to say that pilot attitude as a contributing factor in accidents has gone unnoticed in aviation medicine. The FAA doctor talked about Dr. Gibbons, formerly with the FAA in Fort Worth and now with the City and County Health Division of Salt Lake City, who has done research into actual suicides by aircraft.

He also said that the Navy conducts an after-the-crash study called a psychological autopsy. Dr. Roger Reinhart has attempted to establish behavior patterns by reconstructing those pieces of the pilot's psyche that might have contributed to the crash, much as the FAA today reconstructs pieces of the airplane. And the Feds have a man in Washington, Dr. Robert Yanowitch, a psychologist and a pilot with the Office of Aviation Medicine, who is researching along the same lines but has no way to implement his findings yet.

My FAA spokesman also mentioned a committee of 28 psychiatrists from the ranks of the Flying Physicians who are urging psychological testing to screen out the immature and unstable pilot applicants, but the FAA medic added wistfully, "It would cost money." The FAA public-affairs officer worded it differently: "We haven't overly worked this aspect."

Back to our hero of the night skies, who seemed to be speaking from two minds: "I was playing a delightful, secret and dangerous game, and I really wonder why. I presented the story to my wife that night as a tale of my great skill and nerve, without which my precious body would have been strung out in the trees. Human behavior is very much a part of flying, but I never heard or read a word about it during all my instruction as a student. Why?"

Well, I am in no way qualified to enter into the bushes of psychology, but I have lived for half a century and been around airplanes and pilots a lot of that time. The very personality traits that make for a dangerous pilot in today's cabin planes and closely gridded skies were, it seems, the same forces that drove those early pioneers who carried aviation forward out of its unsafe and unprofitable infancy of biplanes and barnstorming. With boots and jodhpurs, they set themselves apart from the common crowd; lowered the level in the brandy bottle, then set it in the cockpit as an artificial horizon; they brought in the mail, laughing at the night's storm.

The heritage of the *macho* pilot is waning now, as any frontier yields to the homesteaders. On any Saturday, a man in a tie and jacket will teach you to fly a civilized airplane in a civilized manner; but down at the saloon, if you could sit in the corner with a group of good, gray airline captains off-duty, you would sometimes hear the same hair-curling tales of narrowly missed disasters that you hear back in your hangar. Not one element of the aviation community is willing to admit any of this to outsiders; so with the exception of the air shows, where it belongs, flying for the hell of it has gone underground. And that, I suppose, is some small measure of progress.

LaLa "Oshkosh," which we printed in November of '75, comes as close as I will ever get to saying all the things I feel about the Experimental Aircraft Association and Paul and Tom Poberezny. I had tried it before and have since. Should have quit on this one.

Oshkosh: Fun Flying's Supernova

Oshkosh is America at her best. Each year, we swarm there, fill her skies, fill her greensward, brim it wing-and-wing with airplanes. Fifty thousand strong we come, drawn up from beyond distant mountains and over checkered fields. From 200 miles out, all the airplanes in the sky pour into the funnel to Oshkosh.

No other airport in the world, not O'Hare, not Reading, not even

Da Nang at its worst, has ever seen a stream of over 8,000 aircraft a day pouring out of the sky. That's Oshkosh, the greatest aviation picnic on earth.

We come to Oshkosh laughing, laughing at those mad chefs in the tower who make a tossed salad of us, mixing and melding lightning bolts of fighters, forking in fat-tomato Cessnas and ripe Pipers and strange, stringy homebuilts. And they slide us down the runway, sometimes three at a time, like the bartenders of the old West who sizzled schooners of foaming beer down the bar top and never sloshed a drop.

"Mooney at the gravel pit."

"C'mon, Mooney, I see you, Mooney, folly that Cessna."

"Which Cessna?"

"Any Cessna, c'mon, c'mon!"

And later, in the rows, parked in the weeds, when the excitement of having done it is still high, we climb out stiffly and grab at each other. "You the Mooney?"

"Yeah. You the Cessna?"

"I'm one of them, har har." And we clutch each other laughing. Brothers. We have landed at Oshkosh together.

And that night, when the field is sleeping and I lie rolled up in my blanket beneath my wing and the summer stars, I am comforted by my brother's campfire over there. I hear the low sound of his laughter and murmuring voice. I want to lie beneath the wing of my own plane on the heartland prairie, like Lindbergh did when the world was young. I want to soak up all of this.

From across the field float the sounds of applause and laughter. They are still giving out awards in the open-walled assembly pavilion. They sit row on row in their little white dickie-bird caps, and the awards go on forever. Do not laugh. May you someday be good enough at whatever you do to have your work judged well at Oshkosh.

Somewhere in that enchanted night, between midnight and dawn, I awakened; iron ore was digging into my back. Wisconsin may be the land of milk and butter, which they get from one cow or an udder, but her men and her soil are like iron. I don the old hobo trick and rummage through Basler Flight Service's trash for soft, luxurious cardboard. Oil cases, flattened out. And in dreams

I hear the cough of the night mail plane come to life, twin P&W 450s rumble, catch and fade in the night's gathering storm. Some lonely kid, challenging lightning. Then the light rain begins, reaches under, finds me, and I retreat inside the Mooney. You ever sleep in a Mooney? A candid photo of a man trying to sleep in the Mooney he loves would pass as a low-grade porno flick or the rarest of silent comedy.

The Blue Goose arrived at dawn, thundering and reversing twin Rolls-Royce turboprops and sounding reveille for 18,000 campers just before my legs broke off and fell into the baggage bin. I joined the long lines of good-spirited men standing in light rain, awaiting fat, steamy Wisconsin food served by fat, steamy Wisconsin blondes. The EAA feeds its own.

Oshkosh asks only that you bring your own bedding, the rest goes off more smoothly than Patton's army in the field. There must be an oligarch at Oshkosh, someone brilliant and tough, to plan the logistics of how many gallons of milk and eggs to truck in and how many trucks and crews to haul the sani-cans out. But the hand that plans Oshkosh is open, never a fist.

The place is a swarm of humanity, but without disorder, drunkenness, trash or theft. A city of strangers—of men, women and children who move onto the world's busiest airport and live in peace along its runways for a summer's week. I tell you, Oshkosh is the best of America. And always in the near distance, you can hear laughter, music and the sweet sound of airplane engines running.

Oshkosh is contradictory and invites analysis from the Freudian thoughtful. It stands as a tempting morsel to the avaricious, although no one has yet discovered how to cash the check of Oshkosh.

The General Aviation Manufacturers Association gives the Experimental Aircraft Association only a most guarded, token recognition. Yet, of all the 8,000 aircraft parked on the field, GAMA products outnumber all others 10 to one. GAMA, you are strong at Oshkosh, but where are you?

"Kooks!" mutters the Establishment. "We can't make money off pop rivets and VW-engine converters."

Kooks? Yes. Beautiful kooks. Here sits a new Chevy pickup, all power and loaded, a walk-in camper body on the back, and it's towing a travel trailer with a canoe on top and a motorbike strapped to its rump. The lady of this house is enclosed in a white picket fence and is cooking steaks on a propane gas grill under a blue-fringed awning; the children are bicycling. On the rooftop, her husband has Oshkosh Tower tuned on the portable stuck in his ear, and he's watching the landings with expensive binoculars while he builds a model airplane.

Mentally masturbating aviator, you say? Listen, this kook represents almost $20,000 worth of rolling stock and hardware. "Yes, but how are we going to get him to quit playing at it, come down off the roof and buy a Beechcraft?"

That, sir, is a problem you should be working on. Are you perhaps being too formidable? At the Reading Air Show this year, I heard one of the largest makers of avionics for general aviation introduce his product by saying, "Now that we are outgrowing this nonsense about fun in flying . . ."

Oh, how I wish he could have seen just one of those 65,000 airplanes that came to Oshkosh for the fun in flying. It was an old, blue Apache, parked right in front of my faded Mooney. It had about as much of this very same company's avionics in it as the boxy ole twin was worth. And the guy was tenting with his wife and three kids. He was the kind of a daddy who buttoned up the kids' pjs, and those little rascals held still by the morning-coffee camp fire while he brushed their hair. Okay, so what if the guy was 25 years old? That family has put its treasure into aviation, and they did it just for life, liberty and the pursuit of fun.

Some writers among us who are always driven to try to analyze Oshkosh, are starting to murmur that Paul Poberezny is turning the EAA into an instrument of his own creature comfort. Hah? Say again? Are you speaking of our own Pope Paul, our own good-hearted bohunk, ever one of us? Where were you back when he was holding all of this together with his own two bare paws?

And what of Tom, the young Prince Valiant of the EAA? Is he hollowed out and stuffed into it by a dominant dad in the classic boss' son situation? Nossir. Tom went it alone in another profession and slashed his own mark high on the tree, where daddy never prowled. Then Tom came back to aviation, to the EAA, and made his mark here as one of the 10 best aerobatic pilots in this country. Came back to the EAA for the same reason the rest of us do, for the love of it. It's that simple.

So I said to the everlasting Golda Cox, about whom the media swirl smoothly, "I have walked the line with the warbirds, I have run my fingertips across the homebuilts, I have shared your night and your soil and your huddled masses. My story is in the sack. Now I need to be put with the High Honchos." Golda said, "I'll get you Paul or Tom."

That Paul and Tom have become interchangeable is good and as it should be. Tom solved the "what to do with the guy from *Flying*" thing neatly. He cut me into the deck for the VIP luncheon. He sensed what I needed and took his chances.

The most influential aviation congressmen had come down off the Hill and flown out to Oshkosh: Dale Milford, of Texas; James Lloyd, of California; Gene Synder, of Kentucky. And add Joe Del Riego, of NASA, as cream to the pot. We gathered at the airport inn.

I sat on the edge of my chair, ready to whip out my pad and take notes when they got down to the heavy stuff on who will run the FAA, what about fuel and the cost allotments. And what did Dale and Lloyd and Tom do? Hangar flying. Pilots, all of them, telling the same kind of old war stories you can hear in the back of any good hangar, while outside, the mighty turboprop N-3 stood at the ready, nostrils flared, crew up, to fly these movers and shakers back to Washington when this vital conference was done.

I got edgy. "Tom," I whispered, "when do we do our number on these guys?" Tom looked at me with those ace-blue eyes, "We don't. We just invite them here, let them see who we are, what we do. They are not stupid." And neither are the Poberezny boys.

I have written before that the EAA is the cutting edge of development in general aviation. The man who wears "experimental" on his cockpit is free to design anything, so long as he agrees to kill only himself over some uninhabited airspace. So there lives among us the continuing hope that another Clyde Cessna, Walter Beech or Bill Piper will emerge among us at Oshkosh, maybe arrive some year with the ultimate airplane tucked under his arm and blow us all away.

For a few years, Jim Bede carried that star over his head. This year, there were those who predicted that if Bede held a public meeting, someone would come forth from the crowd with a new rope. Listen, don't you guys know yet that given an hour alone with Pug Piper, Bede could sell him a kit?

The new hope at Oshkosh is Burt Rutan, and I never even saw him or his plane. They were out doing what aviation had to do in the '30s, trying for endurance and distance records to prove that what they had was good enough for the public's money. And I guess that is a sort of type-certification program in itself. Rutan wasn't ready. Little stuff still plagued him: bad plumbing, blown oil cooler. The Rutan brothers probably welcomed finding weak links, even in public, for it is their philosophy to release nothing to the public until they have utterly tested it with their own hides.

Even the Wright brothers were willing to admit that they were not yet sure which end the rudders or elevators ought to be on, and the Rutans are back into that area with their VariEze. Competent engineers will tell you, as competent engineers have always been willing to tell you, that everything that can be invented for lightplane design has already been invented. The Rutans, Burt and Dick, being unaware of this, are pressing on into unknowns.

Such folk heroic derring-do always attracts the mobs, and thus it was for the VariEze at Oshkosh. By the time I got there, they were lying on the ground under the cowling at Green Bay, leaving Mrs. Rutan, who looks like a home edition of Katharine Hepburn, to mind the booth. And although there was much panting and stamping around the booth and folks willing to press money upon them, the Rutans seem to be holding off until they are satisfied that the slender, swept wings aft, VW-powered, swift and stable VariEze can be homebuilt and safely flown by a 40-year-old man who wears bifocals and knee-length short pants.

Ideas still flow freely in the EAA, as they once did in a bicycle shop in Dayton, Ohio, and somewhere, someday, someone will make a breakthrough in the frozen art of aircraft design. These people, in their silly badges, patches, jackets and dickey-bird caps, are not satisfied with the hard professional evidence that it cannot be done. And that, dear hearts, along with the fun of being there, is the sort of stuff that is the best of America.

Let "The Christmas Chicken" stand to offset some of the silk scarf, ace-of-the base grain that stains through in much of my war stories. Here the pilot figures his odds and goes out and buys an airline ticket.

The Christmas Chicken

Nobody ever says anything about the terror factor in flying. In the hokum-macho world of men, such admissions are allowable only in the framework of gallows humor. Tom Block, my friend the airline captain, says, "I want all the help I can get. All the engines they can line up on that wing, all the people they can get on this flight deck, all the radio and radar I can stand." Or the British Red Arrows, when I was sent to ride with them, asking, "How do you feel about tight-formation aerobatics?" "Terrified, sir." "Good. You'll do."

In the accident-report series we publish, what they never seem to measure in are the "ulps" and "gulps" on the tape that is played back after a poor bloke has stewed around up there in it the last few minutes before finding his hillside resting place. Scared witless but can't say so. Cowboys never cry.

I've been flying for 17 years, and I do it because I love it, but some parts of flying just scare the b'Jesus out of me. Instrument work. Let me come clean here: low approaches. Man, that is scary. And ice. Ice scares me so bad I don't even want to think about it. In case you are new here, an airplane is a beautiful case of form follows function. Its shape is meant to make it fly. An airplane will pick up ice in flight, and ice will grotesquely malform those subtle shapes of wing and propeller. Ice will close the windshield to outside view, and then it will seal off the little openings that let the instruments tell you how to fly when you cannot see out the window. And what you will have then is a glittering crystalline shape falling from the sky.

These were the thoughts threading through my Christmas Day plans. We were going to fly about 300 miles to my wife's family home in Dallas and return that same night after the party. And my

Christmas prayer was for moonlight and stars.

I have a horror of the Christmas Day crash, and we've had one here. Three men in a slick retractable single, just before Christmas, leaving a swath of raw, torn pines, the hot shambles of aluminum and bodies and Christmas packages all mixed in the oil and rain, soaking.

And what did this guy say on the tape just before he vanished from the scope? "We are having a little trouble . . ." Lowtime pilot, professional man, 0.8 hours' check-out time in his new plane, non-instrument rated and trying to run the ridges in a stalled cold front. Poor guy. Yeah, he was "having a little trouble here." If only he could have allowed himself to grab approach radar by the lapels and cry out, "Help me, man, talk to me. Which way is out of here?"

Christmas Day, and the stalled cold front still hung over us, but Dallas was reporting 1,800 scattered and 15 miles, so I elected to go. Here comes my wife, all rosy in the cold rain, hurrying to duck under the wing and get the bright packages into the back. I look at her fragile beauty and her trust and at those low, rolling clouds that I've got to punch out of in a few minutes, and I think, oh Lordy.

It was only a thin layer, but no pilot ever made a more detailed preflight or nosed up into the blind stuff sitting up straighter and paying more attention than this one. We popped right out. Got a sandwich layer and could see 100 miles. I sent pireps about it, and my wife opened up the coffee and squirmed around in delight at the unearthly blue beauty of our wide clear tunnel world and said, "See there?"

There was surprisingly light radio traffic. Houston Center was quiet and good humored, passed me and some unseen Commander 1,000 feet apart over a VOR, and we wished each other a Merry Christmas.

Then came the long leg, and I sank into the enchantment of it, and it was a long time before I realized that I had not heard from center and was well past the point where they usually hand me off to Fort Worth.

How do you say this? "Er, Houston, this is 690, have you forgotten me?" What I did do was ask for a radio check. That prodded them. Faintly and from far away, Houston asked my position. That meant I was off their screen. A long pause and they handed me off to Fort Worth. Forgot me and lost me. Helluva note. And me supposed to be in a tightly controlled little boxcar of moveable, protected airspace.

Suppose I had been in the blue stuff, with hail and lightning forking all around, with me clutching over the wheel. I tell you, there is no good scheme without a few flaws.

Fort Worth had to fish for me, too, then said to report Scurry VOR for radar identification. Isn't it neat how two souls and $15,-000 worth of airplane and a backseat full of gifts of life and love can enter into a busy air terminal with just 10 seconds' worth of words? I mean, this part of our art is good.

"690, Scurry at four."

"Contact. Cleared to Love VOR."

That's really all we needed to know about each other for them to admit me safely into their multimillion metroplex at 100 knots.

Love Tower was coasting. They asked if I wanted to continue the ILS approach, although I had visual contact. I thanked them, yes.

Man, do you realize that a 31L approach to Love puts you within a twitch of the tallest bank building in Dallas? For over a quarter of a century, at one-minute intervals, every approach to Love has had to be a perfect one. The day somebody got 400 feet low or a quarter-mile offside, the Dallas *Morning News* would be worth about $5. That's a lot of confidence to put into some wiring and plumbing.

At Mustang Aviation, the gaffer who drew the short straw for working Christmas Day told me I'd better go out and buy a toothbrush.

"Why?"

"Because we've got an ice storm coming in you won't believe. You gonna be in Big D for a while, boy."

And that's the weird part about weather briefing. We've got holes in weather briefing. Before I left, all I got on Dallas was good news—8,000 and 15 by nightfall. Suddenly none of this is any good, and it's just three hours later.

There is one more succulent part of this. I waited until late at the Christmas party, harboring my pilot's secret, then called the

Dallas FSS and got me a good briefer. Now this man is forbidden by what must be rules made of good, two-sided reasons from just coming right out and telling me, "No, don't go." But he did everything short of that: "True, it's only 40 degrees in Dallas now, but we've got reports of patchy, freezing rain all the way down to the coast, temperature inversions, sleet, ice balls, lowering ceilings, and it's getting dark, too, sir."

And he told me of a helicopter that had been forced down by ice from 1,500 feet and of a twin Baron that had barely made it in to a strip south of here with a load of ice. He was almost wheedling me not to go, though ceilings were still good and the whole state was about to freeze solid for the next two days. When I told him thanks, I wasn't gonna try it, he almost gripped my hand.

Again, we seem to have this gulf between pilots and ground people that is there when we need it the least. I have read the FARs, and I think they were written more to stand up in court than in the sky.

We went home on a Braniff Boeing 727 that was piloted by three brave men who are professional pilots and are aided by more deicing equipment than my Cessna was worth. And when we got home, I paused at the flight deck and told the skipper I had left a 172 in Dallas because of reported freezing rain, and how about it? "We used deicers all the way. You done good."

Then I called Pappy out at the grass airport and told him we were home but that his Cessna was welded in ice to Love Field, and he said that would be the easiest place he could think of to go look for it.

7.

A Little Orange-and-White Airplane

I n January of 1976 they took away my title. No more "Associate Editor, *Flying* Magazine." They bumped me and Tom Block all the way back down to what we were when we came in, "Contributor." Actually that's all we ever were, and sometimes I had felt queasy about being listed on the masthead as Associate Editor with Norbert Slepyan and George Larson, who really were editors and stayed cooped up in that rabbit warren of the New York offices catching all the schlock details and turning out huge amounts of writing. But still, it was a point of prestige to us—it sounded good in introductions, even though we all knew it was only a gift from Bob Parke.

As I understand it, we lost the title through lawyers. One of ZD's legal eagles decided that since we were not on the payroll and not really associated with the company except as outside vendors, there would be some legal liability. It has been my experience with lawyers that if you go to one for advice on a borderline matter, the only thing he can tell you and still be a lawyer is "No."

I missed Stephan. He was still down the hall trying to instill his fine sense of the literary into those animals at *Car & Driver.* My feeling of being "in" on the flow of things at *Flying* had dried up. Since July 1975 nothing had found its way out to my Texas outpost that was not a Xerox copy, which added to my sense of being disenfranchised.

Adding to the pressure was a growing air-mail and telephone relationship with Keith Connes, who heads up *Air Progress.* Keith's frank word that he needed me was everything I was not getting from *Flying.* Many times I have jokingly introduced myself as the *"Air Progress* writer who writes for *Flying."* And that is about half true, with my "gee whiz, ain't this wonderful, me and Joe" stories. Both Keith and I know it.

I decided it was time to lay it on the line with Bob Parke and wrote him a carefully worded memo trying to sound neither pitiful nor threatening. In truth I was never sure of what corner to come out of. I suspect that most of this was my imagining. They were simply busy in New York and unaware that I needed to be patted on the head now and then. My quip about writing for love not money may have been truer than any of us knew. I was making a fortune in broadcasting, anyhow.

Dear Bob,

I need a bit of your time, your mind, and some consideration from what I hope is more than just a business relationship between me and thee.

It's the *Air Progress* thing again.

Keith Connes called me the other night and sounds like he needs me. This is flattering. Like most romantic writers, I want to please editors and find more and more of me in print.

It comes at a time when my last direct contact with you was in July of '75. A kind but firm rejection of a story. It was a sorry story anyhow.

Am I getting out of touch with your needs?

Or are you in another economic crunch?

Wish I knew.

Coming up on six years with the prestigious *Flying* is something I don't count lightly, but since the lack of even a dollar a year token salary cost me the only title I ever earned, am I a captive free lancer? Is there any justice in restraining my output only to *Flying*? I would like to see a more relaxed attitude about that, or be bound up closer to you. And there is personal affection in this.

Do not read this as some kind of an ultimatum, I'm not that silly, but I do need some consideration from you.

Bax

Parke didn't write. He called. I made notes. "Money is not the problem, yes you should be your own man, but we do want to keep you exclusive. Your material is *good.* We will have a meeting in March, you, Block, Peter Garrison. And I have been gone most of the fall . . ." I wrote me a summary under the phone call notes: Don't write for AP.

Meanwhile, back on the printed page, in the January *Flying,* I carried out more explorations into the world of learning to fly when you can't see out the window. I was learning the tight jargon of real aviators, and enjoying it.

Conversation Piece

The language between pilots and controllers must be swift and clear, a ritualistic exchange that by its very nature creates a perfect stage for occasional humor or pathos.

Once, on a busy weekend, I heard St. Louis Center ask the pilot of a Cardinal RG for his groundspeed.

"One-sixty-one knots," sweetly sang the wheels-up Cessna.

There was a deliberate, drawn-out silence for about a five count; then St. Louis drawled, "Aw, c'mon." And a score of amused pilots heard St. Louis haggle the proud new owner of the RG down to 141 knots.

I got an unexpected name call once in the congested Dallas TCA. I had encountered cloud, filed en route, got cleared for 3,000 and was a little flustered copying clearances and getting my IFR senses settled down. A deep voice said, "Hang in there, Bax."

I looked across to my wife in surprise, and she said, "Bill," recognizing the voice of a mutual friend she had flown with during her stewardess years. I picked up the mike and said, "Bill?" and the mystery voice said, "Come up a hundred feet and ride in the sunshine." My rudder must have been cutting the cloud surf like a shark's fin. Fort Worth let us get away with all of that.

Sometimes the system nearly breaks down in the search for official terminology to cope with hard-to-describe situations. Houston Hobby was having a busy day, mixing the swarm of general aviation with a Braniff 727 whistling inbound through the smog.

HUD—Ah, Braniff, there seems to be an object which is moving on the active . . . it seems to be, ah, a small cow . . . a heifer.

BI—(not concealing obvious mirth) Ah, roger, copy heifer on the active.

Then somebody mooed into his mike, and there was more laughter until HUD came in with, "Aw-right you guys, cut that out."

At least one airline, whose name I won't mention so as to protect those obviously rotten with guilt, has developed the highly secret "800 code." This is a list of things you always wanted to say back, but in language acceptable only in a Marine Corps mortar squad. But as such things tend to do, the 800 code has leaked to centers, so when a line captain vents his frustration at an awkward approach set up by replying, "815—(B.F.D.)," center may come back with an 816—(hang it in your ear).

What I have sometimes wished for is a code way to tell a controller I'd like to send him a bottle of Scotch. As in the time Chicago was swamped with traffic and prowling thunderstorms, and I hit an imbedded cell while in solid cloud. As the hail hit the windshield, the Jepp charts hit the roof and my heart hit my boots. What I wanted to do was yell, "He-e-elp! Get me out of this!" But with that perverse pride of dying pilots, I held off the wing-bending panic and said something official, like, "Ah, Chicago, Twenty-Seven November is in heavy precip, hail, turbulence and lightning. I will accept any reasonable suggestion."

Chicago, whoever he is, and may his shadow never decrease, laid aside his other traffic, got an ident and after a deliberate scope-searching pause, advised me to come left to 90 degrees and said, "You ought to be out of that in three minutes." After exactly three minutes of being grateful that Al Mooney had designed the wing spar in one solid chunk from tip to tip, I burst streaming out of the well of it and into light air. Before I could report, Chicago called me and quipped, "Seemed like three years, didn't it?" That's when I needed the "I will send you a bottle of Scotch" code.

Now here are two instances of the most ruthless disregard for a pilot in trouble. As the 1975 Reading Air Show ended and the great exodus of aircraft began, I was among those in the full cabin of a scheduled de Havilland Twin Otter commuter airliner. A ground delay developed, and much twitching spread among the passengers about missing connecting flights.

The young skipper of the Otter was obviously in on whatever was happening, listening intently on his headset. So I leaned forward from my front-row seat and told him that his load consisted of nothing but licensed pilots, so he might as well let us in on it and forego the usual airline song about something being wrong.

The pilot looked back at us, groaned, shrugged and fed Reading Approach into the cabin speakers. The delay was a real emergency: a VFR pilot, lost and trapped on top between layers, blocking hundreds of IFR departures from Reading. The response to one pilot's hour of terror from 18 of his fellow birdmen on the ground was calloused braying: "Oh what a yo-yo!" "I hope he runs out of gas before I miss my connection." "He should, he's been up there lost for 40 minutes now, he's got to fall out soon."

I presume this luckless aviator was vectored to sunnier skies; at least, I never read about him in the papers.

The other incident is unfortunately typical of overcrowded airspace and overloaded controllers, a system that must grind on, and woe to the halt and the lame who get in its pathway.

A 310 pilot at 8,000 in cloud broke in on New York Center with a report of heavy ice and an immediate altitude-change request. New York, up to his ears in traffic, gave him a cold "stand by." Two pilots at lower altitudes cut in and reported no ice at four and at six. New York, who had the unfortunate grating accents of a Manhattan cabbie, cracked down on the Good Samaritans with a rulebook reminder about improper use of the radio for personal communications. Our pilot growled to himself, "Why that creep! Watch for traffic—it will be a 310 dropping through encased in a solid block of ice."

In contrast to the cold hard world of the metropolitan skies, where they say, "G'day," and it sounds neither good nor day, there is the easy midnight mood down in the warmer climes, where there are long stretches of silence on the graveyard shift and the pilots use the romantic, "S'long." I usually say, "Thank y'all."

Here, over vast mid-America, the night-mail pilot and controller come to recognize each other, and a terminal forecast may include some ball scores and where the bass are hitting. I know of one grizzled corporate jet jock—and so do the Feds—whose call sign within 50 miles of home plate is to ring his cow bell over the mike.

Richard L. Collins courts the rare thrill of personal recognition in his name-branded Cessna Skyhawk "40RC." Collins' watchdog vendetta about the proliferation of controllers is widely known among the boys in the towers. So at Oshkosh '75 I met a controller on the ground who said, "We had your buddy, Collins, in here yesterday. The gun was in place, but we were real busy and he got off before anybody could find the clip."

As the skies get fuller and the radar gets better, we feel ever more the close, hot breath of the controller over our shoulders, even out where VORs and filling stations are 100 miles apart. I always blush and smart when some radar voyeur tells me and the rest of the world that I'm four miles south of the centerline. Back in the good ol' days, sloppy flying could be just a personal thing.

And in some areas, I'm hearing a new, devastating phrase that the ATC uses to herd some drifting pilot along. They say, "Where are you going?"

That is so bad. It implies that the course keeper is so hopelessly mixed up that radar is no longer certain of which city he is aiming at. I'm still trying to think up a real good flange-him-up reply to that one.

Many strange and wondrous things happen in the never-never land of publishing a great international aviation magazine. Some I will never understand.

Once I attended a press conference in which a new money man was taking over the franchise of a very expensive bizjet from another money man. I asked the new man what had happened to the other money man and he said, "He ran out of

money." We printed that and shortly thereafter Parke called to
say that I had just set the Ziff-Davis all-time record for law
suits. The other money man was suing us for six million dollars.
And did I have my copy of my notes? (I'm not sure about that
amount. Anything over a hundred thousand dollars is not real
to me, anyhow.)

I had my notes. Just then they were stuck to my hand.

On another occasion I found a wonderful old Dutchman who
had in his barn, in mint and flyable condition, the original
biplane with which he started business at that same little grass
airport in 1929. He opened up and talked to me and what a love
story I wrote about that wonderful old guy and his cherished
biplane.

He asked for, and we did, something we seldom do—we
showed him the story in advance. And would you believe he
nearly killed it? Completely deballed the story. Cut all the
great and generous things he had done in his long and
splendid life.

At the magazine, we were just heartbroken. Even Parke got
on the phone and tried to fix it up, to no use. I suspect the old
guy was a fighter pilot in World War One, but on the other side.
And Lord knows I would give my eye teeth to interview a
Fokker pilot. But America treated him badly when he first
came here and again during World War Two. This old man
who had made his life in America and brought aviation to many
who are airline pilots today, we treated him like a spy and an
alien and in 1942 practically made him a house prisoner when
he offered to form a Civil Air Patrol unit to defend this country.
I think the key feeling that drove him to kill our story was in
his words, "I don't want to be the Hun again." There was no
way we could reach him to tell him how America's heart had
changed and how ashamed we were of how we treated the
Japanese- and German-American people back then.

In the March issue of *Flying* they ran the stuff I do best,
romance. Although I think they could have picked a nicer title
for it.

Garbage

We were inbound to Montgomery County Airport, at Conroe, Texas. I had told my wife about the long lines of surplus airliners parked there, old Convairs and DC-3s, parked nose to tail in elephant rows of dull aluminum. In her 10 years with Braniff, Diane had started back in the old Convair days and had bid for them right up to the end. "One girl, one cabin, my airplane."

Then we were over the rows of pines on approach, and I was searching for the rows of Dumbos we had planned to visit, when out of the corner of my eye I saw something that stirred in me a sinking kind of horror. It looked like a giant air crash. The bodies of the airliners were broken and spilled, the silver wings lay torn off. The neat line of transports had been reduced to an aluminum garbage pit. People were cutting them up. Some junk dealer had bought them, stripped the engines and instruments and was cutting them up for scrap aluminum. Tossed around, the carcasses lay in pools of black, dried oil blood and bright shards.

We parked the Mooney and walked slow and silent among the dead sky queens. A few DC-3s reared up in their final agony, wings grounded and trampled, empty windows gaping at the sky. All that was left of the Convairs were the midsections of the cabins: "Mohawk" in black peeling letters, and ice dimples in the skin from winter storm battles over the Hudson Valley. One lay on its back; wind tinkled dangled aluminum strips in the ghostly cabin. "Somehow, I never thought of a Convair like this," Diane said in a tiny, controlled voice.

As we moved to another gutted cabin, her face was a study. She reached in and touched the bare floor stringers that once held her flying feet. "Stout built, weren't they . . . they seemed so much bigger then . . ." *On the ramp under the lights, all snorting and smoking with power and a very young South Park High School girl standing in the doorway. So serious in that old black motorman's uniform, and all those important places to go.* She reached up into the wreck and touched the boarding-stair lever. It moved strongly, as always. The last girl's hand to touch it.

A little apart and at the far end of the carnage, stood a lone DC-3, not yet savaged except for the engines. It stood proudly, still burnished aluminum. The hulk called to us with a very special dignity.

We entered and I made my way up the slanted deck of the stripped-out cabin, looking for the name plate. I used to do this in gentler times when Trans Texas Airlines flew DC-3s. The game was to read the manufacture date and then ask the copilot how old he was. The Gooney Bird was nearly always older than the kid flying right seat. And this one looked even older, something about it, worn smooth as a plate.

I found the stamped numbers, rubbed away the grime and looked again in the faint light: 1936, serial number five. Good grief, this was the fifth DC-3 out of over 10,000 made, and it had flown here. Donald Douglas himself had once stood where I was standing, fresh back from receiving his Collier Trophy from President Roosevelt for this revolution of the skies. C.R. Smith, president of American Airlines, had taken delivery of this one, named her for some proud American city and painted "Flagship" on her. The airlines were being born. She had seen ribbon cutting, flashbulb popping, and had taxied up to the terminal crowds with movie stars aboard and little American flags whipping in the window brackets.

And God only knows where she had been after that, wandered all over the world, through three wars. Thunder in distant mountains, lightning slashing her old vee windshield, and now to earth, in this oil patch in Texas, waiting for the cutter's torch, to become beer cans. Flagship Sixpack, and one last flight, out the speeding window and into the roadside weeds.

We came down. Diane carefully latched shut the cabinet doors swinging slack in the galley. We walked under the nose, and I looked back and said, "Lady, I wish there was something I could do . . . I really do . . ." And the winds blew through the myriad empty holes and slots, and the DC-3 whispered, sighed and murmured something to us, waiting, staring at the sky she had opened to us all.

Going back to our plane, past the Convair corpses again, Diane recognized something, a battered rectangular aluminum box, and lifted it by its carrying cut-out. "This is a Convair garbage container. It had to last us eight hours, 40 people per flight. I'm keeping it. A good stew was recognized by how well she managed her garbage. Sorted it. At every stop, I got off looking for a place to dump my sack of dry stuff; the wet stuff went in here. This thing is Convairs to me."

We left this graveyard, thinking how strange that we outlive these marvelous modern machines, and so quickly, too.

In the April issue, almost a year after I bought our Mooney, we ran my first story about the joys of owning your own airplane.

I Wanted Wings

Hot damn! I done bought myself an airplane! A used Mooney. A hangar queen. It had 700 hours; it was seven years old. I bought all that trouble and glory. My own flying machine. After having the airplane crazies since I was a kid and renting airplanes for 20 years thinking I couldn't own one, my Diane cut me loose for it.

"Go on, it's only money. You're 50 years old and you got about 20 good, juicy summers left. When they pat you in the face with that shovel, you can't come back and wish you'd bought an airplane. Airplanes have always been so much of your life. Go on, enjoy, enjoy!"

I made serious work out of shopping for the plane. Nearly took all the fun out of it. You ever notice how when you look up after reading *Trade-A-Plane* for a few hours, the world looks blurry and green?

I read old *Flying Annuals* as far back as I could find them, comparing all those lying figures. Then I went out and found me a banker who used to fly bombers in the war and could talk airplanes. From him I found out how much money I could stand. And from my tax man I found out how much of this I could write off. It's better than you think.

What I was shopping for was speed. If you ain't hauling freight, an airplane's only excuse is to go fast. Anything else is saner.

From my tip sheets I narrowed it down to a Bellanca, a Cessna 182, a big-engine Comanche, a 20-year-old Bonanza or a Mooney. I also considered and looked up the numbers on the fast exotic antiques like a Staggerwing Beech or a Cessna 195, but I soon dropped this option because I was holding in reserve the idea that I might lease out my plane now and then, and none of today's pilots can land those headstrong old taildraggers. I also negated the idea of a partnership. Might as well go back to renting stuff from the madam again as have to book my own airplane.

What I kept getting was a gut feel for the Mooney. It was partly out of "What if the fuel scare comes back again?" It was partly because I like their sharp and wicked looks and mostly because I admire how tidy Al Mooney's mind was when he designed this simple, strong and functional thing that goes like the hammers of hell. I was also influenced by finding out that a good used Mooney is second only to the Bonanza for being a hot, scarce item in the used-plane market.

Any contact with Mooney people brings up the name of Charlie Dugosh, who runs a Mooney service shop across the field from the factory at Kerrville. Dugosh is a living legend among Mooney owners. He worked with Al; he was quality-control inspector at the factory, and most of his people once worked there during the Mooney Mite and wood-wing days. I called Mr. Dugosh, and in his voice I heard a man without guile: "Look for corrosion in the tail cone or around the battery box and buy a Ranger. I think you'll like the 180 Lycoming better than the fuel-injected jobs. You'll get nine or 10 gallons per hour, and that simple engine runs 2,000 hours as compared to about 1,200 for the big fuel-injected 200 hp. On an average 300-mile cross-country, you'll be in the pattern while the faster bird is taxiing up to the ramp." So I gave up the eight knots' difference and went Mooney Ranger hunting, mostly on the strength of all the good things I ever heard about the simple everlasting four-banger carbureted Lycoming 180-hp O-360-A1D.

And right here at home, in Beaumont, Texas, I found a Mooney Ranger in my favorite passionate orange-and-cream paint. Her story was typical: born 27 February 1968 (Pisces, compatible to us Capricorns); she was bought new by a couple of doctors back in the Every-Man-a-Mooney-Dealer days. After that bubble burst, she languished in an open-front T hangar in the Gulf coastal dews and damps until a contractor bought her. He replaced one rusted jug and gave her a flurry of flying, but his kid threw up in airplanes, and his wife never liked it. So N6727N drowsed once more in the dirt-daubed and fog-ridden hangar.

He still had her picture on the wall when I made him the bluebook offer. He agonized awhile, then said "sold," and I was at last an airplane owner.

With trembling hands, I signed that mortgage, then threw a party for the airplane. We had a wax-in. I invited all my grown kids and freaky friends, and we laid out quilts on the grass and brought cheese and wine. Don Jacobs, the Fluke of Anchor Street, brought his Mattel guitar and sang an original ballad:

"Oh you can't get me up in that Mooney,

You can't get me off of the ground,

I've seen all I want to of Beaumont,

And I know that the planet is round."

Abstaining from the fruit of the vine, but high on airplanes and love, I flew each of them long into the red rays of the sunset to the day's end. And they gathered there in the darkening hangar, and we feasted our eyes upon my airplane squatting low and glowing in the last light of day.

"Speech, speech!" they cried, "Speak to us, oh wild ol' Mooney man." And full of pride and happiness, I stood and gazed upon those I love, but words would not come. It was better than my electric train Christmas when I was 10, better than the first bike Christmas when I was 12. I was holding hands with Orville and Wilbur, with Captain Eddie and Mr. Lindbergh and with Al Mooney. I get a lot out of owning an airplane.

Alone at last with Diane, I took her aloft. But first there was one more ceremony, in private. I knelt to all the fuel drain humblings. The floor drain is just long enough for one Hail Mary. Then I committed a private and personal deed upon each of the three tires, while Diane giggled and vowed that I was one of the world's original dirty ol' men. (I had been a dirty little boy.) Then side by side, we flew.

I asked her, "How do you really feel?"

"Like the first time we made love after we were married."

I asked her what would she like to do.

"Only one thing left to do. Let's fly it down Main Street as low and as fast as it will go."

That night, wondering what was the first Mooney I had ever flown, I got out old logbooks, and back in March 1968, I found it. A Mooney 20C, N6727 November. Our airplane was the first Mooney I had ever flown.

Later, I went out to "explore the performance envelope," as my starchy friends, Collins and Olcott, would say—or just go out and see what she'll do. Stiff as a preacher's nose at a double wedding, that's how the Mooney handles. The ailerons are so heavy that I still can't be sure whether or not I have the PC wing leveler punched out or am just overriding it. But I like the device. It will do course keeping for miles or hold the wings level in cloud.

Trim is something else. The Mooney tail is hinged at the cone. Trim moves the whole works up and down, and it's tender. If Diane leans back and stretches, we ascend 300 feet. But after she curls up in back for a nap, if I can ever find that exact pinpoint, the Mooney will fly flat and level for hours on end. Or at least until the temperature changes two degrees or a bird dropping blows off the wing; then we go phugoiding along again.

Landings also are something else. That Mooney will float like a T-Craft in July until the wing pays off—then it's all through. At the Mooney convention in Kerrville, I learned a trick you may not approve of. Just as the Mooney's low-hung flags go into ground effect, which you can feel like rolling up on a bale of hay, just flip the flap lever to "up" and the sink rate is exactly in time to the normal flare movement, and the Mooney can be painted on.

I have the old Johnson Bar model. The landing gear is operated manually by wrestling down a great iron lever at center stage. Being of the generation who toted our own water and chopped our own firewood, I prefer this to the modern labor-saving devices with which nothing can go wrong . . . go wrong . . . go wrong. . . . I pry my wheels down. When they are down I know it. Wheeze, slam, click. The only gear failure ever recorded in such a Mooney was when a crystallized Johnson Bar broke off even with the floor. Wouldn't you love to have been there?

I also include in my checklist "Floor clear for gear handle." *The*

International Mooney Society Log, printed in San Antonio with the
blessings of the factory, tells many tales that every Mooney owner
should know, and I proved this myself. Didn't fasten the right seat
belt and did tangle the gear handle on the floor with much loose
belting. There I was: Mooney nose up, me nose down, nothing I
could turn loose from with either hand.

And Diane, who has not yet learned the flip-wrist trick of quickly
cycling the gear handle, got caught with it halfway down, gear and
doors out, Mooney gaining speed. It lifted her up against the belt,
and between her shouting and me giggling, I can see how the
power gear on the new Mooneys is a sane thing.

Stalls were a surprise in the Mooney. Not even the old aileron-
knocking Stearman can equal the commotion of a fully stalled
Mooney. It will hang, then dip, and I can feel hard lift pop back
over those long laminar-flow wings. I was thinking this thing would
stay in the air forever until I noticed the sink rate was 1,000 fpm.
And once, checking out a friend who insisted on very deep stalls,
the Mooney did all that shuddering and bobbing, but still he held
the yoke back. Without warning, but very deep into a secondary
stall, she snapped over and gave us a heart-stopping half turn
before spin recovery. The Mooney is not to fool around with.

The more I fly this airplane the more I like it and begrudge
myself the wasted years of not owning my own plane, any plane.
I beat airline schedules' door-to-door times. I find my work ex-
panding to meet the abilities of my time machine.

Owning your own airplane is nothing like flying somebody
else's. It has put a whole new meaning into my life, but not without
many unexpected expenses. I had to scrap all the ancient avionics
in it and went all King Silver Crown. It costs, yes, but what's a life
worth? And the Mooney panel does not allow room for a T layout. I
have more of a Z panel. But at least I don't get a fixation on one
instrument while something else is going to hell a yard away. I
mean, I got a real scan. The instruments on the panel that can't
be moved are the wing leveler coupled to the rate-of-turn indicator and the EGT that is right in the middle of the panel. I may not
be shooting the sharpest approaches, but I'm the only guy on final who could report exactly what his exhaust gas temperature is
if they should ever ask.

I go to sleep at night dreaming of my little time machine. I have learned to fly her high and hard to get the book numbers, and I can fly her at 65 percent and get eight gallons per hour. I like her looks, standing out there with her pert little tail perked up. It got so bad that my Diane declared a one-day moratorium.

"Me. Think of me for just one day. King's X on that airplane, and I know you got that owner's manual hidden under your pillow."

"Diane, how could you?" And I took her by the shoulders like I saw Gregory Peck do in the movies. "Look into my eyes. . . . What do you see there?"

"A little bitty orange-and-white airplane, *that's what!*"

In November of 1976 Stephan Wilkinson came back to *Flying*. As Executive Editor, whatever that is. And those crisp little chickenshit pink memos began to liven up my rural mailbox again.

12 Nov. 76

Bax—call me asap. We want to see if you can go to the Bahamas for the Treasure Hunt. Nov. 27–Dec. 3, though you don't necessarily have to be there for the whole ridiculous thing. What we have in mind is you Showing The Flag and getting, at the most, A "Bax Seat" out of it. No unnecessary hooring.

S.

And in rejecting a story about carburetor ice, Stephan wrote:

15 Nov. 76
Dear Gorn;

I hate to be the prick who does this to you, but I don't think the carb-ice manuscript makes it. For several reasons: It is about too many things, and it's not about enough. And it's in the format that's getting a little too familiar —Bax takes a trip in his Mooney, moons about his Diane and is scared/edified/delighted/awed by what he sees/hears/experiences.

You give a clue to it yourself in your covering letter when you list all the things that you've rung into the article—intercollegiate flying, Alcor, the youth of America, low lead fuel, etc. The story is far too diffused, leaping from one theorization about the state of the young, to the state of your engine, to praise about a mechanic who worked free. There's little focus in the piece.

As for the familiar-format gripe, we will have "Night Fright" coming up in January, the cross-country piece in February, two me-'n-my-Mooney pieces in a row. And I remember others in the past. Remember how tired we all get about hearing about a trip. Reject the obvious, because if you don't I will.

Having said that, the cross-country piece was brilliant, a little too loose, like somebody so caught up in something that happened to them that they can't stop talking about it—but charming and evocative nonetheless. I am taking the liberty of sending it to *Reader's Digest* on your behalf. Enclosed is the manuscript that I edited, in case I did damage the piece. If I did, *tell* me; this airway goes both ways.

It's so good to be among all you warm people again.

Best
SW

Executive Editor Wilkinson's chair was hardly warm before he was on with more executing. Instead of sending in our stuff rambling free form all over nice white sheets of our own grocery store typing paper, we now had to use official manuscript paper, all gridded into characters 70 letters wide and lined from 1 to 28.

Bad enough he's hounding us for good and original material —and correct spelling; now he has marked off the size of the squares we can write in. Forty-five wide, 28 deep.

I whipped out a poem of outrage, called "On Flying & Lovin."

We come to such a sad state with *Fly'n*
Center requests 45 inch's per line.
Omnis, transponders, TCA and Stage III
Grid out the pastures where once I was free.
Through shuttered skies I sullenly rage,
But throttled to 28 rages per page.

Back, turn backward
Groupthink in your flight.
Orwellian be monitoring
My bedroom tonite?

Bax

Susan Crandell posted it on the bulletin board. She also pins up a collection of the kids of the Staff.

Susan Crandell is beautiful. She could be one of the Breck Girls, the one with the slender body, Valentine face, eyes you could drown in, and a fall of shoulder length dark hair. Susan is now Managing Editor, and that is serious. But so is Susan. She came straight out of Middlebury College to *Flying,* and ran hot and true to the top. She first surfaced in my mind when the word got around among stringers that if you sent copy or photos to her, things would quit getting lost. This as compared to Stephan Wilkinson as Managing Editor, who worked on the once-a-year "we are really going to reform and shovel this place out" plan. Crandell also impressed us during the infrequent weekend staff gatherings. My wife said it best: "See there, a woman in a man's world can overcome the handicap of being beautiful." True. Furthermore, Susan is a pilot and on her way onwards and upwards through the ratings. But I still feel funny sometimes, having my real keen airplane stories thrown out by just a girl.

8.

Just One More Hour . . . Solo

Ole Steppin' Wolf was right about too many me-'n-my-Mooney stories appearing in the magazine, but they sure sound sweet if you are writing a book about what it's like to be a pilot. I can land better than him, too.

Night Fright

Mr. Robert B. Parke
Editorial Offices
Flying Magazine
One Park Avenue
New York, N.Y. 10016

Dear Bob:
This is one of those stories that just poured forth the morning after. Shouldn't send unfinished work like this, but I had to get it down.
Best, Bax

The trip was a showcase to set out the solitary brilliance of what you can do only with little airplanes. And in the shadows all around it were the classic warnings about how to kill yourself in one.

It was a two-day trip that involved my getting up at four A.M. on Friday, doing my radio and TV shows until 11 and being in Oklahoma City by three P.M., a banquet that night, and being back, 400 nautical down to Beaumont, Texas by nine the next morning, to emcee a tractor-store opening. That's right—a tractor-store opening.

There just ain't no other way to get all that done except with a little airplane. Beaumont is favored by a visit from an airliner from time to time, but I doubt if you could fit together a schedule like that even if you lived next door to JFK. Anyway, what airline will let you watch the sun come up through the windshield?

At 3:20 that afternoon, I was in Oke City. Now all I had to do was keep a clean head and be wheels up for Beaumont at 4:30 the next morning.

But I was pretty tired before I even started this marathon. I could see that marked down on the left-side page of the NTSB investigator's notebook: "Pilot was tired."

And then there is the strong peer-group pressure in being at a party, among people you really enjoy, where the hospitality is rich and flowing. You must remind yourself that while all these other troops are snoring in the barracks, only you will have a call to arms at three A.M. There is also a section in the investigator's notebook on what they found in the pilot's bloodstream after the autopsy. Eight hours from bottle to throttle, or is it eight feet? Har de har har. Well, that's why I sneaked out of the party at 7:30.

Third, the weather. A good old Texas-Oklahoma blue norther had met me on the way in, and by next morning, it would be stalled, clagged up around my home plate down on the Gulf Coast. I won't fly ice, and I won't fly a line of thunderstorms, and the idea of a long night, IFR in cloud and rain, alone in a single-engine airplane, turns my lower digestive tract to stone.

To this problem I applied Collins' Law—one of a set of principles I have put together out of reading what Dick solemnly writes about IFR flying. My Collins' Law for assessing weather is that the FAA can only give you lots of reasons *not* to go. The time you will spend not going can just as well be spent setting stern limits and then going as far as you can within your limits. Often as not, the sky will have opened some. If not, wherever you quit is that much farther down the road.

So with the dark and unfriendly road I had to travel very much in my mind, I took comfort from the forecast of moon and stars as the journey began in Oklahoma, to be followed by daylight before I got to the front, plus a stack of approach plates for airports where I could chicken out along the way. And then I dismantled the git-home-itis apparatus. Hell, anybody can be late for a tractor show.

"Pilot made a careful weather briefing at the Wiley Post FSS both upon his arrival and before his departure at 4:40 A.M." I hope they put all that in the notebook, too. Not even the tower guys stay on at Wiley Post that early in the morning. They just leave the lights on and go home. One lone FAAman unbarred his door and went over the wavy bars of the weather map with me. Yes, it would be solid all the way down to the coast. And rain. But no ice and no thunderstorms. Nothing to do but go. He was also clearance delivery, ground control and the airport advisory, and he bid me good-night in warm and solemn tones as my winking lights curved out and away from Oke City.

I would not kid you a moment and say there was anything at all I liked about hauling out of there cold, alone and in the dark. I was intensely aware that any item overlooked, any silly daytime slipup, could loom up like a monster in the night. The preflight, the placing of things in the cockpit, the careful folding of the chart . . . all of it was a lonely High Mass for the serious ritual ahead. Somebody to talk to would have helped. Oke City Departure was chatty, as centers sometimes are before the day shift comes on. He said my radios sure sounded good and they must be Kings.

After a while, Departure came back on: "You reading Oke City VOR?"

"Uh, yeah. Why?"

"Well you've gone ten mile past it. Will you accept my vectors?" I told him I was scrambled up. No lie in the sky.

That's when I realized this thing had me bunched up enough to be making basic errors, and there was no comfort in knowing this was my state of mind when the first clouds slid below and friendly Ardmore winked out. I found myself turning the panel lights up full bright for their cheer. Then my new set of strobes began to bat at me off the clouds. Well, that's what they said they'd do, so just turn them out.

Now I was just a dark little Mooney shape out there north of the Red River, known only to God and Center. I backed off and looked at this scene—this beautiful little cruciform of frail aluminum hurtling through the wet bellies of giant clouds. Why was this giving me the clanks so bad? In 20 years of flying, I'd never had such a night flight before. Sure, the first 15 were all pasture-pilot fun—nuzzling yellow Cubs, green fields and one wing in the sunshine—but there had been a few hundred hours of instruments and nights. Yes, but nothing like this. Ever.

Reasoning with myself helped. I relaxed, opened up the cheese crackers and a can of tea. Began to experiment to learn. Found that I couldn't tell if I was in rain or not, if it was light stuff. And that a flick of the strobes was a sure way to find out if I was in cloud or between layers. Found that when there was nothing to do but look at the panel and fly it, the Mooney was more stable than I'd ever known it to be.

The night went on. Occasional unseen terrors came in and pressed around me. Twice it was vertigo. The real leans. I had to call up everything I had in me to make the literal translation of the bar on the horizon a matter to dominate my senses. Well hell, why not? Those senses have kept me upright a hell of a lot longer than any message from a gyro has. And once or twice, there were lumps and thumps in the night. "Light chop" I think they call it in the airline trade, where they do this sort of thing all the time and, I suppose, get used to it.

Then I should get used to it. C'mon, Bax, the Mooney doesn't know if it's night or day; it can only respond to your nerve, your hand.

But even at best, night solo IFR still has some element of seat-of-the-pants in it. If whatever unseen cloud castles I was punching through jarred my spine too hard, or if I saw lightning, I was going to put out the fire, call the dogs and head for the nearest barn.

Once, south of Dallas, I asked if they were painting anything down the road I ought to know about. "Oh, we don't have radar coverage out there." So it really was just me and God, and the ramparts that guard the Gulf Coast were coming up soon. I'd never seen a night so long or a daylight so slow to come. Once or twice, I got glimpses of ground lights and was ashamed of how I longed to see familiar things again.

Looking out for a strobe-light cloud test again, I finally saw the faint outline of my wing. The night was going to pass! These endless hours of forcing my mind to control my body and my fears. Basic primitive man, all hooked up to transponders and VHF radios, breathing his own sweat cool because he could see the first hint of light at the mouth of the cave, and at least he'd be able to see the tigers.

Then another cloud break, this time with wisps of dawn streaked in the distant layers. *Layers.* Something horizontal to see. I felt like I was leaning on them, laughing. Already it was hard to recall the near edge of panic in the belly of the night back there. Already it was memory, hero stuff for my own sorry trophy wall. Beaumont Approach was an old friend, calling me down through layers. "I show you a little left, Bax."

"It's been a long night."

"I bet it has."

Now it was a gray, rain-washed dawn. Other airplanes were waking up and taking off. The day shift was coming on. I got permission for a low approach and took the fix to scud-run 20 miles over to Orange County and parked near the tractor store.

It was a four-hour stand-up broadcast, and all that time I was looking out the showroom windows and watching the sky fall in. Rain, fog; visibility went down to nothing.

So I had barely got in after all. I left the plane at Orange County Airport and suffered the humiliation of bumming a ride with ground wheels back home. And all the way, I kept looking at the sky and thinking, maybe I coulda been a hero and made it. Then the radio came on with a bulletin: "A family of four has been killed in the crash of a lightplane in South Texas."

So the long, dark night had selected someone. I looked out through the car windshield at the rain and fog, thought about my Mooney tied down, thought about those folks, and I grieved. I thought about the sunshiny days I have flown under the hood, over and over, to teach myself the final end of this exacting and demanding learned skill. I thought about a corny ad in a gun magazine I read, which says, "No second-place winners." There's no comfort in any of this, except to respect this air ocean we fly in, these good and noble machines and the hard-and-fast rules.

Big Sky

My throat was full of wanting to go home—to see my own familiar patch, my dog in my lane. It was a thousand miles or more from Oshkosh down to the curve of the Gulf of Mexico, so I went out to the field and touched my airplane. Walked all around her and asked if she was ready to vault the broad belly of this nation. One does not lightly mount the step and ask the little engine to run eight hours, or close one's mind to what nuts and bolts may have shaken off during the night. Even though cars do it all the time, pulling off the side of the road in a little airplane nearly always gets your picture in the papers.

Oshkosh fell below at 10 minutes after nine in the morning and became a memory. I took off my shoes and leaned back to the soft rumble of the cruise setting for 1,500 feet and set a course line for Janesville, wherever that is. The airplane was strong and steady, my heart was full of the freedom of flight. I was low enough to see what was in a pickup truck, to tell how old the kids were by the wash on the line, to see the green richness of Wisconsin and the fat cattle always facing the wind. Little clear lakes kept coming up in surprise, piers stepped out over the water from shaded homes on the shore.

And this must be Illinois; it's changed. The first settlers here had time to lay out the section lines, and the roads run to the squares. Mile after mile of these squares, rich in crops, and in each square, the little quadrangle of trees that shade the house, barn and silo. I wondered how it looks from down there living in that sea of grain with only the distant silo to break the flat horizon.

I wondered about the details of life under each farm roof. Was there love in there or desperation? Were they sitting across the corner of the table not speaking, getting nothing but bad news and crime shows on TV? How I wish they could see from here.

Sometimes the scars of factory sites slid beneath my wings, but even the cities were dwarfed and all their suburban dottings made small by the limitless prairie sea. And the Interstate system that looms so large from your car is only a faint etching. The land doesn't make the press wires or the nightly dispatches except in dry commodity figures, but it lies out there in the silver looping of broad rivers. The land reaches a thousand miles in any direction, the pattern of slow tractor wheels, the careful tending of a man's hand slowly pumping its life toward the screaming cement of the Las Vegases, New Yorks and LAs.

I flew enchanted, held in the bright crystal of sunlight. Midday heat baking up from the fields jostled my wings, then settled into the cockpit to stay. The course line to Capitol's beacon lay right over the dome of the old Gothic statehouse of Missouri. Harry Truman and hanging judges. In the distance, the purple folds of the Boston Mountains promised Arkansas. Better not stretch it the extra 100 miles to Little Rock, because the tanks are getting light and I'm getting a little crazy and want to embrace all those people and paint murals in their post offices and tell them how great they are. So tip back the wings and hello, Walnut Ridge, Arkansas. Halfway. Inside the old-pilot-scuffed building, the delightful surprise of a little calico-curtain restaurant and a sloe-eyed girl who brought me a hamburger right off the grill.

It felt like it should have been more than halfway. I had spent myself in the glories back there. Now the sun was hot brass in the windshield and the legs between VORs were 100 miles or more. I picked up a freeway that looked like it went to Little Rock and cheated along that until a big blue thunderstorm woke up and nudged me out of its pasture.

Now the country was pines and red gullies and desperate little strip towns and a newer breed of man, who has much to learn about his stewardship. He was out there bulldozing great swaths of the forest and laying bare more reddening gullies. I tried not to hate him until he learns. And I sneaked past Little Rock without breaking my long silence on the radio, but I listened and heard them talk about me: "Traffic, southwest heading, altitude unknown."

The 100 miles or so down to Shreveport took about a month, and that little airplane and I squirmed and sweated until we didn't have anything that fitted each other anymore. Oh, how I wanted Shreveport. Shreveport is almost home. From there, it's all downhill. I decided I'd better work Shreveport Approach, but working the radio meant breaking the spell, letting the ground people in. The song was ended.

The heat had fried my radios as well as my brains. It was 95° in the cockpit. Shreveport Approach talked some gibberish until I was able to squeeze out of their grasp, and then I was alone again.

It's nearly all lakes south out of Shreveport, lakes and cool water and bass boats in shaded coves. May the Corps of Engineers fry in hell for wanting to pave the rivers, but these lakes are their masterpiece. Manmade lakes, so huge that they show up in photographs made from halfway to the moon. A bittersweet tradeoff: the old truckpatch farmstead buried beneath the waters for a place in the sun where its children's children can play.

And then the sawmill stacks of home were coming up, and yonder lay a gap in the forest—Eastex's secret strip, smooth concrete known only to the jet of Time, Inc. I could see my own sandbar down there, Village Creek waiting for me, to bathe away the day in the shade of her willows. Pappy came up on the unicom and told me Diane was waiting with a Mason jar of something full of ice, and at 10 minutes to six, I taxied up to waiting arms.

I have lived when a trip of 50 miles meant the entire day, counting waiting for the river ferries and changing a tire on the old Dodge a time or two. But Daddy didn't mind; it was so much better than the horse of his childhood. He said we were lucky—that the car would change our lives. Now I live in an age when a man who works for wages can own a small airplane and in one day unfurl the width of this continent and see things that Carl Sandburg and Thomas Wolfe could only dream of.

No matter how far down you may be on the pecking order, if you write for an aviation magazine long enough, sooner or later you get to make your trip to the Bahamas. I can still shut my eyes and see some of those stretches of clear water between islands. But I did lampoon the Bahamas Treasure Hunt in this story, and one of the contestants who was with us, and who did really follow all the rules, wrote me a testy letter about my flip attitude.

I always answer my mail. For one thing there ain't that much of it. For another, I enjoy people. I wrote this gentleman and said that next time I go on a fun trip with him, I sure would try to be more serious about it.

Islands in the Sun

Many strange and wonderful creatures inhabit that shadowy zone where land, sky and sea meet and wash together. They adapt to this shifting shoreline, each finding the narrow band in which he can survive. They feed upon each other and migrate unknowingly, answering some eons-old timetable, guided by a mysterious sense of direction. They are the rock louse, the phantom crab, the big-eyed gobie.

More recent evolution has added the vee-tail Bonanza, the straight-legged Piper, the svelte-winged Cessna. These are hard-shelled, winged creatures that are capable of brief periods of noisy but spectacular flight. Their migration from Northeastern America to the Bahama Islands lasts but one week, the signal for their swarming coming when ice forms over the bridges in New Jersey and the snow is navel deep in Montreal.

Their rallying cry is "Bahamas Treasure Hunt," a call heard only during harmless blizzards of brightly colored pamphlets borne northward on trade winds from the Bahamas Ministry of Tourism. The call sets up an itch in the wallet so irresistible that many creatures make the arduous migration repeatedly. This year, the flock was so thick that many were turned back at the shoreline; all the roosting trees were full.

Since all of these birds are land creatures, there is a great ceremony prior to their launching from the continental edge outward over 60 miles of relentless ocean. They flock into such favored Florida sanctuaries as Tilford's and Dan Darling's, where their pockets are emptied and their aircraft filled with bright yellow flotation objects. The purpose of these objects is to prolong drowning should one of those flimsy little wires come loose.

The flock quiets its nervous clackings by the dipping of beaks in alcohol. This is a quaint custom by which its members can later be identified anywhere among the island roosts. They depart at daybreak, flying forward but looking backward and crying "omigod omigod" until they can see land no more.

In the Bahamas, the natives are noted for their great sense of humor. Their wit is dry and droll, and an outstanding example of it was in naming one roosting spot "Freeport." There is nothing free in Freeport. Freeport is a city on the Grand Banana Island, a fact that comes as a shock to most of the flock, who thought the whole area was named Nassau (from the Grecian Emperor Nassaus, who threw up at orgies). The flock roosts noisily together in Freeport at the Royal Pilfer Hotel, gets one last chance to show off its expensive luggage and then is scattered to the Doubt Islands.

The quaint Doubt Islands got their name because of doubt over whether they actually existed. Columbus discovered the first Doubt Island and named it San Salvador, which means, "Thank God we found something out here." But when he got back home, people doubted his story. Same thing still happens.

Doubt about the islands also exists in the hearts of the treasure-hunting birds as they leave a coastal departure point flying low enough to look for clues and find nothing but sea in the direction of the next island. They do have migratory aids, of course. One is a Jepp chart that has so many compass-rose marks on it that it has finally reached the point of being totally unintelligible. There is another chart, furnished by the flock leaders and The Minister. Just where you need them, it has no compass roses at all. But on the back, there is a comforting message from Bahamas Minister Maynard to read while you fly a blind heading wishing you had asked someone about the wind.

Those feeling the block of panic rising in the throat can call up Nassau Radio, whose frequency is improperly listed on the Treasure Hunt chart in order to create an eerie silence and perpetuate that legend of mysterious radio failures in the Bermuda Triangle. Some will find the correct frequency—it's only two clicks away—but no clue-exchanging, please. Once you reach Nassau Radio, they will give you a squawk code, though there is no radar for little birds down low. As you talk to Nassau, you can hear calypso music and laughter in the background, and that is a comfort. I envisioned a limbo contest going on at Center and said to myself, "Why should I be an uptight American and miss all the fun?"

I was still laughing and singing when I found the Island of Urethra. What matter that I was aiming at Greater Eczema. We are only here to have fun. I tossed my treasure map and all its pesky clues away, as most do by the second day. Why not? Now that you are there, who needs the excuse anymore?

There are 700 of these islands scattered over 100,000 square miles of crystal-clear ocean, but the total population is smaller than that of Houston. Nicer, too. There are no two islands alike, though the trend is that the eastern fringe is more New England coast, with rocky limestone cliffs, and the western group is more South Seas, with crescent beaches of warm sand and swaying tall palms. The names are quaint. Bimini was named for the sound of steel drums, which on a clear night you can hear from Miami. Small Hope Bay was named from what Morgan said to Teach after they buried their treasure there, slaughtered the crew and were rowing back to the ship: "Small hope of seeing any of that again." Hard Bargain Bay was named for a man who had the plugs changed in his Cessna 172 there.

There are services available in the Bahamas. The Bahamas have, in fact, always existed by the ready availability of services. The first trade route from the early Colonies was a triangle of rum, sugar and slaves between Georgia, Africa and the Bahama Islands. The place has always been handy for operations that others needed to conduct but not close to the house. The Queen based her pirates there and later sold Enfield muskets to the Confederacy via the Bahamas. There was rum during prohibition and gambling today, and the future is trending toward tuck-away banking. In the Bahamas, you are never far from an airport or a bank. Good thing, too.

And in these islands, I found my own island paradise, to which

I shall return as soon as I finish this story. It is right out of Michener and *Tales of the South Pacific*. I will not name it but will let you hunt for it. That lets me tell the story without clinging to the facts.

The Viking founded my paradise 16 years ago. He had reached the male menopause and did not like who he was or what he did. Casting free of briefcase, wife and kiddies, he came to this place of clear seas and crescent beaches. Still suicidal, he strapped himself, an observer and 100 pounds of stone to a plank and shot frothing down to 462 feet, setting an unofficial scuba record and experiencing every known human emotion in those five minutes. He survived, vowed never to do that again and began building stone-and-wood lodges.

Years passed, and a luxurious yacht put in with Mr. Rocks and his lovely bored wife, Ms. Vassr. Six days elapsed. Ms. Vassr announced to her hubby, who was *so* busy with his vast toys, "Dear John, this terminates my part of the cruise and our union." Today, she is the Viking's wife, and the heart and intellect of the place.

It is a spot where you forget your shoes and watch after the first day, and the kitchen help and boat hands come sit at the table with you. Air conditioning is by trade winds, television is the tidal rock pools, great books and brave ideas come in the still nights.

Our treasure hunt ended there. There was hugging and weeping when we left. I dipped low with orange wings flashing in the sun, looked long and thought of what one island philosopher told me: "You can use it all up, but you can't take none of it home with you."

There are many strange and wondrous creatures that survive in this ever-changing band between sea, water and air. The female horseshoe crab comes ashore, dragging her mate along. The whelks cruise for clams at the gaming tables, wrap a muscular foot around their trophy and rasp out a neat hole with their radula to extract the succulent meat inside. The Bahamas have always existed by the ready and cheerful availability of services. And the place is only 30 minutes away in a Cessna 172.

The springtime of '77 found us all easy with each other at *Flying*. Change was in the air. We were as busy as a one-armed paper hanger in a windstorm, working on the fiftieth anniversary issue of the magazine, due in September, and all of us knew that after building that monument, Parke was going to ease up and declare himself a sort of Editor Emeritus. The everyday Staff would get a new Ed-in-Chief.

I got myself fired from the radio station in Beaumont. I closed the mike key on 31 years of broadcasting, to move to the woods and get serious about writing. I asked Stephan for permission to go through the seven years of our memos so that I could abuse him some, and he replied, "I give you all rights, North American, Samoan and Sicilian, to reprint my memos to you, per your request."

That permission for further folly came in a memo that has within it the one perfect jewel of advice to any column writer, aviation or not:

> I have always felt that columns should be concise, self-contained, easily digestible, with a beginning and a middle and an end—the short stories among our pilot report novellas.
>
> If you want to see how a column should be done, take a look at what Patrick Bedard does in *Car and Driver*. These are finely crafted little morsels that tell a story, read like they were meant to do exactly that in as little space as possible, and are full of information.
>
> If columns were comedians, I'd rather they were Woody Allen, doing one nicely-formed monologue, than a whole bunch of Henny Youngman one liners and take-my-wifes.
>
> SW

While school is "in" for would-be writers, I would like to pass along the same thought, more directly viewed, by the Good Grey Bob Parke. While shredding my Tullahoma story, which Bob termed a "disaster," he said, "Baxter, stay on the airport. The trouble here is that you got fascinated with Tennessee, the hill country, the history of the Parish family [they used to make buggy whips], the nearby Jack Daniels distillery. [It's a dry county. I asked the whiskey makers what they did if they wanted a drink. "Same thing we always done."]

Parke illustrated his memo with a cartoon. Me by the wind sock, labeled "Stay here." And a sign pointing to town and a caption, "Do not go here." He suggested I get a tag made to wear around my neck that reads: "I am an aviation writer. If found please return me to the airport."

I wasted a lot of years in my "wonder if they still love me" attitude, hoping that some super-intellect in New York had the magazine's future contents all cut out and dried and that they would send me out on assignments. In truth that rarely happens. The editorial staff meets regularly, has a firm idea of where it's going to be six months from now and reviews the strengths and weaknesses of what it has been doing. But the powers are always open to fresh ideas. In fact, Parke, Collins and Stephan sometimes go fishing among us for ideas: "the guy who uses a Cessna 310 as a crop duster, the rodeo ace who flies from gig to gig in a Pitts, the weirdo who has restored a Champion Lancer twin, the man who's trying to market a steam-powered ADF . . . gimmi some ideas. . . . SW"

They sent me on one assignment in '77 that was like sending a rabbit out for carrots: Go out to Sacramento and find John Schafhausen, the guy who flies the Pappy Boyington Corsair for the TV series, *Baa Baa Blacksheep.* John Schafhausen and I knew each other the minute we met, and we danced paw in paw by the light of the moon. The key idea in the Schafhausen interview was his realization that the Corsair pilots and the show were bringing back to a dulled and anti-hero-minded generation of American kids a little bit of what we once felt about Rickenbacker, Lindbergh and Doolittle. What cynics might call the old heroic virtues.

For me the Corsair story was my chance to lean back and really sling the old baloney like I read it in my formative years. The story opens like that, ideally framed by the true event of Lt. R.R. Klingman, USMC, using his prop to saw down an enemy fighter plane. The Corsair story pulled as much mail as anything I had done up to then. One of the most moving letters was from Mrs. Klingman, expressing surprise and gratification that anyone remembered the caper.

The usual careful nit-picking by *Flying's* staff saved me from several gaffs. The Corsair went through several mods and growths in its long career through World War Two and Korea and into peacetime use. Schafhausen's is a fairly late model with a four-bladed prop. In my rush of enthusiasm I assumed they all were. Somebody questioned that, and it was back to the old books until finally I found a photo of Klingman, just after landing, standing by his chewed up three-bladed prop.

Stephan and I also got into it about the hairy landing and takeoff characteristics of the bent wing bird. I guess I wanted to believe it was wild. Schafhausen encouraged me.

But Stephan had arranged for Wolfgang Langewiesche, probably one of the most sensitive pilots in the world and the author of *Stick and Rudder,* to do the "companion piece to your F4U revel . . . Wolfgang flew hundreds of them as a production test pilot, is a lot calmer about the Corsair's flying qualities . . . says it was quite an ordinary airplane to fly and was a piece of cake to land . . . make it a little clearer that the kids who torque-rolled in at NAS Glendale did so because the Corsair was a bear and they didn't entirely know what they were doing. Up to you, but I don't want it to seem that Wolfgang is coolly contradicting everything that foam-flecked wild man Baxter has to say.

SW"

We laid a little more stress on the inexperienced young pilots, and I stood firm on the rest of my foam-fleckings. Stephan always has a ready pin for my hot air balloons. After reading my statements that no Stearman can be considered landed until it is tied down, he got checked out in one and wrote that it was "a pussycat to land." I wrote back and told him that if he flew one long enough, to send me a piece of the fabric from the wingtip he tears off and I would autograph it for him.

Corsair

The broad bent wings of the Corsair flashed once in the sun, then blended into the deep blue of the ocean as the giant bird swooped down, talons out. The rear gunner of the fleeing Nick pounded on his pilot's shoulder, and the two stared for a frozen moment at the vee-winged death.

In the Corsair cockpit, Klingman jacked his seat a notch higher to put his eye exactly in line with the electric gunsight and swept his engine instruments with a glance—all in the deep green. There wasn't a Japanese aircraft in the Pacific that could outrun an F4U, and flattening out of his dive, he was almost idling up on the Nick. Klingman sawed the rudder lightly, felt the huge, beautifully balanced fighter waltz daintily, watched the Nick's tracers coming up and going wide. The twin-engine Japanese fighter filled his sight. Blood of the meatball. Now. The Marine squeezed the gun button, waited for the bucking roar of those six .50s. Nothing.

Klingman's eyes darted to arming switches just ahead of the stick—on, ready—and back to the skimming Nick. Now! Should have been about a 12-second burst. Silence. Far below, more American destroyers were sinking in their own oil, Marines were dying on the Okinawa beach. Maybe Lt. R.R. Klingman, USMC, never thought of the strategic elements of this particular Japanese air attack; perhaps it was just the simple rage, the elemental aggression, that makes a good fighter pilot. He deliberately urged the hog nose of his huge fighter in toward the thin rudder ahead.

The two Japanese airmen looked right into the airscoops at the muscular shoulders of that drooped wing. Felt the shock as rudder parts were chewed and spat away by the huge, open-mouthed engine. This was no way to die, eaten by a giant blue manta.

The F4U fell back a few feet, then the mad Marine urged the brutal snout of his fighter into the tender parts of the Nick again. Three deliberate passes he made, sawing the Nick right up to the rear gunner's doomed eyes, then fell back and watched the shredded plane spin away.

From the Corsair's battle debut on February 13, 1943 until the end of the war in the Pacific, the aircraft flew 64,051 combat missions. They shot down 2,139 enemy aircraft. And sawed down one. The 2,000-horsepower beast came into service when the Navy shipboard fighter, the Grumman F4F Wildcat, stood nine feet tall in its stocking feet and grossed out at about 7,000 pounds. The Corsair towered to 16 feet and weighed 11,500 pounds. That's about as heavy as a Cessna Citation. The Corsair had only one seat, but it could skip two 1,000-pound bombs at you and then go about a thousand miles home.

But the Navy didn't like it. John Schafhausen, of Spokane, Washington, who keeps one as a pet, says that in '43, when he was a brand-new shave-tail lieutenant with a grand total of 280 hours, he went to Naval Air Station Glenview, north of Chicago, to get carrier-qualified in field landings. The green Corsair pilots with only 70 hours in a retractable advanced trainer—the SNJ—would turn base to final with everything down and dirty, hanging on the prop and waiting for the landing signal officer to give them the paddles to plop it down on the carrier deck outlined on the field. When they got a wave-off, and most of them did, the new pilots only recently acclimated to 600 hp, would turn on that 2,000-hp mill and start a left breakaway, and that three-blade paddle prop would torque the Corsair lazily onto its back and drop it straight in. (Turning right in the carrier Navy is forbidden: that aims you at the skipper and the bridge.) He said he saw two of them go in on one afternoon.

Nor did the Navy appreciate the long, springy oleo legs of the Corsair. They would soak up the shock of a five-and-a-half-ton no-flare landing, but they'd also start the plane galumphing across the deck, the bouncing tailhook skipping every wire until yet another F4U had shredded the barrier and stacked itself among the parked planes on the deck ahead. The Navy's solution: give it to the Marines.

Schafhausen's Corsair is the one that Pappy Boyington flies in TV's *Baa Baa Black Sheep*—one of the five movie-star airplanes that are cleverly filmed and shuffled around to look like Pappy's old Marine 214th Squadron of 15 planes. (There's not but a dozen Corsairs known to be still flying.)

The Corsair and the Marines were made for each other. Said

Pappy Boyington, "The Corsair was a sweet-flying baby if I ever saw one. No longer would we have to fight the Nips' fight, for we could make our own rules."

Schafhausen said that part of the rules they made up had to do with the unlimited gear- and flap-lowering speed of the Corsair. Even if a Zero got on your tail at 350 knots, you could pop the switches. (As he told me this, his left hand made little twiddling motions on an imaginary cockpit console.) "The gear would start forward and down, and so would the flaps, and the slipstream would stop them, as it was designed to do—you couldn't hurt anything—but the F4U would stop like it was sandbagged. The Zero would skip by, and then it was your turn."

Schafhausen says you pick up a Corsair the same way you pick up a cobra: behind the ears, very gently, but firmly in control. Tailwheel locked, rudder six degrees right, right wing four degrees down, set brakes, bring up about 1,400 rpm, release the brakes, and very slowly come to full throttle. "If you slap it, it will turn full left and go into the hangar." Same if you touch the brakes. But you must tap the brakes after the 1,000-foot takeoff run, because the centrifugal forces will expand the tires enough so they won't fit into the tight wheel wells, and you can smell rubber for hours.

In flight, it's the most stable airplane in the world, Schafhausen says. "I felt like I could get out and walk around on it. After all, its purpose was to steer six guns around the sky." Boyington agrees. He used to envy the bomber crews with their automatic pilots, so Pappy rigged some strings and rubber bands from the stick. He'd then undo his seat belt, slip out of the chute harness and catch a snooze on the way into combat. He said the Corsair wandered very little, and it took only a tweak on the strings to swing her long, noble snout back to true flight.

Landing was something else. You see mostly wheel landings in the TV series, because the location set is an old California duster strip about 3,000 feet long with no discernible edges to separate the runway from the rest of the desert. With the nose lifted and a yard-wide engine hanging out on 14 feet of nose plus the gill flaps sticking out six inches on each side, you come over the fence at 90 knots looking out of the sides of your eyes. Thus, wheelies for TV. John says the big bent-wing bird quits flying at 76 knots, gear and 50 degrees of those huge flaps down, "and from there, you will need all the rudder and brakes you got."

Schafhausen says the only real TV trouble comes from trying to stay within camera range of Frank Tallman's B-25 camera ship and maneuver with the T-6 Hollywood Zeros. A good T-6 will hit 200 knots tops and does aerobatics best at about 120. At those speeds, slow-rolling a Corsair that is nibbling the ailerons requires a fine touch. A stalled Corsair spins over the top, and requires 7,000 feet of recovery room, and the book says that if normal recovery is not attained in seven turns, leave it. Schafhausen wears a chute.

At 53, John Schafhausen is getting some of what he missed in the war. Trained in Grummans and Corsairs, he was one of those frustrated young fighter pilots who always ended up in a unit held in reserve. The closest he ever got to combat was to be poised on the West Coast in a replacement squadron for a carrier that finally came in—the *Franklin,* utterly destroyed from internal fires and bombings. John got back into the F4U when his sons, looking at an old photo album, asked, "Dad, don't you ever miss those great old warbirds? Why don't we get one?" He got two; his P-51 has won many EAA warbird awards, but the Corsair is a true affair. (And any good folly is worth what you are willing to pay for it. John just changed the plugs on his front nine: it cost him $500.)

Today, the smoke of these strange, hose-nose throwbacks to another age has drifted across the land and into every living room. *Baa Baa Black Sheep* has risen to third place in the bloodiest battle of all: TV ratings. The series has been renewed for another season. Ten-year-old kids sit in front of TV sets and build models; others have to wait until the sold-out hobby shops can restock. Schafhausen says this is the most satisfying part of it all. How long since the kids have had a hero? A whole generation knows little but the crippled mewlings of the Dustin Hoffman antiheroes.

The *Black Sheep* plot is thin and corny and nothing but *Dawn Patrol* warmed over: "I can't send the kid up in a crate like that . . . the Major is going to ground you all . . . devil with the regulations, we got a war to win. . . ." But it also couldn't be more timely. It's Carter in the White House, it's a nation sickened by its own lies and finding itself at last in the truth-fantasy of knights on noble steeds riding forth to do battle against the forces of darkness.

Pappy Boyington knows this and loves it. He came down to the set, climbed into Schafhausen's cockpit, fitted his hands to those familiar controls, smelled the old smells and heard the thunder of 18 cylinders again. One need say no more—not if you are in the mood of this thing. And if you are sneering now, there would be nothing more to say anyway.

For the same June issue I sold them another "Me 'n my Mooney" story. Or Bax makes a trip. Bax finds/peace/beauty/-terror/humor/great wisdom. I'm getting a little self-conscious about this, but nobody else does it, there is always a moral to the story, and anyway it's fun and folks still seem to enjoy it.

"Unpadded Cell" is unique because in it we broke the "shi-yut" barrier in the magazine. You would be surprised at how much flak mail we draw for the use of "filthy language". But not a peep about it this time. I guess it was because the word was pertinent to the story, humorously presented, modified and explained for. Even though it was said by a 16-year-old maiden. In the "author's copy" that Susan Crandell sent me, she had changed the spelling of the word. I wrote back and explained that while Yankee girls might say "shi-yet," that little Southern girls, properly brought up, say "shi-yut." Like I say, *Flying* is carefully researched.

Unpadded Cell

This is one of those hair-raising stories that you know will turn out all right in the end. I didn't know that at the time, though, and man, oh man, what a ride.

I had launched from home plate on the Gulf Coast of Texas, to fly the coastal crescent, fuel stop at Mobile, then on to Florida in 27 November, my 1968 Mooney with the faded orange paint,

180 engine, hand-fired gear and more King IFR stuff than the hull is worth. With me were my two teenage daughters, both of whom think the ol' man is neat, and who will trample each other for a chance to make a trip—any trip—with me. All that is as good as it can get, thank you very much.

The FSS briefer spoke of a stalled cold front on that early winter morning. The front, one of the first that would freeze you poor Yankees' behinds, reached from the Great Lakes down into Tennessee and was influencing weather along the coast by backing up some warm tropical air masses that were trying to get ashore. The forecast said that I would break out of the clouds about halfway to New Orleans, encounter scattered layers and showers, then fly into steadily improving weather. My "aw shucks, you know better than that" feeling was confirmed as we continued through solid but stable cloud and light rain beyond New Orleans. A good standard westerly was giving us the coveted three miles per minute, and I was enjoying the gray and doing a pretty professional job.

But my mouth was all fixed to break out before Mobile, so the report from Mobile Approach to expect ILS 14 with 200 and a half sort of grabbed me in the belly. That's minimums.

I had been lollygagging along, expecting sunshine, and hadn't done my usual rehearsal with the Jepp plates. Radar was already turning me for the interception and giving me descents when I was flipping pages in the book. Not good. It was a wiggle-waggle approach, and the cloud had turned that deep-green bottom-of-the-sea color that means you are near the ground when the lights appeared, right between a wiggle and a waggle. The kids said I sure was good. Yeah. Heh, heh, heh.

Mobile FSS advised me of continued low ceilings down into central Florida, strong southerly winds and a sigmet for turbulence below 7,000, but with a flourish of satisfaction, the briefer pointed out that I would be well clear of the cold front, which was moving a little now but was still north of us. Not a word about a warm front, and me too dumb to recognize it.

Mobile had gone down with fog and light rain. I enjoyed taxiing out past that dead-still flight line for a just about zero-zero takeoff. A few landing lights, zip, zip, and we were on the gauges.

I had filed for 9,000 to top the reported turbulence. They cleared me for 7,000, and I settled down to holding about 25 degrees right drift. It was really blowing but still smooth. Then near Gleet Intersection, the man at JAX Center said he was painting a little heavy weather across my course. Did I want radar vectors? Sure, I need all the help I can get since I quit flying railroads and water tanks.

Right 10 degrees didn't do much more than ooch me back onto the centerline; that invisible wind was really pouring in. Gleet is between Destin and Panama City, north of both. That's the last place I knew where I was for a long time. At Gleet, I drove right into the freight elevator.

It didn't start out with a wham; in fact, there were only one or two whams all the way through, but each was like lifting the Mooney about 20 feet and dropping it on the ramp. We whooshed right up at about 2,000 feet per minute, then in less than a minute, we were headed down at 2,000 fpm. No warning. Usually if you hit an embedded cell in the daytime, the cloud color changes to dark blue or bile green; this one just went darker gray. It was like trying to fly up a fire hose. I would never have dreamed an airplane could swallow that much water.

I was still pretty cool. Then we flew into the inner chambers, and I felt ice cold in my guts. It all took place in less time than I need to tell it. JAX was on the horn trying to tell me something, my backseat daughter, who had been stretched out asleep loose from her belt, was hitting the cabin roof, and the Jepp book was beating us badly up front. "Grab that thing," I yelled at the front-seat kid, who was hanging by one hand, clutching the door strap, legs and arms flying; she looked like a rodeo rider.

Suddenly I realized that the rate-of-climb needle was all the way over, and I didn't know whether it had gotten there climbing or diving. We hit hail and shocks that blurred the rest of the panel. I don't know why, but I started putting it all on the tape at JAX Center. I've been a broadcaster all my life; I guess doing a play-by-play of our own disaster afforded me some small measure of sanity.

"JAX, 27 November is in a cell, I am getting over 2,000-fpm changes both ways, heavy rain and hail."

"Daddy, I'm going to be sick!" The daddy instinct is strong. I laid a comforting hand on the kid in back, dumped out sandwiches and Fritos and gave her the empty bag. When I turned back to the panel, the horizontal situation indicator looked as though it was tumbling.

"Marginal control of the aircraft, JAX, one passenger sick, the cabin is a shambles, am reducing power . . ."

Maneuvering speed is 132, but I had no idea what our airspeed was because the needle was swinging. Gear-out speed is 120, but us old hand-operated manual-gear Mooney owners know that it will stand whatever it takes.

Slowing down and dropping the wheels quieted the spearing lunges at sky and earth. Now the Mooney just whipped and floated like a leaf at a windy corner. Then the engine quit. Ice!

". . . and partial power failure, JAX, unable to hold altitude or maintain normal attitude. Falling through 5,500." All on the tape.

In the seconds it took for that little Lycoming to drink all the ice water melting out of the carburetor, the prop seemed to flick still for an instant. I knew by now that I was in a fight for life. An attempt at a 180 would be suicide. JAX had taken the friendly concerned attitude of an old uncle at the deathbed. "You'll be out of it soon." But when that prop ticked, with us falling and flipping, and the hail roaring, the little darling in the front seat leaned over to the daughter in back, and, in a voice sweet as Tinkerbell's, said, "Oh shi-yut."

She said it so calmly, and my kids never talk that way in front of Dad. I felt a well of laughter bubble up in me, got the outloud giggles looking at that surprised little pug-nosed freckled face. That made the whole day. Everything outside was still going to pieces, but something had changed inside me. I put on my Ernie Gann face, heard the engine pick up its full hearty roar, remembered that the Mooney wing is made in one piece and that I have never heard of one breaking up in the air, whispered thanks to old Al Mooney and settled down to fly right on out of there.

We never did break out of cloud, but there was no doubt when we flew out of the cell. I told JAX they'd better clear me for 5,000 because that's where I was, and man, don't send anybody else through there.

We fought headwinds down past Cross City and scud halfway across Florida before we saw orange groves, lakes and sunshine. But let me tell you something. When that briefer tells you where the cold front is, and you see those wind shifts and rain to the south, ask about the warm front, too. It'll eat your lunch.

Reader reactions in the form of letters to the editors are more important to most publications than you may think. The really good ones get handed around, anonymous ones get scrapped, nearly all get answered. The sum of the mail reaction is one of the inputs by which the worth of a story, and sometimes the author, are weighed. "Please withhold my name" is always honored, and short pithy ones have a better shot at being among the few selected for print.

In one letter, I was hee-hawed for my country-boy observation in the "Big Sky" that cattle face into the wind. To the reader who advised us they stand rump to the wind I wrote back and said, "No wonder I keep running through that fence."

But the longest run of letters, still on at this writing, was from a mere technique piece called "In A Flap," which ran in June 1977. It is included here to continue the fun. Our letters ran about even on to flap or not to flap, but the agin'ers were personally mad: "meddling with a flight instructor," "a god-like writer from *Flying*," "of course if all of us had a cozy 'in' with the FAA . . ."

We printed Diane's flight instructor's letter defending himself, but the one thing I did leave out was why Diane has not yet gone back. We were in a hazardous pregnancy and have since had our lives filled with our first-born, little red-haired Jenny.

In a Flap

The 35-year-old housewife was on downwind for her first solo landing. Her instructor's words came through clearly. "Reduce power, carb heat on, 10 degrees flaps on downwind, 20 on base, maintain 70 to 80 mph, go to full flaps on final when you see you've got it made."

She was also thinking, "I am really on my own, and if I don't do all this right, I can get myself killed." She knew that she didn't scare easily. She had flown 10 years and 8,000 hours as a hostess for Braniff. "But now I am the pilot," she thought.

Banking easily onto final into gentle winds with 7,000 feet of broad pavement ahead, she applied full flaps, as ordered. The nature of the docile, lightly loaded Cessna 150 changed at once. She was still adding power to overcome the shuddering drag of 40 degrees of flaps and jockeying with abrupt pitch changes, when suddenly it was time to flare and unload all that roaring engine. This was simply more than she, at 11 hours, could manage. The 150 dropped in, sprang hangar-high and quit. She was set up for a crash, and she knew it. As she applied full power, she saw the runway lights pass under the sinking airplane, and she knew there was no hope of flying it out with all those flaps hanging down.

She still does not know how the airplane came to a stop, upright, in the center of the runway. But at that instant, she still believed it had been a crash. She switched everything off, made an emergency cabin evacuation, and looked around to see if the fire truck and TV cameramen had arrived.

It's really funny to hear her tell it, except for one thing. She never went back. She quit.

By now you must be thinking, "Why, for God's sake, were they telling a very low-time student to use full flaps?" Same thing I asked her. (She's my wife.) "Because my instructor said so— that's why. And he's good. I've never landed that Cessna 150 *except* with full flaps."

Not feeling at all good about undercutting her instructor, I took her to another airport, rented a 150 and talked her through the sheer delight of gliding one of these stable little trainers in with power off and no flaps or floating it a little using 10 degrees. She made a squeaker every time. "But," she said, "we are paying an instructor, and I will do it the way he tells me."

Now really feeling rotten about this, I went to her instructor, who said, "Except in gusty conditions or crosswinds, all normal landings will be made in a normal manner. Forty degrees of landing flaps are provided on the Cessna 150, and they will be used."

I told him that was idiotic. He said he knew that, but his boss, who runs the FBO, is the local FAA designee. "He's a friend of yours, and you know what a stickler for the rules he is."

I went to my friend, who spread his arms like a Cessna with 40 degrees of flaps. "You know it's crazy, I know it's crazy, but it came out of the GADO and there is nothing I can do."

I called the general aviation district office, talked to the general aviation operations inspector. Same story: "We are teaching standardization. Normal landings under normal conditions." He made the same obvious exceptions for gusts and crosswinds but refused to listen to anything about the rather extraordinary performance of which the 100-series Cessnas are capable under full flaps. "The equipment is on the airplane, the student will know how to operate it, and we must never be drawn into special types of instruction for each type of airplane. We consider the Cessna, Piper, Beech and Grumman American trainers as single-engine, light, fixed-gear landplanes."

"Where is all this stuff coming from anyway?" I persisted.

The GADO man motioned off in the direction of Oklahoma City.

Within a week, while attending a meeting of aviation writers, I met the legendary, lovable and crusty Pete Campbell, chief of the general aviation branch, Southwest Region, FAA. Cornering Pete after his speech, I related my sad story.

"What? Where is all this stuff coming from anyway?"

"Your office," I told him.

"The devil it is. What we've got here, I suspect, is a lack of communication. Give me some names and stand by."

There was the distant sound of heads knocking. Not everyone within the FAA is passive. The inspectors who operate out of the district and regional offices are not your everyday white-shirt, narrow-tie office runners, but the most highly qualified and experienced bunch of pilots you could hope to assemble. And there was lively contention among them, as one shot back to me, "There are some boys up there that could teach old Pete a thing or two about flaps." That remark, when I relayed it, was like putting out a fire with gasoline. I was beginning to enjoy this.

Our flap culminated in a conference call among Pete; the GADO office; Paul Baker, chief of flight standards; and me. We established that in no way does the FAA advocate full-flap landings every time. "A normal landing is a full-flap landing" is a quote out of context. A student certainly should be able to demonstrate proficiency in full-flap landings on his or her flight test, but when to start making full-flap landings is a judgment call for the instructor. At no time will the FAA advocate any procedure that is contrary to the owner's or operator's manual.

With the true meaning of the owner's manual in mind, I called Cessna. The manual for the 150 only says "flaps as desired below 100 mph," and in another section, "surface winds and air turbulence are the determining factor for the most comfortable approach speed." They never come right out with anything like "10 degrees on downwind, 20 on base, full on final."

What I wanted to learn from the Cessna factory was what the designers were thinking when they put such flap power on their 100-series airplanes. And I might have found out if I hadn't gone out of the way to tell the Cessna feller that all this had developed out of a hassle with the FAA and would be reported in *Flying.* All he was willing to risk was reading to me out of the handbook.

Generally, under "normal" conditions, the FAA does recommend the use of flaps for landings (Circular SW 8000–19–13), citing the advantages of slower touchdown speed, shorter roll-out, less wear on tires and brakes and more controllability on the ground. Yet within our own little nest of vipers who fly and write for *Flying,* there is lively debate. One of our pros stood off another during proficiency rides in the company's heavy and headstrong Cessna 310: painted on no-flap landings with only gradual power reductions that never affected pitch or exaggerated the flare. "They never should have invented flaps for light aircraft," cried he, setting off an uproar that would make another story.

So now with thundering clarification from the FAA, my wife can return to the airport and build her confidence, floating lightly to earth in a power-off 150. The only trouble is, I can't persuade her to go back to the airport.

So the best result of all this is the closing remark of Pete Campbell: "I only wish that more people, finding themselves in contention with the FAA, would call it to our attention. Our only reason for being is to foster and encourage every safe aspect of aviation, not drive people away."

The springtime of '77 must have been hectic in our New York office. Parke was rounding out his long career as Editor-In-Chief by producing the Fiftieth Anniversary issue for September. And that 432-page book was sucking everybody's brains out. Then Parke was slated to become "Vice President for Washington Affairs." Dick Collins was to become the new Editor. You may notice that Ziff-Davis seldom fires anybody or lets the good ones go. They either get promoted upstairs, or moved to *Psychology Today*. The day they got word that I was out of radio and a steady income they even offered me a paid staff job in New York. That meant a lot to me, but I had already clutched my typewriter to my chest and jumped off the cliff to see if it alone would support me.

My assignment for the Fifieth was air racing, to go find Jacqueline Cochran, that beautiful lady who set all the records just before and after the war, and Cliff Henderson, the man who invented air racing, the 99s and Los Angeles International Airport. I found them gracious and delighted that we all still care and remember. But even more exciting to me was to go find and interview my hero, Al Mooney. And that led us into a funny little side-bar event. It was one of those things that there just is no place for in a serious aviation magazine. Parke had sent me a thick manuscript by famed aviator Ed Lund, who was Howard Hughes' co-pilot on Hughes' record breaking round-the-world flight of 1939. Lund is a fine gentleman, and his story will be valuable to aviation history, but his attempts at writing it were about the same as mine would be if I tried to fly his Lockheed Electra around the world.

Parke asked me to interview Mooney. I laid Lund's manuscript on the floor by my desk, and the rest of the story is told in this memo:

Got so excited about actually meeting Al Mooney that I was half-way to Marble Falls when I realized that I had left my camera, recorder, notebook, canteen, cup and cover in my unlocked truck back at the grass airport.

Got lost. Landed at the wrong strip. Found right strip, saw Al Mooney himself waiting, bounced hangar high. The interview was a love fest, wants me to come back, go fishing with him.

Meanwhile back home, the cat had kittens under my desk and one of them crawled out and shit in Lund's manuscript. With love, bax.

The response from New York was immediate. The staff wanted the cat flown to the City to be exhibited as a four-legged literary critic. But Art Davis, then art director, hastily wrote, "Save that cat! That is Howard Hughes come back!"

There is one unusual aspect to this next yarn. It was rejected once. Usually when they send one back I just take it personal, grieve awhile, then go read it a few months later and see that they were right. But a story about a guy's wife suddenly taken with the idea of going wing riding on a Stearman at an airshow is too good to quit on. I waited a few months, rewrote it and sent it back.

Stephan said, "I liked it better this time, and if all you did was retype it clean and spell it right, I'll never forgive you."

Riding High

The Lake Charles Air Show was over, the day had been long and hot, and the crowds were good. Now they were going home with their heads all bored out and feeling fine from watching the Blue Angels and Wayne Pierce and all the others making bluegrass music in the sky.

I had been the announcer, and a bunch of us were sitting around the dying embers of the day when Wayne came taxiing up in his hairy old 450 Stearman and asked Diane if she would like to ride the wing. She said, "Yes, I believe I would."

You know, a fella can be married to a woman for years, feel like he knows all about her, then a thing like this happens. I asked her later why she did it. "Because nobody might ever ask me again."

Wayne's act is that he ties a beautiful woman to the post on the top wing of his Stearman and does loops and rolls with her up there, streaming and screaming, helpless. Not a man in the crowd that doesn't feel that right down here.

Pierce does not think of this as a daredevil act, and he abhors the hint of blood at air shows. He used to fly indoors, in the cabin of a transport plane, delivering people safely and on schedule and making money on a regular basis and doing air shows with the Stearman for fun as a sideline.

One day, the airline company called him up in front of the Big Desk and said, "Choose one." Wayne has a crooked smile but even teeth and he looks at home in the cockpit of a Stearman. He made one of those elusive "quality of life decisions" that a lot of people talk about but not many do anything about. He ran off with the circus.

His wife, Sandi, was his first wing-rider, but one day after the act, he parked in the pits, went off to get coffee and left Sandi out there in the sun tied to the wing. She quit him, learned to fly aerobatics, bought her own clipped-wing Taylorcraft and has an act where she ties a man under the fuselage and flies low and slow over fields while he picks cotton with his teeth. "Sandi and the Cotton Picker" is how she bills herself, and there's not a woman in the crowd who doesn't know what she's saying.

Naw, seriously, Sandi has become a great show pilot, and she works her little Taylorcraft in low and slow, close to the crowds, and they love her. Wayne features Sandi and her T-Craft in his shows and has had a series of other lady wing-riders.

I have often wondered how he communicates with the girl on the wing—I mean, in case she has something to tell him. Arm-waving and shouting would be lost in all that arm-waving and shouting. Diane later told me how Wayne briefed her. Simplest and most practical thing you ever heard of: he told her if she had a bad bug strike, or couldn't breathe, or the wind got into her flight jacket and was choking her, just to turn up a heel. Show the bottom of her foot. That's the part of the girl that's closest to Wayne's line of sight, and the effect would be the same whether she did it intentionally or if she was passing out and buckling at the knees.

Diane said that she had a little trouble breathing at first, standing up there on the gas-tank center section a few inches behind that big old 450 engine and that whirling silver saber. "But it was beautiful! I have never experienced such a total feeling of flight!"

She was telling me this right after they landed. I wish you could have seen her face—rosy, glowing, eyes like searchlights. "I felt like I had wings on my feet. I could look down and admire all the lovely lines of the Stearman. The rivets on the nacelle stood out in the sun, I could see the shadows in the hollows between the wing ribs. I could *feel* that airplane strum with lift and power. Looking out when the horizon was tilting, I have never experienced so deeply the patterns and colors of the fields. I could smell the earth. And when we came over the airport, the rows of parked planes, I could pick you out in the crowd."

I had had some pretty strong mixed feelings of my own when they roared out on takeoff. There was a little old lady in what was left of the crowd who turned and said to nobody in particular, "I just can't believe it. Only a few minutes ago, she was sitting right here, crocheting, just like an ordinary woman." Yeah.

Now I was watching the Stearman circle in the distance, a tiny figure standing up there on the wing. The center of my universe. Now Wayne was boring in on us. He made a low pass, and there was my wife going by me at 100 feet and 100 knots, waving.

A beer-sodden drunk in the crowd felt it too. He leaned against me and said, "Mr. Bashter, she ain't *never* gone be the same after that."

And you know, he was right.

Suddenly, on a day in September, I woke up in the hospital. At 53, an age when most men are concerned about a heart condition and high blood pressure, I am as hard and healthy as I was in high school. I even came to feeling good, ready to go home. What was all this about anyway?

What they found was a very slight malformation of two capillaries, a defect that was old and calcified, but within the left occipital lobe of my brain. No operation called for, no growth, but it had flickered me lights. And might do it again. The doctor, an old flying companion, stood at the foot of my bed with his face long as Bob Wills' fiddle. "Name your two favorite things." I did. "Now choose one." And that's how come I gave up flying.

The response from the New York office was instant and full of compassion. Parke and Collins called. Ed Muhlfeld, the VP in charge of aviation at ZD, wrote a chin-up and cheers note. Susan wrote, "What awful luck, you just get your new daughter out of the hospital in time to check yourself in." From Stephan, a long scrawled letter, and with it the most complicated and detailed kit to build a plastic model of the Gee Bee racing plane.

Dear Gordon,

You have the love and support of us all . . . the enclosed is intended to keep your hands busy until we can come up with yet more enigmatic article ideas for you to tackle while temporarily grounded. . . . call at any hour of the day or night if you get itchy and just want to talk. . . .

Fondest,
Steph.

I am still fighting the sensuous pleasure of just wallowing in it. And still have to put aside the shirt tearing rage to just go out at dawn and steal my Mooney and fly it south until I come to some place below borders where they do not ask who you are or where you come from, but can you land short. That I can do.

I fight irrational behavior, like the pilot's habit of stepping outside first thing each morning to look at the sky. I still carry my license and my still valid medical. It is a self-grounding. And I too know of lots of pilots who just ignore ailments and

go on and fly. I am not sure of why I don't, for I agree with
Nevil Shute who wrote, "When it comes I would prefer that it
should be in an airplane, since airplanes have been the best part
of my life."

There have been a few very sharp moments. Once, driving
home at sunset I saw a sleek little monoplane flying the freeway,
low over the forest. I used to do that, "give them a thrill, let
them see how beautiful an airplane in flight is."

The shape quickly grew larger, more familiar; the pilot was
holding off to one side to pass between me and an absolutely
gorgeous sunset of flames and silver cloud. In the instant he was
silhouetted I saw the sharply upturned tip of a Mooney. I pulled
off to the side of the road, beating my fist into the tears falling
on the steering wheel, "Gah-DAMN, I didn't need that!"

We had a long serious discussion around the chairs in New
York as to whether or not to go public about it. The story was
printed in the January, 1978 issue.

It Only Hurts When I Flap My Arms

The last flight couldn't have been as perfect had it been scripted
as romantic fiction. It was home from Houston on a clear night
alone in my own plane. A passage of places as familiar as the feel
of a loved one's face.

I had spent the long day at Houston, frying out on the ramp at
Hobby Airport, doing videotape interviews of teams of pilots who
had been invited to come fly a new three-engine $6,000,000
French bizjet.

The interviews were being conducted on a ramp teeming with
expensive hardware—Lears, Citations, Falcons and other exotica
wheezing by. So many little expensive hard rubber tires nibbling
at the cement that all the ordinary old fat-wheeled flying machines
like mine had been shunted out of the way and left out in the high
grass, like extra cardboard boxes.

And all day as I interviewed keen-eyed, carefully spoken corporate pilots, I was looking over their shoulders at my own airplane

sitting out there, all sun-faded and oil-streaked, and daydreaming about her. She is a disgraceful-looking airplane compared to all this bright jewelry around us, but unlike these other creatures, she belongs to a single person. To me.

You ever notice how an old Mooney sitting out in the grass always looks like her socks are down around her ankles? If you opened-the door of my Mooney's cabin, it would smell like old tennis shoes stored in a filling station, but there is a document inside a yellowed plastic frame on the bulkhead that says I am the sole owner of this frazzled little beast. They got a piece of paper like that on the bulkhead of every one of those jets, but you won't find any of those pilots' names on them.

We edited film until midnight. It was a really sharp crew with some space-age computer-edit, split-frame stuff, but even with all those whiz consoles going for us, my eyeballs were flat as fried eggs by midnight. I got to thinking about all those accident reports where the Feds peel back the layers and find out how fatigued the pilot was, and I decided to play it cool and hang it up for the night in Houston.

I spent 90 minutes trying to acquire a cheeseburger and a cab across town, and still hadn't made it but was zingy enough mad to know that in 40 minutes I could be home, could get there in my own plane and not have to wake up still in Houston. Part of the decision to go fly myself was the moonlight and stars; I could see all the way to El Paso.

The old Mooney was glistening with dew as I felt around in the wet cabin and brought her little starry panel to life. She was fresh and feisty from her annual at the healing hands of Charlie Dugosh, who happens to be the world's best Mooney mechanic.

Now, in the center of the night, the whip-crack urgency of daytime Houston radio traffic had snoozed off to the secret compacts of those who keep the night watch. "You don't bother me, I won't bother you." Two-Seven November became a set of winking lights curving away, monitored only from the dark windows of the tower that watches over HOU.

The little airplane settled down at once. You ever notice how old engines seem to run fatter at night? And there were none of the daytime pranks of an airplane that sometimes wants to skew along sideways. My backbone and my old airplane's spine lay in perfect alignment in the purple night.

The white-shafted San Jacinto battleground monument and other favorite sights drifted into view. I thought of Sam Houston's army camped down there, where Interstate 10 now carries a bright berry row of auto lights, and where more Texans and Mexicans kill each other with their cars every year than did all those armies combined. That's a part of the smugness of flying your own plane over the Interstate.

The heading to home cuts across Old River, lost and old, and the Trinity River bottom lands where pirate ghosts lie in the permanent fog wisps. Some of the first stories I sold to *Flying* were about sneaking through there in Cessnas.

Then the flight path quarters across the terraced rice fields where the broad-wing Stearman biplanes will bank their greetings to the morning sun. I have come this far flying a 450 two-holer. I've looked at the world from every conceivable angle from between those taut wings, and I've shouted in the slipstream for the joy of it. I don't think I was ever more alive than those summers when I groaned around in those old biplanes.

Then it was time to start letting down for Pappy's grass airport. Go on, drop the nose and don't throttle back; let her sizzle some, but don't play with it out over that black-hole north approach. Gear down, green light, really an instrument approach, though no longer as hair-raising as it used to be before we got lights and pavement. We used to sink into the dark grass and wonder where they left the tractor.

The landing was a kisser. A no-brakes rollout and swing round by my old tin stall. I sat there a minute with all the switches off and listened to the dying whine of the gyros. What a rich feeling of accomplishment. I breasted the cowling, spinner nuzzled under my arm, and rolled her in, then spent my shameless magic moment with this molded warm-smelling airplane. I said to her, "Thank you, Mooney, for bringing me home again. You're a good airplane." Then I walked to a pay phone for the swagger call to Diane, "Hi babe, once again I have cheated fate." Our private thing. We both know airplanes are not like that.

A few days later I was slated to fly solo to Memphis for an

interview. I had the seizure that midnight, in my sleep. Woke up
a day or so later in the hospital. The prognosis is good, all but the
pilot's license. But you know what's funny? I still carry it. I cherish
the 21 years I was a licensed pilot. The richest years of my life.
I only owned 27 November a year and a half. And this is only the
first month of building a documented record to someday apply for
the waiver and get it all back.

   The responses came from all over the world. Some wrote me
poems, many sent medical advice, all sent love. Two even wrote
"Bax Seat" stories about me to offer to the magazine. I answered them all and kept them all.
   To the one who wrote "Come with me, fly beside me, use my
airplane, anytime, anywhere," I answered, "I will be with you.
When you are flying into a sunset and the golden light is level
with the chord line of your wing, shadowing the lift curve, and
every rivet head stands in its own little shadow of strength, I
will be with you then. We won't have to talk."
   Out at the grass airport, Pappy Sheffield said, "Whatever you
need." So I tried one trip with a really nice young kid flying my
left seat. It was like watching another man dance too close to
your wife.
   On the long ride home the kid said, "You want it awhile?"
I told him to cinch up his belt, I was going to do a wifferdill.
And laid hands upon the stiff little yoke of my Mooney, let her
dive down into the yellow arc, then peeled her right up into
heaven. When she got slow and a little heavy and a little over
on her back, I kicked some relief into her and I guess you could
call it a hammerhead-wingover. Then let her get howling down
and stiff again and pulled up firmly but gently and did the other
half of the flower. When we coasted back up to the same altitude, same heading and to cruise power, I elegantly raised my
hands off the wheel and turned to the kid to take my bow.
   He was looking at me. "Golly, you should have seen your
face." "Pretty dramatic, eh?" "Oh nossir, your ears. They got
long. The G loads pulled your whole face down and your ears
got long. Sure looked funny."

Yeah, kid, when you get old you get a lot of slack in your hide.

There were other sharp little pangs that came in the most unexpected ways. Take the business of the Jepp charts. You would think that being free of that insistent pile of brown envelopes would be one big relief. But I kept my stern discipline of updating the same day I got them, knowing the folly. It took two and a half months before I wrote Cap'n Jepp a personal letter cancelling the service:

> Unbuckling this tidy way of life that has become so much a part of flying. I am surprised at the reluctance to let go. . . . it was like a party line, reading the updates. How's it coming with the expansion of Atlanta? I see where the Feds made ole Petersen put a beacon in at Plains. . . . Will we ever have a week with no change at Miami? And I learned a lot about geography just hunting pages. And some plates, stained with fog, sweat and smears remind me of the times when I bet it all on you. Some pages ought to be framed or put in the family Bible. I guess all I am trying to say, Jepp, is that you'all were good to me—and thanks—and so long.

It's not all that final, of course, but I think the solo-pilot part of it is. Down the road somewhere, when our little red head Jenny does not require so much of her time, Diane plans to go on and get her ticket. I can see this generating a lot of good copy for *Flying*. "Student Wife," and later, "Wife-In-Command," and then Jenny growing up and continuing this soap opera, starting with "I was the kid in the baggage bin."

Good things are already starting to fall into place. Just as we were most worried about how much money we were spending each month for transportation we could not use and being concerned that the Mooney needs flying, not sitting and soaking in an open T-hangar, there came a knock at our door. It was a young, and highly nervous couple apologizing for the intrusion and even more for the sacrilege of asking us if we wanted to sell our Mooney.

I could never tell you why, but both of us took an instant liking to this slight-built and shy young couple. Elmer Lee Ashcraft is a Certified Instrument Instructor and a bricklayer. Elaine works the front desk in a plastics company and is a licensed pilot. They stood, sort of hanging on to each other, and I offered to sell them half of it, if they would take the half that eats, right now. We all got to laughing, and we got a partner.

After the serious Ceremony of the Lawyers we all went our separate ways, but Diane and I wanted to go out to the darkened airport and tell the Mooney. There was a car parked by the hangar. The door of the airplane was ajar. We walked up, feeling sort of uneasy, and there, like a couple of squirrels in a nest, were Elmer Lee and Elaine cuddled up in the cockpit with a bottle of champagne.

After the rush of "excuse us" and "aw gol-lees" they told us the most beautiful thing we could ever hope to hear. That this was not just an airplane, and it was an important moment in their lives, and being partners in old 27 November really required some ceremony. The four of us stood there, awkward and full of the moment beside our old sweet-running, faded Mooney, and the night grew as still as only a dark and deserted airport can be.

So now we have a flight instructor in the family and another pilot and plans for where the four of us will go and future stories for *Flying.*

But if the Good Flying Fairy were to come shimmering and hovering down, right here, right now, and grant me just one more hour of solo time, you know what I would do?

I would go out to Pappy Sheffield's grass airport and get the yellow J-3 Cub and go fly it in the heat beneath puff-ball clouds as their shadows drifted across the field and do touch-and-goes. I would throttle back and do long, delicious side-slips back to earth. With the side open, the window pinned up under the wing and the door let down on the landing gear strut, I would feel the warm wind on my face as I looked out and saw when the wheel touched. If you bring the Cub in just exactly right, descent rate, speed, pitch, all of it just exactly right, the three wheels will touch at the same instant, and that fat tire never lifts an inch from the first contact. There is not an ounce of lift left in that wing, and the little airplane just starts rolling, if you do it just exactly right.

And with your head out like that, you can smell the tires crush the clover.